Disturbers of the Peace

New World Studies

J. Michael Dash, *Editor*

Frank Moya Pons and
Sandra Pouchet Paquet,
Associate Editors

Disturbers of the Peace

Representations of Madness in Anglophone Caribbean Literature

Kelly Baker Josephs

University of Virginia Press
Charlottesville and London

University of Virginia Press

Printed in the United States of America on acid-free paper
First published 2013

9 8 7 6 5 4 3 2 1

Library of Congress Cataloging-in-Publication Data

Josephs, Kelly Baker.
Disturbers of the peace : representations of madness in Anglophone Caribbean literature / Kelly Baker Josephs.
pages cm. — (New World Studies)
Includes bibliographical references and index.
ISBN 978-0-8139-3505-8 (cloth : acid-free paper)
ISBN 978-0-8139-3506-5 (pbk. : acid-free paper)
ISBN 978-0-8139-3507-2 (e-book)
1. Caribbean literature (English)—History and criticism. 2. Mental illness in literature. 3. National characteristics, Caribbean, in literature. I. Title.
PR9210.J67 2013
810.9'9729—dc23

2013007094

A book in the American Literatures Initiative (ALI), a collaborative publishing project of NYU Press, Fordham University Press, Rutgers University Press, Temple University Press, and the University of Virginia Press. The Initiative is supported by The Andrew W. Mellon Foundation. For more information, please visit www.americanliteratures.org.

For my parents,
Ruby Baker and Bruce Josephs

Contents

Acknowledgments

THESE FEW PARAGRAPHS of acknowledgments have proven most difficult for me to write. It is impossible to express in words the debts I owe to the people who have made this book possible: the generous scholars, supportive institutions, helpful friends, and patient family members who have enabled my work over the duration of the project. Thanks first to Brent Hayes Edwards, whose unstinting attention and counsel helped this project grow from seminar paper to dissertation to book. I can only hope that the following pages evidence even a little of his brilliant guidance.

There are two people crucial to this project and to my intellectual, professional, and personal development who do not fit easily into the groupings below. David Scott, thank you for your time, for your patience, for your timely impatience. Your work inspired me before I met you, and I continue to be awed by your genius and generosity. If I had your gift for words, I could thank you properly. And Tzarina Prater, thank you for conversation, commiseration, and companionship across countless diner tables, café couches, living room floors, and now Skype sessions. For reading and commenting, for reality checks and credit to dream. Thank you for then, thank you for now, thank you for the work to come.

I am deeply grateful to the scholars who helped shape the early stages of this book during my time at Rutgers University: Marianne DeKoven, Abena Busia, Daphne Lamothe, and Simon Gikandi, each of whom encouraged not only this project but also my potential as a scholar; Cheryl Wall, who always asked the right questions and made the answers seem possible just by being the amazing scholar and woman that she is; and my fellow graduate students, especially Soyica Diggs Colbert, Jeremy Glick, Krista Walkes, and Richard Mizelle, for our dinners, discussions, debates, and friendship.

Many other scholars and friends have been generous with their time and intellect during the postdissertation revision process. Thanks to my readers at University of Virginia Press; to my editors, Cathie Brettschneider and J. Michael Dash; and to my copyeditor, Kelly S. Martin. I thank my colleagues at York College, particularly Linda Grasso, Mychel Namphy, and Rishi Nath, for their early enthusiasm and continued support. Thanks also to the members of the Africana Colloquium Series at York College and the Atlantic Contexts seminar at the CUNY Graduate Center for their personal and intellectual encouragement. I thank Barbara Webb, Christopher Winks, Herman Bennett, and other members of the Caribbean Epistemologies Seminar; their passion and engagement with Caribbean studies continuously remind me why we do this work. Thanks also to the members of the Transnational and Transcolonial Caribbean Studies Research Group for their comradeship during the homestretch of this project.

Portions of this work have been presented at past conferences and lectures, and I thank the audiences at each of these events for their comments and suggestions. In particular, conversations with the following scholars have influenced portions of this work: Michael Hanchard, Charles Carnegie, Carolyn Boyce Davies, Evelyn O'Callaghan, and Raphael Dalleo. Chapters 2 and 4 also benefited from reader reviews and were published in earlier versions in *The Caribbean Woman Writer as Scholar* (edited by Keshia N. Abraham) and *Small Axe* 32 (July 2010), respectively; I am grateful for permission to reproduce that material here. Support for this project was provided by a PSC-CUNY Award, jointly funded by the Professional Staff Congress and the City University of New York.

This project was also supported by a postdoctoral fellowship at the Center for Africana Studies at the Johns Hopkins University. Ben Vinson's energy and enthusiasm inspired me to accept the position, and the year I spent teaching, researching, and revising during this fellowship was transformative, primarily because of the people I encountered. I am especially grateful to Franklin W. Knight, whose generosity, on every level, continues to influence my intellectual and professional development. I was very fortunate to have Reanna Ursin and Brian Norman at nearby institutions during this fellowship year, and their friendship and steadiness as scholars helped keep me grounded and focused.

For my family and friends who have held me in their hearts and hands during this process and before, nurturing me emotionally and physically, my gratitude is truly greater than these words can express. Special thanks to my aunts, Thelma Baker and Lorna Down, who introduced me to Caribbean studies and make it not only possible but also desirable to continue this work, and to my sisters, Taja and Lydia Josephs, who remind me of the importance of life beyond this work. Above all, of course, I thank my parents, Ruby Baker and Bruce Josephs. You make this and everything that is good and worthy in me possible. I am grateful for the opportunity to dedicate this book to you both.

Disturbers of the Peace

Introduction

Madness, Caribbeanness, and the Process of Nation Building

Yesterday
Ah was mad mad, mad mad,
Mad mad, mad mad mad, mad mad,
Mad mad, mad!
Stark ravin' mad!

—Paul Keens-Douglas, "Jus' Like Dat"

MAD MAD, MAD mad mad, mad mad . . . Paul Keens-Douglas's rhythmic repetition illustrates both the complexity and the consistency with which literary artists appropriate madness to represent Caribbean life. The poem reveals the ambiguity of the term *mad* as each repetition confuses rather than enlightens the reader.[1] The poet leaves his audience to ask not only why the speaker was mad but also what he means by *mad*. Is *mad* the same as *mad mad* and *mad mad mad*? By the end of the piece the reader can infer that the speaker was temporarily insane during the bacchanal of carnival and has now come to his senses. Throughout the poem, Douglas repeatedly plays with the performative aspects of "losing one's mind," using the slippages between insanity, anger, and excessive gaiety to recreate the physical and mental experience of carnival.

On a larger scale, Caribbean literature repeats the use of mad characters in the same way Keens-Douglas repeats the word: constantly changing intensity and meaning. The bulk of *Disturbers of the Peace* traces this repetition of madness in Caribbean literature written in English between 1959 and 1980. During these politically turbulent years in the anglophone Caribbean, writers in the region consciously attempted to make their literary tradition as independent from British literature as they hoped to be from England. One of the distinguishing features of literature produced during this period of upheaval is the ubiquity of madmen and madwomen. While representations of madness were prevalent in Caribbean literature across the anglophone, francophone, and hispanophone traditions throughout the twentieth century, they increased markedly in anglophone writings during the latter half of the century. I connect this increase to the concurrent shift from colonial to postcolonial status. In contrast to the Spanish, French, and Dutch islands, the British islands experienced a relatively homogeneous struggle to establish their collective and individual independence from England. The theme of madness—whether central, as in Jean Rhys's *Wide Sargasso Sea*, Derek Walcott's *Dream on Monkey Mountain*, and Erna Brodber's *Jane and Louisa Will Soon Come Home*, or seemingly supplemental, as in V. S. Naipaul's *Miguel Street* and Sylvia Wynter's *The Hills of Hebron*—permeates literature from the Caribbean and serves as both a social critique and a form of literary innovation in these texts.

Despite the preponderance of "mad" characters populating the Caribbean literary canon, little attention has been paid to their presence. Literary and historical scholarship on writing and madness, though extensive and long-standing, has focused primarily on European writers. This scholarship has recently begun to include francophone Caribbean and African literature, expanding and enriching the field with insights from postcolonial and race theorists. The result, however, has been a collapsing of Caribbean representations of madness into a larger postcolonial discourse. Although criticism on individual texts sometimes includes attention to the characters' mental disorders, madness has not been examined as a significant element in the anglophone Caribbean literary tradition. With mad figures frequently appearing in Caribbean literature from the French, Spanish, and English traditions—in roles that range from bit parts to first-person narrators—madness should be regarded as a significant part of the West Indian literary aesthetic. This prevalence raises the question, What function(s) do these figures serve for the writer and the represented communities? If, as Kenneth Ramchand writes in his study of the West Indian novel, Caribbean writers were especially concerned with representing "the social and economic deprivation of the majority; the pervasive consciousness of race and colour; the cynicism and uncertainty of the native bourgeoisie in power after independence; the lack of a history to be proud of; and the absence of traditional or settled values," then how does madness figure in these varied interests?[2] My object in the following chapters is to answer these questions by drawing connections between the writers' representations—and repetitions—of madness and the issues inherent in decolonization, including those noted by Ramchand above.

In asking what madness *does* for these writers and these texts, I find the repeated representations of madness at the juncture of creative expression and political and social commentary. Mad figures (whether marginal or central to the text itself) work as plot devices and creative gambits not only on the level of artistic and aesthetic choices but also on the metaphorical level of the concerns Ramchand lists as crucial to West Indian writers of the period. So, for example, Naipaul's Man-man adds to the development of the narrator's character and that of Hat, and helps to round out the "character" of Miguel Street; thus Man-man's madness provides a platform for the narrator's and Hat's continued philosophizing about life and people. But Man-man's ambitions to political power also contribute to a larger discourse on the contemporary discussions of federation and independence. The distinction I make here is in some ways unnecessary, because aesthetics are never ahistorical; however, because madness has not yet been studied as crucial to both a burgeoning Caribbean aesthetic *and* the representations of a Caribbean political identity, I wish to emphasize both valences at work in writers' turn to such representations, particularly in this midcentury period of political and social flux.

A major premise of *Disturbers of the Peace*, then, is that the slow but relatively condensed decolonization of the anglophone islands during the 1960s and 1970s makes literature written in English during this time—what Mary Lou Emery describes as "the closing of the era of empire"—*especially* rich for an examination of the function of madness in literary critiques of colonialism and the Caribbean project of nation making.[3] The crux of my argument concerning madness in anglophone Caribbean literature requires that the reader conceive of this "closing of an era" as a prolonged process, more like the slow, cautious progression of an electronic security gate than the definitive slamming of a front door. In the 1960s, 1970s, and early 1980s, there was a "rolling out" of independence among the formerly British-owned islands in the Caribbean. In his introduction to a multidisciplinary anthology of essays, *Jamaica in Independence*, Rex Nettleford writes, "Independence is more than an event, it is a process."[4] This "process" started long before Jamaica became the first of the anglophone islands to receive independence in 1962. For the West Indies, there was no watershed moment after which everything changed, and, as the other authors in Nettleford's anthology conclude, it is difficult to determine when (or whether) that "process" (has) ended.

The appearance of early strains of independence in the Caribbean can arguably be dated as early as 1871, when the Leeward Islands Confederation was formed as part of an attempt to unite some of the smaller English colonies.[5] These first efforts to consolidate the English islands into a region continued to spread; from 1882 to 1938, British-sponsored delegations to the Caribbean regularly suggested building a federation among the British islands. Despite these efforts and the islands' common colonial culture and geographic proximity, the West Indies was slow to think of itself as a region. The islands shared some social, commercial, and political institutions, but these associations did not immediately confer a West Indian nationalism.[6] In 1958, talks culminated in the formation of the West Indian Federation between Jamaica (with the Cayman Islands and the Turks and Caicos Islands as dependencies), Trinidad and Tobago, St. Lucia, Dominica, Barbados, Antigua-Barbuda, Grenada, St. Vincent, St Kitts-Nevis-Anguilla, and Montserrat. A major goal of the federation was to provide more political power for the region, but it created a tension between individual self-government and regional self-government. Trinidad and Jamaica, two major islands in the federation, soon found themselves on opposite sides of this divide. Trinidad pushed for West Indian independence, with the federation as the governing body for the region, while Jamaica, which John Mordecai describes as making "a strange and schizophrenic late entrance to West Indian Federation," pushed for less power for the federation, without quite aiming for independence as a nation.[7] Although in 1959 Jamaican prime minister Norman Manley could still conceive of a "West Indian nation," in 1961 Jamaican nationalism warred with West Indian nationalism, and, by a slight margin, the former won.[8] Jamaica left the federation and obtained independence in 1962. Trinidad's prime minister, Eric Williams, described Jamaica's defection as a great loss to the federation. Indeed, Williams's oft-cited comment that "1 from 10 leaves 0" marks the federation as pointless after Jamaica's exit.[9] Soon after, Trinidad also withdrew, gaining independence in 1962. The federation, without these two powerhouses, disbanded, and over the following two decades the other member nations began seeking independence as well.[10]

The beginning of independence for the anglophone Caribbean, therefore, was steeped in the islands' failure to organize politically as a region, but this did not mark the ideological end of a West Indian nation. Mordecai's use of the term *schizophrenic* illuminates the near-debilitating divided loyalties that characterize this often contradictory split between national and regional identities. It is not surprising that an increase in anglophone writing accompanied this fragmentation as writers attempted to decipher and represent the social effects of political turmoil. Reading the products of this increase, Ramchand concludes that "West Indian novelists apply themselves with unusual urgency and unanimity to an analysis and interpretation of their society's ills."[11] Many of the writers grappled directly with the meaning of independence. V. S. Naipaul's *Mimic Men* is perhaps too ideal an example here, but his narrator-protagonist, Ralph, accurately describes the chaos of the moment: "Given our situation, anarchy was endless, unless we acted right away. But on power and the consolidation of passing power we wasted our energies, until the bigger truth came: that in a society like ours, fragmented, inorganic, no link between man and the landscape, a society not held together by common interests, there was no true internal source of power, and that no power was real which did not come from the outside. Such was the controlled chaos we had, with such enthusiasm, brought upon ourselves."[12] Naipaul's novel centered on a fictional island in the years surrounding its independence from England, but Ralph's summation of the gap between the leaders' promises of independence and the society's fragmentation is echoed by other texts of the time, including those that appear less concerned with the political aspects of independence. Ralph describes the disparity as a "vision of hysteria" and utilizes several such terms of madness throughout his narrative.[13] As Mordecai's quote above and the various texts in the following chapters indicate, such connections between mental disorder and the disorder of decolonization abound in both fictional and nonfictional writings.

Disturbers of the Peace focuses on texts from this historical moment, which also saw an increase in literary production in the anglophone Caribbean. The seeming concurrence between the increase in literature and the "process" of independence provides fertile ground for a study of the variable yet pervasive usage of madness in Caribbean fictions; but the discussion cannot end there. Thus my epilogue considers how we may read the trope of madness in more recent Caribbean fictions. These twenty-first-century fictions by writers of the Caribbean diaspora situate madness as central to representing both the still-ongoing process of decolonization and the (more) contemporary concern with the residues of migration.

Madness in a Caribbean Context

The juxtaposition of the texts included in *Disturbers of the Peace* not only furthers critical engagement with the trope of madness in Caribbean fictions but also frames such figurations of madness as necessarily linked to the peculiar existence that is the postcolonial Caribbean—with its histories of displacement and imported cultures, forced and free migrations, and the psychic landscapes that these histories fashion. Although I have narrowed my focus to texts published midcentury in order to think madness more particularly in connection to decolonization, there is a larger context of Caribbean writers' preoccupation with characters who may broadly be described as people "whose mental state is often, and for deeply complex reasons, just the wrong side of a thin dividing line from 'normality.'"[14] In addition to the texts considered here, there are minor characters described as mad in much earlier works, such as in Claude McKay's *Banana Bottom* (1931) and Miguel Angel Asturias's *El Senor Presidente* (1946). In works published later in the century, one can find narratives with the mad character as protagonist, such as Myriam Warner-Vieyra's *Juletane* (1982) and Anthony Winkler's *The Lunatic* (1987). The epilogue of this book, which looks at twenty-first-century novels by David Chariandy, Marie-Elena John, and Zadie Smith, argues that the preoccupation with mental abnormalities still exists, whether for the protagonists themselves or the people with whom they interact. But the lack of criticism on this aspect of Caribbean literature relegates it to a position of exclusion, or at best marginality. Very few critical articles or full-length books focus on insanity in Caribbean literature, despite its being as prevalent as, say, autobiography (a common concern in Caribbean literary criticism) in the works of contemporary and earlier writers alike. Even treatments of what may be deemed canonical texts of madness, such as *Wide Sargasso Sea* and *Dream on Monkey Mountain*, either consider madness a given fact that does not need to be explained or hurry through it in order to discuss the texts' representations of other issues (race, gender) or their connections to literary movements (modernism, postmodernism). While these concerns are certainly part of how the particular figurations of madness work in these and other texts, the inescapable repetition of such characters across the Caribbean literary canon demands more connective critical engagement.

Some writers, such as Erna Brodber and Michelle Cliff, repeat this preoccupation with madness across their oeuvre. I focus on Brodber's *Jane and Louisa Will Soon Come Home* in chapter 5, but her second novel, *Myal*, also explores the mental and physical breakdown of the female protagonist. Cliff, beginning with her first book, *Claiming an Identity They Taught Me to Despise*, and carrying through to her most recent publication, *Into the Interior*, displays a fascination with characters legendary for their abnormalities, namely, Bertha Rochester and Annie Palmer (the White Witch of Rosehall). But Cliff also creates her own mad characters: for example, she ends her first novel, *Abeng*, with Miss Winifred, an old Creole woman who has retreated mentally and physically after having a child for her family's black servant. In *The Store of a Million Items*, Cliff continues her exploration of madness with two stories, "Contagious Melancholia" and "Stan's Speed Shop." In the latter story, a conversation between the young narrator and her aunt Cliff raises the question of defining insanity: "'You said he was crazy,' I reminded her. 'There's crazy and then there's crazy,' she said, and I wasn't sure what she meant."[15] For the young narrator, the meanings of *crazy* are not clear; for her aunt, some eccentricities are expected from the rich (particularly the white rich), but even they can cross into an unacceptable form of *crazy*.

This "continuum" of crazy is magnified when one turns to the discursive usage of the word *mad*. In fact, I rely more on the term *mad* than on *crazy* because of the former's multiple meanings. The *Oxford English Dictionary* lists fourteen definitions for *mad* when used as an adjective, with an additional seven entries for the verb, noun, and adverb forms. I refrain from attempting my own definition of madness because the term's plurality provides fertile ground for literary analysis. Any such attempt to circumscribe the term would, in any case, be destined for failure because it constantly resists and subverts imposed limits.[16] *Mad* also has a wide range of meanings in Caribbean usage. To return to the Paul Keens-Douglas poem that opens this introduction, *mad* can equal angry, crazy, and even happy. It can be both derogatory and desirable, both criticism and commendation. The recognition of these various meanings of *mad* can also be read in the various phrases used to avoid using the term at all. Whether conscious or not and whether motivated by political or social motives or not, phrases such as "lost her head" or "touched" or "a little different" indicate a related range of meanings and a similarly complicated nomenclature surrounding abnormal behavior. The linguistic variations surrounding madness as both term and concept makes it simultaneously extensive and elusive.

Descriptions of madness lurk in definitions of Caribbean culture even when writers do not utilize specific or clinical terms of insanity. For example, in a 1989 essay included in Nettleford's anthology on independence, Erna Brodber proposed that Jamaica's "socio-cultural history" is the history of European attempts at dominance over nonwhites, "the history of the resistance of Africans to strategies to keep them in place and a history of African anger at the system's constancy." Brodber notes that this "anger and frustration translated themselves into sporadic outbursts of violence."[17] She also refers to this anger as "traditional anger" and describes Afro-Jamaicans as "angry and alienated," emotions that were "heightened" after independence.[18] Madness can describe this state of turmoil, since it refers to both anger and alienation. In a plenary speech at the 2006 Caribbean Women Writers Conference, Brodber refined this idea under the heading of "ancestral anger," describing this with terms similar to "traditional anger": for example, both are attached to the black Caribbean population and have existed since the Middle Passage. But she inserts a class dimension into her configuration of ancestral anger. She describes, for instance, the abolition of Emancipation Day as a holiday in favor of Independence Day in Jamaica as one of the additional reasons for this anger. Here it is fueled not by colonial or racial discrimination but by a decision perpetrated by the "college trained" sector of Jamaica. Brodber's formulation of ancestral anger may be considered relevant to my study (more so than traditional anger) because she adds that ancestral anger has not yet had a chance to be resolved and, therefore, appears as occasional violent breaks in history *and* literature. One possible way of reading madness in these texts, then, is as representations of this repressed anger and alienation, as the repeated ("mad mad mad") eruptions of ancestral anger. Not only a range of meanings of the words surrounding madness (*mad*, *crazy*, *schizophrenic*) but also a range of theories on the Caribbean flirt with notions of madness, whether read as inescapable difference, psychological damage, anger, or some combination thereof.

The plurality of meanings and usages of madness in Caribbean literature presents both opportunities and risks for a project such as *Disturbers of the Peace*, interested as it is in reading across a disparate array of texts—fictional, critical, and theoretical. Definitions of psychological aberration, any aberration, are based on an idea of normality. Therefore, while *mad* can define a person, situation, or event, it more often describes the person attempting to define said person, situation, or event. That is, the term says as much, if not more, about the subject employing it as about the object it attempts to label. How then, without definitions, do I decide that a character is mad (and that, therefore, the text in which said character appears is appropriate for this project)? There must be some parameters. For the most part, I leave this up to the texts themselves. The productive aspect of doing so lies in the tension between the label of madness and the actions and interactions of the characters labeled as mad in the texts. The characters in the various texts share some similar traits but experience madness differently; hence, my use at times of the plural, albeit grammatically questionable, term *madnesses*. The authors whose work I examine in the following chapters are less concerned with defining than with *utilizing* madness in their texts, to varied ends. Thus my aim is not to define madness but to examine the ways madness defines—defines community, defines gender, defines the form of the text, and, for some characters, defines reality itself.

In the following chapters, I rely more often on the term *madness* than on *insanity* or *delirium* because it more clearly incorporates both anger and alienation; but, along with the authors I study, I am careful of the various connotations of these terms. With such complex and nuanced representations of madness, this collection of works avoids a simple reversal of value, with madness as a desirable trait, or "more sane than sanity." Neither is madness utilized as an automatic symbol of rebellion. Yes, some of the characters designated as mad do challenge the status quo, questioning especially the norms surrounding race, class, and gender. And the texts certainly explore the creative powers of madness. However, neither the texts nor the characters valorize madness. In some texts, it does signify resistance, in others, just the opposite. In *Wide Sargasso Sea*, Christophine, often a voice of wisdom in the novel, describes her mistress's madness: "They tell her she is mad, they act like she is mad . . . In the end—mad I don't know—she give up."[19] Annette's madness becomes a retreat, a "giving up," indicating that even with roots in resistance madness can shift from solution to problem. In a chapter on three Caribbean novels of madness, Evelyn O'Callaghan writes that as a "defensive strategy [insanity] is ultimately counter-productive as dissociation occurs, and even the 'inner self' is fragmented in madness."[20] In Annette's case, then, madness corrupts the very part of the self that aimed to utilize it as a shield. Thus while madness is often read, even in Rhys's novel, as providing a means of interrogating the hierarchies, assumptions, and values of colonial societies—and in some cases it is this questioning that incurs the label of madness—*Wide Sargasso Sea* also resists such a reading, because in the novel madness is not presented as powerful enough to successfully undermine these aftereffects of colonialism on anything more than a psychological level.

But this form of mental decolonization cannot be overstressed. It is here that representations of madness often serve writers' creative and political ends. For Derek Walcott, it is in art that Caribbean writers "imitate the images of [them]selves."[21] He is speaking of the theater here, but his words could easily be applied to the various forms of literature from the Caribbean. In the "images" conveyed, the actors and the literature are aspiring to portray Caribbean life, not necessarily as it is objectively, but as they imagine it is, as they perceive it to be. The images that they imitate become indicative of their own diagnosis of their community. Thus the schizophrenic quality of West Indian life and the unsuccessful repression of potentially disruptive psychological resistance to colonial conceptions of "natives" become integral parts of the artistic images. We can perhaps think usefully of Brodber's theory of "ancestral anger" here. Walcott's choice of the word *imitate* adds another layer of imagination between the real and the reproduction (in drama or print) of Caribbean life. This term is reminiscent of Jean-Paul Sartre's statement in the preface to Frantz Fanon's *The Wretched of the Earth* that "the same violence is thrown back upon us as when our reflection comes forward to meet us when we go toward a mirror."[22] Although Sartre's "us" is certainly not Walcott's "we," the shift turns on the anger that Brodber describes. In their anger, the colonized will begin to imitate the colonizers' violence. But what happens when the artists begin to imitate themselves, the colonized? For Walcott, part of the artists' work involves a similar violence, that of hurling these imitative reflections back upon society, enabling the artists to meet themselves coming back. The schizophrenia that features in *Dream on Monkey Mountain* and other Caribbean literary works lies in the violence and anger embedded in the split between the real and the reflection.

Not surprisingly, the representations of madness increased as, with the process of political decolonization underway, writers began experimenting with routes to social and mental decolonization. In *The Empire Writes Back*, Bill Ashcroft, Gareth Griffiths, and Helen Tiffin position the growth of postcolonial literature as dependent on not only state sovereignty but also "the appropriation of language and writing for new and distinctive uses."[23] Various terms of insanity became part of this search for new forms of expression as writers contemplated communal neuroses and schizophrenic existences.[24] The writers utilized such terms in their creative and critical works to describe Caribbean cultural and political realities. As politically engaged intellectuals, most of the authors I discuss in *Disturbers of the Peace* have produced significant bodies of theoretical and critical writings about colonialism, independence, and postcolonialism. These texts are invaluable in my reading of the authors' fictional and dramatic works and my situating of their work within contemporary discourses. Erna Brodber's sociological study "Perceptions of Caribbean Women," for example, provides a ground for my reading of her protagonist's madness as occurring in the interstices between her gender, class, and color. Such an approach to Caribbean narratives of madness facilitates an enhanced synergism between fictional texts on madness and critical writings on Caribbean culture and postcolonial identity. Thus reading Édouard Glissant's *Caribbean Discourse* and

Frantz Fanon's brand of anticolonial psychology alongside Naipaul's "sketches" of Trinidadian life or Rhys's revision of *Jane Eyre* clarifies the Caribbean resistance to European pathologizing of colonial behavior.

Relying on work from Fanon and Glissant may seem questionable in a study of anglophone Caribbean literature; but the two devote large sections of their writings to madness in the Caribbean context. To theorize the psychic disorder that colonialism renders, they each grapple with what colonial repression does to the colonized psyche. Both Fanon's study of the mental effects of colonialism and race in *Black Skin, White Masks* and his more scorching attack on colonialism in *The Wretched of the Earth* consider the psychology of oppression. Though the former would seem to be more useful for my study because it is a premier psychoanalytic text, I turn more often to *The Wretched of the Earth*'s focus on nationalism and the building of a national culture, a process in which many of the authors of the texts I study here were highly conscious of participating. Although *The Wretched of the Earth* was written in response to the Algerian fight for independence, I draw parallels to the Caribbean process of decolonization, despite the absence of physical violence there. Glissant's collection of essays in *Caribbean Discourse* (*Le discours antillais*) is, as the title indicates, more concerned with the Caribbean situation. He looks toward a regional consciousness, though writing from a Martinican standpoint. Glissant links madness to language and class through a hierarchical system of what he terms, at various points, mental anguish ("la misère mentale"), delirium ("le délire"), and verbal delirium ("le délire verbal").[25] Glissant's theories are especially useful in considering Naipaul's and Walcott's representations of the charismatic sidewalk preacher who gathers followers with dramatic speeches of new worlds.

In addition to works that focus directly on madness in the Caribbean, I utilize theoretical concepts about the Caribbean in general, throughout the body of the book, and about the Caribbean diaspora in particular, in the epilogue. Fortunately, in five of the six chapters I can turn directly to the authors of the fictional text under consideration for complementary critical material. The notable exception is Jean Rhys, who migrated to England at age seventeen in 1907 and returned to Dominica only once for a brief visit in 1936. Distanced by time and geography, Rhys did not participate in the lively discussions taking place in West Indian intellectual centers—universities, writing circles, conferences—and in regional journals and newspapers. There is, however, evidence that she regularly read newspapers from Dominica and was concerned about political affairs there. Interestingly, she has been included, in absentia, in other writers' engagement with her work. For example, Walcott writes a poem imagining Rhys's life, and Naipaul reviews her novels. There are similar crossings in reviews and literary criticism as the authors become authorities on the emergent Caribbean canon.

Although in chapter 3 I rely on the letters Rhys wrote while working on *Wide Sargasso Sea*, to escape the association of diagnosis of the writers themselves I have generally avoided autobiography.[26] I have also used less formal literary theory than perhaps expected in a book on madness in literature. Taking my cue from other studies of madness, I attempted to utilize psychoanalytic, postmodernist, and poststructuralist schools of theory but found that for my framing of the project and the individual chapters I kept returning to where I began—Caribbean texts. The meshing of madness in Caribbean literature with such schools of thought is possible, however, as evident in Valerie Orlando's francophone-oriented study of madness, *Of Suffocated Hearts and Tortured Souls* (2003). Orlando's focus is on the insertion of a postcolonial representation of madness (she reads both African and Caribbean works) into a larger feminist canon (she concentrates on women writers). Therefore, she relies heavily on European and Euro-feminist theorists; Fanon does, as expected, figure in her readings, but Glissant is conspicuously absent, as are any major anglophone Caribbean theorists.

I approach the topic of madness from a differently located (though not oppositional to Orlando's) position vis-à-vis the spectrum of formal literary and postcolonial theory. In *Disturbers of the Peace*, I situate madness in a Caribbean context, drawing not only on writings on and from the region during the years immediately preceding and following independence but also on work from later years as academics, intellectuals, and cultural critics began to consider the ramifications of independence, themselves often drawing on and responding to formal theories—such as postmodernism, feminism, postcolonialism—that did not adequately address the Caribbean. Antonio Benítez-Rojo's "final comment" in *The Repeating Island*, where he addresses the lure and the lack that constitute his usage of postmodernism, resonates with me as I work to balance this methodological approach. Benítez-Rojo feels, he writes, "the uncertainty that every Caribbean person must feel in trying to write about the Caribbean, especially when suspecting that any chosen rubric is never one's own but rather realizes itself wholly in some alien language, in some ordering code that comes from over *there*."[27] I am less uncertain, less unstable in my readings of these texts when I read them against the rubrics developed in direct theorizations of the Caribbean situation, particularly those concerned with the possibilities of sovereignty. Although his text is also heavily informed by francophone literary examples, Michael Dash's description of his goals in *The Other America* also helps to explain my own methodology here in situating madness within a Caribbean web of tradition. Dash describes "the more generalized all-encompassing theories of Third World culture" as dangerous because they tend to "undervalue what is concrete and specific in Caribbean writing, and in so doing blur the particular ideological and historical circumstances that give rise to ideas, movements and ideologies."[28] While it might be productive to examine how these and other Caribbean texts trouble European, feminist, and general postcolonial theories of madness, my focus here is on madness as part of a Caribbean aesthetic. By focusing on the writers who are trying to determine what "Caribbean" means—primarily during decolonization but also in diaspora—I demonstrate how that meaning dovetails with the representations of madness at this time. In a larger sense, via such a focus I also consider how these representations trouble the "ideas, movements and ideologies" of the independence period.

The Intertextuality of Insanity

Rather than relying on "traditional" readings of madness, which privilege particular ideological formations, my emphasis on Caribbean texts as both primary and secondary sources not only lessens the uncertainty described by Benítez-Rojo but also facilitates the productive intertextuality of madness as a Caribbean literary trope. Dash argues that "the only useful approach to Caribbean literature is an intertextual one." He draws on Glissant's claim that the Caribbean is "a multiple series of relationships" to argue that Caribbean literature itself is "a multiple series of literary relationships."[29] That madness spans ethnic, gendered, and national boundaries implies that this is yet another of the "multiple" defining relationships forming the Caribbean literary canon, drawing together a range of texts and writers whose most visible connection is the Caribbean. Although the increase in the use and exploration of madness is marked in the period surrounding anglophone Caribbean federation and independence, madness does not suddenly become an issue during decolonization. Claude McKay's novel *Banana Bottom*, first published in 1933, provides a good example of an early literary representation of madness that is similar to those I examine here. Kenneth Ramchand, in his study of the West Indian novel, dedicates the last chapter to McKay's work, specifically *Banana Bottom*, because "McKay seems to anticipate patterns in West Indian writing" in several ways, one of which, I would argue, is the pattern of mad characters to come in later texts.[30] Often regarded as McKay's literary "return home," *Banana Bottom* indicates that madness is by no means new to Caribbean texts. A brief look at McKay's novel will help support my claim here and give some indication of my approach to the later texts I study in *Disturbers of the Peace*.

In *Banana Bottom*, madness defines the community but is still included in the community, not (r)ejected. The novel tells the story of Bita Plant's return to Jamaica after seven years of education in England. Many of the characters that reconnect with Bita have their own histories and storylines, rounding out the novel until it resembles the village from which it takes its title. The narrative begins with Bita's first public appearance after her return but shifts suddenly to the event that precipitated her departure to England, when the village madman, Crazy Bow, raped the prepubescent Bita. The rape leads the Craigs, rich missionaries in nearby Jubilee, to take her under their wing, eventually sending her to England. Crazy Bow's crime is crucial to the novel's plot because it initiates the action in *Banana Bottom*; but the description of the rape is set within the community's acceptance of Crazy Bow's "harmless insanity."[31] Crazy Bow is a source of entertainment for the village because of his talent for playing music on many instruments. He is sentenced to the madhouse, but both text and community excuse his actions. Despite the narrator's initial use of the term *rape*, the textual treatment of the rape exculpates Crazy Bow. Mrs. Craig describes Bita as having been "abused" when she first hears of the event; but in relating the happening to her husband, Mrs. Craig likens the happening to the "girls who had been wantonly introduced to the ways of womanhood before maturity." When Malcolm Craig considers the occurrence in the very next paragraph, however, he thinks of it as "the rape of Bita" (17). Even grammatically, Crazy Bow disappears as the perpetrator, while the other characters vacillate on the terms with which to approach the rape. Crazy Bow's mental imbalance is necessary for the commission of his crime and for the dismissal of it for the rest of the novel. The crime itself is only a trigger for the action in the text, not the focus. Therefore, Crazy Bow needs to be somehow pushed to the background, disregarded while the reader focuses on the resulting events. His madness allows the novel to reposition him in this way without diverting any attention from the rest of the narrative.

Ramchand characterizes Crazy Bow, whom he describes innocuously as "the wandering flute boy," as representing the "protest against civilization" evident in McKay's previous works, but here refined so that the protest (and the protesting character) is "neither over-insistent nor . . . central."[32] However, Crazy Bow's very marginality is central to the novel. He is part of the history and the future of Banana Bottom. Although Crazy Bow is "light-headed," the people of Banana Bottom are attached to him. McKay describes the relationship in terms of acceptance and homage of roots: "The village was sentimental about Crazy Bow because of his antecedents." The story of Crazy Bow's great-grandfather as the founder of Banana Bottom is legendary: "Every Banana Bottom child was acquainted with the origin of the Adair family, the story of which had been told from generation to generation. Of that taciturn tradition-breaking European who by one great gesture created Banana Bottom and placed it among the first of independent expatriate-Negro villages" (9). The community's reaction to Crazy Bow is tied up in race, colonialism, and ideas of success.

Crazy Bow himself becomes a legend after he rapes Bita. The villagers compose a song about "the rape of Bita" that, in a reversal of Mr. Craig's and other narratives, centers Crazy Bow and leaves Bita nameless:

> You may wrap her up in silk,
> You may trim her up with gold,
> And the prince may come after
> To ask for your daughter,
> But Crazy Bow was first. (14)

In a practical sense, Crazy Bow is also "first" in the narrative, propelling Bita into her newly possible future. He makes only one more appearance after he "sets up" the plot of the novel. His second and last appearance in the novel positions him as the savior of the community. He appears when the country is experiencing a drought. Because of the drought, the villagers have turned to revivalism to "blow off their emotion whooping and wailing" (233). Crazy Bow appears in the schoolroom, empty but for Bita and Teacher Fearon during choir practice, now deserted for the revival church. Bita does not directly connect Crazy Bow to her past except to think that she "really never felt any resentment towards him at any time." Even Bita, then, accepts Crazy Bow's insanity as pardon. Instead of righteous anger or psychological torment, Bita feels only "a deep sorrow that a human being, a rare artist, should be deprived of the ordinary faculties" and envy at "the magic of his natural genius" for music. Crazy Bow's playing draws the villagers to the schoolroom, making them "happy that the Good Spirit had visited their great musician and brought him home to them" (257). Crazy Bow appears in time to recapture the attention of the villagers. His performance in the schoolroom is described as "his grandest and last in Banana Bottom and it broke the spell of the Revival" (258). Shortly after that performance he is once again put away in the madhouse and conveniently dies there a few weeks later.

In *Language and Literature in Society*, Hugh Duncan concludes that "once we make a person into a pariah, he becomes a possible bearer of evil who may be sacrificed for our purification."[33] Crazy Bow plays this function for Bita, Banana Bottom the village, and *Banana Bottom* the novel. There is no psychological damage from the rape for Bita because it was committed by someone who suffered the psychological damage in her stead. Readers never discover Crazy Bow's name. He is simply referred to by the moniker that the village has given him. He is known only by his insanity and his talent for fiddle playing. He never becomes a character of his own—indeed, he cannot become a multidimensional character because he needs to be dismissed. His raping Bita needs to be simply an unfortunate accident so much so that the other village women, the ones whose sexuality has been "wasted" by their choices in lovers and subsequent childbearing, can look upon Bita and be jealous of her rape. All the families in Banana Bottom wished "one of their children had been in Bita's shoes and had been instead the victim of Crazy Bow" (29). Crazy Bow's madness erases any culpability on his part, shifting the focus from the rape itself to the opportunity it provides for Bita.

For Bita, this opportunity is not only adoption by the Craigs but also education abroad, another topic that would become a recognizable pattern in Caribbean fictions later in the century. Crazy Bow "shot right off the straight line" (5) in school, but schooling is not seen as the cause. Even Bita's discomfort with returning home after a foreign education is not portrayed in the light of later literature from the region, despite the narrator's noting that for a girl to receive this form of foreign education was "unique." Bita's reaction to her education is positive and uncomplicated. When she first visits the market after returning, Bita has a "big moving feeling" in response to being among black Jamaicans again. She thinks "that if she had never gone abroad for a period so long, from which she had become accustomed to viewing her native life in perspective, she might never had had that experience" (40). Any discomfort that Bita may feel, any distance between her new English-educated, English-cultured self, can be easily erased. When she is at Kojo Jeems's tea-meeting, Bita "dance[s], forgetting herself, forgetting even Jubilee, dancing down the barrier between high breeding and common pleasures under her light stamping feet until she [is] one with the crowd" (84). Bita's response is a far cry from the similar situation fifty years later in Erna Brodber's *Jane and Louisa Will Soon Come Home*, in which the protagonist Nellie struggles to "keep her head" at a communal gathering. *Banana Bottom* attacks the airs of upward mobility without attacking education as a means toward it. But essentially, like Brodber's text, it does connect madness to education and social mobility through Crazy Bow.

The connection reaches across the century to the texts in this study and those in the twenty-year period I have chosen not to examine, between Brodber's *Jane and Louisa* and Zadie Smith's *White Teeth*. For example, Olive Senior's 1995 short story "You Think I Mad, Miss?" indicates that the Caribbean writers during this period I overlook also turn to insanity to question their society. The story is told through a series of one-sided conversations between Isabella Francina Myrtella Jones, a street woman living at a busy crossroad in Jamaica, and the various occupants of the cars that pause at the stoplight. By the end of the story, Isabella has told of her nervous breakdown at teacher training college and her subsequent retreat to street living. Her life story, or her version of it, ends in questions about sexuality, madness, religion, and her loss of community. Like *Banana Bottom*, Senior's short story demonstrates that representations of madness in anglophone Caribbean literature are not confined to the periods I consider in the following chapters. For example, the noticeable blossoming of Caribbean women writers at the end of the twentieth century gets little to no attention in my study. Another project, perhaps, could productively examine the ways representations of madness, such as that delineated in Senior's short story, have served different functions for writers like Michelle Cliff, Zee Edgell, or Elizabeth Nunez; but I found it most fruitful in this study of the trope of madness in Caribbean fictions to focus on work published between 1960 and 1980, when Caribbean literature begins to grow more sure of itself.

The chapters in this book follow a chronological order, but the varied uses of madness, from Naipaul to Chariandy, are not to be read as part of a progressive narrative, a teleology of a developing aesthetic. Instead, I examine the following texts as providing different viewpoints on decolonization. Chapter 1 argues that madness is an integral part of how Caribbean literature portrays community in the wake of colonialism. Studies of V. S. Naipaul's oeuvre mention his early publications but often begin in-depth analysis with his third novel, *A House for Mr. Biswas*. I focus on the sketches of *Miguel Street* (1959), which offer not only a preview of Naipaul's later themes and literary concerns but also a commentary on the political and cultural state of affairs in Trinidad at the end of the 1950s. Naipaul is cognizant of a transnational Caribbean community—the members of Miguel Street often migrate to, and return from, surrounding islands—but it is the peculiarities of the Miguel Street residents and their acceptance by other members of the community that enable the cohesiveness of the neighborhood. The *Miguel Street* narrator and his neighbors treat the combined neuroses and psychoses of the residents of Miguel Street as normal and acceptable. In this community, madness is difficult to define because the standards of sanity are not clear. In the microcosm of this street, Naipaul highlights the ways Caribbean communities accept insanity and its forms as part of everyday life. Reading *Miguel Street* through portions of Ralph's writings on madness in *Mimic Men*, I also explore the labeling and categorization inherent in both official and unofficial responses to insanity. The young narrator in *Miguel Street* questions the application of the label *mad* and is concerned that Man-man, the only resident to be incarcerated for insanity, seems more reasonable than some of the other street residents. Naipaul's text demonstrates that what it means to be mad depends on much more than the social demarcation between insanity and sanity, particularly in the colonial power structures present in the Commonwealth Caribbean.

The second chapter of *Disturbers of the Peace* examines the anxieties of the independence moment in Jamaica. Although published in 1962, the year Jamaica achieved independence, Sylvia Wynter's *The Hills of Hebron* is set in the early part of the twentieth century, during the labor strikes of the 1930s. I read Wynter's turn to a previous revolutionary moment in Jamaica's history as the foundation for the national allegory she creates in her novel. The developmental stages of Moses Barton's religious followers as they move from cult to community address the avenues through which the new nation could exist and grow. Using selected readings from Wynter's large body of theoretical writings, I argue that in her work madness is positioned as a positive space from which to imagine new forms of leadership in postcolonial Caribbean society. Wynter's inclusion of three mad characters offers the opportunity to examine the function of gender in the community's treatment of madness and its connection to leadership. In *The Hills of Hebron*, Wynter anticipates Michelle Cliff's later theory that "it must have meant something that all those mad were women. The men were called idiots (an accident of birth); or drunks. The women's madness was ascribed to several causes:

childlessness, celibacy, 'change': such was the nature of their native science."[34] In the third section of chapter 2 I explore how Wynter, often castigated as antifeminist, undermines this gendered stereotype of madness.

Chapter 3 examines Caribbean culture's definitions of, and formation by, madness in Jean Rhys's *Wide Sargasso Sea* (1966), a re-visioning of Charlotte Brontë's *Jane Eyre*. Rhys's protagonist, Antoinette, is uncertain of her position in Jamaican society because of her class and color. Unable to position herself convincingly as English or Caribbean, white or black, she can rely on neither culture to ground her when faced with traumatic events. In contrast to Wynter's characters, Rhys's Antoinette descends into a madness that is unproductive on both the individual and the communal level. Although Rhys's earlier novels and some of her short stories incorporate madness and debilitating depression, *Wide Sargasso Sea* is her only full-length treatment of a character's mental breakdown. Rhys's negative portrayal of Antoinette's isolation and mental illness offers a salient condemnation of colonialism's effects on all parties. Rhys avoids the one-dimensional portrayal of madness evident in *Jane Eyre* by switching narrative perspective unexpectedly and often. The closing section of the novel, though short, has multiple narrators and includes dream sequences, underscoring the intimate connection between representations of dreams and madness. Rhys's attempt to delineate the interiority of madness, particularly in this last scene, produces a radical deviation from then current novelistic conventions.

The link between dreams and madness, as well as their influence on literary form, is also the subject of chapter 4. Derek Walcott's *Dream on Monkey Mountain* emphasizes the connections between possible madness and ambiguous dreams in what Walcott terms the "given minds of the principal characters."[35] The mind becomes the connection between dreams and madness because it can envision change—in dreams; but it can also distort visions—in madness. Makak, the main character, praises the power of the mind to create different worlds; but he fails to recognize that he, unlike the play, cannot bridge these worlds. Walcott takes full advantage of the dramatic form to explore the political dimensions of both madness and dream, creating a doubled division for his characters and audience between fantasy and reality, madness and sanity. Walcott's choice of the theater, rather than poetry, engenders a collective response to, and responsibility for, envisioning a postcolonial West Indian community. Although *Dream on Monkey Mountain* was first produced in 1967, Walcott began writing the play ten years earlier. During this time, Walcott shuttled between St. Lucia (his homeland),

Jamaica, Trinidad, and Barbados; he also spent time in New York and Canada. From Fanon to Haile Selassie, and from Japanese Noh drama to the Black Power movement in the United States, the play combines various influences with the representation of dreams and madness to stage visions of Caribbean unity.

The difficulty of representing madness within standard generic divisions—as manifested in Rhys and Walcott—is emphasized in Erna Brodber's *Jane and Louisa Will Soon Come Home*, the primary text in chapter 5. The years between Wynter's novel and Brodber's text saw many changes in Jamaica and the surrounding region, including a wider availability of education to Jamaica's poor and underprivileged population. In a sociological overview of Jamaica since independence, Brodber writes, "It was through education, though, that the greatest number was able to move to a higher status. That this has been the major route to social mobility has had particular consequences on the culture."[36] She examines these "consequences" in *Jane and Louisa Will Soon Come Home*, in which the explicit Jamaican distrust of an overemphasis on academics and studying blends with an implicit skepticism about the Eurocentric curriculum and is articulated in the protagonist's spiraling accounts of her formal education and social interactions. Brodber's training and work in sociology and psychology complicate the generic categorization of the text, which she has described as a "fictional case study." In interviews, Brodber refers to her main character as an example of a "dissociated identity," but she never utilizes such diagnostic terms in her text. The protagonist narrates her own story and is never marked as mad in the novel. Thus this chapter addresses not only the commonly recognized difficulty of describing madness with "the language of reason" and within generic literary boundaries but also the difficulty of writing madness in the first person.

Chapter 5 closes my readings of mid-twentieth-century texts, but neither the independence process nor representations of madness end there (with St. Kitts and Nevis being the last British colony to gain official independence in 1983). Jamaica and Trinidad have, after all, been independent for only approximately fifty years. Therefore, any attempt to present a limited or closed period of decolonization must be seen as arbitrary; the "stark-ravin'" madness in literary representations of independent Caribbean life cannot be safely confined to the "Yesterday" of Keens-Douglas's poetic speaker. My epilogue turns to a consideration of this continuity in the twenty-first century by focusing on three recent first novels by writers from the ever-growing Caribbean diaspora—Zadie

Smith, Marie-Elena John, and David Chariandy. Smith's *White Teeth* (2000) plays on the link between madness and immigration in England—the ways madness in one character can recognize and reach out to variant forms of madness in others, just as immigrants recognize and cling to each other in the metropolis. With its focus on both Caribbean and Indian immigrants in England, *White Teeth* utilizes madness to theorize connections between the two communities. Smith's disembodied narrator offers periodic meditations on insanity as the proper metaphor for postcolonial life in the former motherland. In contrast, Marie-Elena John is concerned with a more overt representation of madness in *Unburnable* (2006), a novel set primarily in Dominica. Like Naipaul in *Miguel Street*, John questions the too easily assigned title of "mad," particularly as it pertains to women, and in a revision of Rhys's *Wide Sargasso Sea*, John's novel explores madness as an inherited method of self-preservation. The perspective here, however, is from the United States, since the protagonists must divest themselves of their American and Americanized ideas of the African diaspora as they encounter (and enact) strategic uses, acceptance, and diagnoses of abnormal behavior. Of the three turn-of-the-century novels I examine in this chapter, *Soucouyant* (2007) by David Chariandy offers perhaps the most literal portrayal of madness. Chariandy utilizes the instability of presenile dementia to explore the fragility of personal and cultural memory for immigrants, particularly Caribbean immigrants in Canada. Dementia, however, interferes with the efficacy of forgetting as a coping strategy, making the sufferer and those around her sometimes "forget to forget." I close with these novels, outside the period of anglophone independence examined for most of *Disturbers of the Peace*, to indicate that representations of madness continue to serve as powerful creative and critical tools in Caribbean literature, which itself continues to engage with the aftereffects of colonization even as it foregrounds new concerns.

The strands that thread these chapters together are varied, but they surround the core questions of representing a Caribbean in the process of decolonization. The texts I examine closely in *Disturbers of the Peace* are exemplary rather than constitutive of my argument. It is never possible to be exhaustive in such a study, and several other texts may come to mind concerning mad characters in Caribbean fictions. Indeed, it is the sheer inescapable profusion of such examples that motivates my project, leading me to question not only their quantity and variety but also their purpose. In other words, the wealth of literary examples moved me to seek to determine how Caribbean writers mobilize representations and rhetorics of madness to reflect, and reflect on, their worlds during the upheaval of independence. My selections represent the breadth of these worlds while working within the relatively narrow chronological boundary of political independence and avoiding critical redundancies. Of the texts I have chosen to examine in answering the questions raised by the proliferation of the trope of madness in Caribbean literature, some—like *Wide Sargasso Sea* and *Dream on Monkey Mountain*—may be recognizable as keystones in any discussion of madness in Caribbean literature; others I single out for attention because of the ways they illuminate connections between representations of madness and various elements of the discourses of independence in the anglophone Caribbean. In this period of seemingly immense and immediate changes, concepts such as gender, community, nation, and race were in flux, or promised to be so, and the shifting presences of mad characters—in their respective texts and in the Caribbean literary canon at large—present one method of weaving together creative, critical, and theoretical commentaries on these concepts. While these specifics of chronological and conceptual framing have shaped my textual choices (along with, of course, some measure of personal aesthetic preferences), my hope is that the broader tenets of my argument about these multiple iterations of madness will influence future critical readings of Caribbean texts, particularly those texts that turn to the trope of madness to represent the peculiar preoccupations of the region and, now, its diasporas.

1 Manias and Messiahs

Man-man and the Madness of *Miguel Street*

In a reverse of the traditional scholarship route, in 1960 V. S. Naipaul returned to Trinidad from England on a three-month government-sponsored scholarship. The stipulated three months stretched beyond a year as Naipaul, at the suggestion of then premier Eric Williams, undertook the project of a book-length essay on the Caribbean. The resulting publication, *The Middle Passage*, chronicles Naipaul's visits to five Caribbean countries: Trinidad, British Guiana, Surinam, Martinique, and Jamaica. It begins, however, with a recounting of his voyage (via ship) from England to Trinidad, and some of the narrative in the first chapter concerns the madmen on board. First, there are the two men who are so deranged as to require keepers; they are mostly kept hidden and thus are the subjects of conversation rather than observation. The two men are black—in the specific racial terminology of the Caribbean—and are being returned to their islands with white guardians, all paid for by the British government. An elderly eccentric black woman and a "tall, handsome Negro [who] had had some mental trouble in England" are also being returned to the West Indies at England's expense.[1] This last character provides some excitement for the passengers when the ship arrives in the West Indies and begins making stops at various islands. On these stops, the ship takes on passengers for its return trip to England, mixing those few passengers "cruising" the Caribbean or returning to an island later on the itinerary with the new emigrants. This mixing requires the erection of physical barriers to enforce the class divides on the ship, barriers that were previously ignored. The "tall, handsome Negro," who has been used to strolling the decks for hours, creates a scene by breaking the newly erected barriers. Several crew members attempt to re-erect the barriers, only to have the man break them again. Ultimately, a loud commotion brings the various passengers to watch as he "walk[s] measuredly round the deck, breaking barriers, his calm stride unrelated to his hysterical words, which carr[y] across the ship."[2] The man is eventually subdued with an injection and caged below, presumably where the black madmen are being stowed. Thus begins Naipaul's return journey to the Caribbean, where the rigid hierarchies of race and class were palpably colonial at the very time the region was moving toward self-rule. As evident even in the microcosm of the ship's "society," resistance to these hierarchies was frequently performative and marked as mad.

In the book, Naipaul later judges his representation of such resistance to be "romantic about the healing power, in such a culture, of political or racial assertion," though *The Middle Passage* is more often than not read as presenting a pessimistic perspective of the region.[3] Taken as a whole, the book is an uneven mixture of Naipaul's initial "romantic" optimism with his persistent criticism about Trinidad and the Caribbean. This contradictory combination also underlies his early fictional work. In this chapter, I examine the connections between this ambivalent view of a soon-to-be-sovereign Caribbean and Naipaul's representations of resistance as minor neurotic manifestations and outright "mental trouble" in *Miguel Street*. It may seem strange to begin my exploration of representations of insanity in Caribbean literature with *Miguel Street*, because of both the author's reputation and the text's disrepute. In his Nobel Prize biography, V. S. Naipaul's country is listed as Great Britain, although his birthplace is noted as Trinidad. He is both praised and excoriated as a writer from everywhere and from nowhere. Derek Walcott writes in a 1987 review of Naipaul: "Despite his horror of being claimed, we West Indians are proud of Naipaul, and that is his enigmatic fate as well, that he should be so cherished by those he despises."[4] I find Walcott's approach useful, even decades later, since it allows for a "claiming" of Naipaul for the Caribbean literary canon without undecidable debates about subject or subject position.

At the time Naipaul published *Miguel Street*, however, these debates were not yet heated. As Naipaul continued to produce an unusually large body of work, critics began to separate his writings into phases, and Naipaul himself began to speak of his work in these terms. In a 1974 interview with Ian Hamilton, Naipaul describes his early work as concerned with a "great sense of the oddity of people."[5] Elsewhere, in an article on Joseph Conrad, Naipaul writes that at the beginning of his own writing career he was preoccupied with "the new politics, the curious reliance of men on institutions they were yet working to undermine, the simplicity of beliefs and the hideous simplicity of actions, the corruption of causes, half-made societies that seemed doomed to remain half-made."[6] As part of this early phase of Naipaul's work, a phase primarily concerned with Trinidad and the West Indies, *Miguel Street*, much like *The Middle Passage* after it, exhibits these preoccupations with the uncertainties—and sometimes the absurdities—of the "new politics" in the West Indies. In the Trinidad chapter of *The Middle Passage*, Naipaul writes, "It was a place where the stories were never stories of success but of failure: brilliant men, scholarship winners, who had died young, gone mad, or taken to drink."[7] In the fictional form of *Miguel Street*, however, some "failures," particularly those related to madness, become detours rather than permanent derailment. In this collection, the stories of characters such as Man-man and Laura question European models of success and sanity.

Like many early works by Caribbean writers, particularly those of the preindependence period, *Miguel Street* is semiautobiographical; it portrays the residents of Miguel Street in Port of Spain, Trinidad. The narrator, who corresponds to a postmigratory Naipaul, often self-consciously switches between an adolescent perspective and more mature reflections in this collection of what he terms "sketches."[8] He has his own sketch at the end of the text but plays a part in many of the previous sketches. Though mostly limited to the actions of Miguel Street, his narrative provides an overview of the "oddity" of the people, politics, interests, and causes of Trinidad at the time. The young narrator of *Miguel Street* questions the application of the label *mad* by both outsiders and residents of the street; his questioning implies the difficulty of utilizing external standards of behavior—particularly European standards of behavior—as a measure of sanity. Given the tolerance of a variety of aberrant behaviors by the residents of Miguel Street, what is the utility of the term *mad* in both this location and this historical moment?

In this chapter, I also examine the connection between madness and the portrayal of these daily existences and resistances in *Miguel Street*. The various innovations Naipaul uses in *Miguel Street* converge to form a complex portrait of a Trinidadian community on the cusp of independence. An understanding of Naipaul's use of form in the text allows for a reading of the cultural implications for madness at this time. Although my main focus for this chapter is *Miguel Street*, my reading is heavily informed by later Naipaul texts, principally his 1966 novel *The Mimic Men*, which is particularly helpful because the reflective form of its narrative provides a broader view of the cultural and historical place of madness in Trinidad. Though the perspectives differ in class and genre, both *The Mimic Men* and *Miguel Street* are set within overlapping time periods, and both exhibit Naipaul's ambiguous appreciation of history and order, place and displacement.[9]

In *Mimic Men*, Naipaul returns to a character type introduced in *Miguel Street*—a religious leader who springs from an uncertain background. This leader, father of the first-person narrator Ralph Singh, takes the name Gurudeva after he suddenly converts to preaching. On his way to work on a seemingly typical day, he begins talking to striking dockworkers, and he ends the day by leading them into the hills to wreak havoc on the forests in protest of their situation. Prior to this conversion, Gurudeva twice shows evidence of madness. In the first episode, he breaks soda bottles in a village shop during an angry response to his son's minute act of indifference toward him. Afterward, he receives respect from his neighbors, particularly the "idlers" of the town, because although "no one had anything against the shopkeeper," he "was rich and the idlers were poor and were glad to see how easily the rich could be made ridiculous." Watching his father encourage the growth of this notoriety, Ralph concludes, "Madness, but there was method in it, even if the method came afterwards."[10] Ralph realizes that madness serves a purpose, especially in a community that respects the anger that it represents.

The similarities between *Mimic Men*'s Gurudeva and *Miguel Street*'s Man-man are striking, and Ralph's meditations on madness and his attempts to contextualize his father's actions are valuable for a reading of the representation of madness in *Miguel Street*. As I indicated briefly in my introduction, the reflective form of *Mimic Men* provides passages on the relationship between madness and the shift from colonization to independence. For instance, Ralph questions whether the success of his father's movement is due to a "quality in the man, or a quality of the time."[11] To narrow the question even further to the specific man and time: Does Gurudeva succeed because of his own charisma, or because his message coincides with the dock strike? Impossible to decide, as in the end the two are inextricable. But even without a definitive answer, the question itself is an indicator that understanding madness, or what becomes labeled as madness, requires a consideration of the "quality of the time." The historical context of the madness represented in both *Mimic Men* and *Miguel Street* is as important as the "quality" of each character. Additionally, the relationship between the two is reflexive:

that is, not only does the historical context tell us something about the character's madness, but the specificities of the character's madness also reveal the tensions of the historical moment.

Although *Miguel Street* is the third major work published by Naipaul, it was the first that he began writing. It was published in 1959 and is set within the preindependence moment in Trinidad, fraught with tensions between US occupation, English social control, and early attempts at West Indian sovereignty. The crossroads of these tensions is often found in the Americanization of the Caribbean. According to Karl Miller, much of Naipaul's later work is "neatly prefigured" in his concern with the world introduced by American advertisements and packaging in his first two novels.[12] And in *The Middle Passage*, Naipaul highlights the negative effects of American technological and cultural intrusion in Trinidad. In *Miguel Street*, Naipaul explores the effects of the war, American occupation, colonialism, and decolonization as both background to and integral aspects of the characters' lives. The variety of eccentric behaviors and neurotic compulsions exhibited by the featured residents make evident the peculiar nature of a Trinidad caught between the American and British empires. Man-man—the designated madman of the street—most vividly reflects the complexities and confusion of these years. In the latter half of this chapter I look at how, with the context of a street full of "odd" characters, the performative and political nature of Man-man's madness foregrounds the instability of a Caribbean at the threshold of a desired yet undetermined future.

History and Order, Time and Place

Miguel Street, published as it was just prior to the official beginning of independence in the anglophone Caribbean, provides the opportunity to examine the literary effects of madness in a narrative not yet colored by the reality of sovereignty. This is not to say that there is no anticipation of autonomy from Great Britain in the collection; one of Man-man's religious speeches concerns this prospect. Man-man's admonishment to his audience to ignore "all the politicians and them talking about making the island self-sufficient" indicates that the discourse of self-rule was certainly in circulation during this time (51). Hayden Williams, who describes *Miguel Street* as a "singularly poignant, painful and disturbing" comedy, finds that "it is not [by] accident that the time depicted is the Second World War, a war that not only brought the United States Army into the West Indies with fateful results, but foretold the traumatic transformation of the 1950s when the islands ceased to be colonies of Great Britain and became independent countries."[13] As part of their response to this political situation, the residents of Miguel Street oppose colonial labels of pathology by accepting behaviors such as pyromania and compulsive repetition as customary. In a line deleted from the published version of Man-man's sketch, the narrator speaks to this familiarity with and acceptance of such actions: "I suppose that many people will think that this habit of Man-man's was a little unusual, but I never thought so, I was too used to it."[14] Thus Naipaul sketches a community of characters who accept each other's peculiarities as part of their everyday lives. Laura's addiction to sex and mothering and Morgan's creative pyromania are placed alongside Man-man's compulsive repetition and Messiah complex as simply their responses to their colonial situation in Trinidad, as their way of ordering their lives.

This collection of stories has received little attention, and less respect, from literary critics. Very few articles, including early writings on Naipaul's work, pay more than superficial attention to *Miguel Street*. Even anthologies and book-length studies of Naipaul and his work grant only a few pages to *Miguel Street*, often in conjunction with *The Mystic Masseur* and *The Suffrage of Elvira*. The few articles that focus solely on *Miguel Street* do recognize its complexities; but those critical texts that mention it briefly often do so disparagingly. In a 1966 review of Naipaul's first five novels, for instance, R. H. Lee describes *Miguel Street* as one of the two "least impressive" of Naipaul's five novels: "The book lacks a developing narrative, and succumbs to bittiness, and to the creations of weird and eccentric characters simply to populate the street, and hold the reader's attention by their weirdness and eccentricity alone."[15] But it is this very collection of characters that makes *Miguel Street* so ripe for exploration. Naipaul showcases a variety of responses to life in a colonial island on the brink of becoming independent. In *Mimic Men*, his interest in such responses to the prospect, and further the reality, of independence continues; but it occurs at the level of people who have some power in this discussion. *Miguel Street* shows the portion of the population that can only respond to the actions of people in power, not initiate the action themselves.

To return to the scene set on Naipaul's sea voyage from England to Trinidad in the first chapter of *The Middle Passage*, the Miguel Street residents are like people on the margins of the class barriers: allowed to see the privilege and power from which they are barred, often encouraged to work toward attaining it themselves, but always physically removed from it. *Miguel Street* presents stories of various responses to this social system: B. Wordsworth retreats to a melancholy life of poetry; Elias makes repetitively futile attempts to do so well on his exams that "Mr. Cambridge go bawl when he read what I write for him" (29); Morgan stages small flashes of rebellion to assert his humanity; and Man-man attempts to break the barriers altogether, first via politics then via religion. Such characters are often defeated by the system when they attempt to work within it and are disregarded (or, in Man-man's case, detained) as delusional when they rail against it. But even when there is some success, the residents remain inhibited by their position in this colonial society dependent on England for definitions of social worth.

In *Miguel Street*, Naipaul exhibits a subtle attention to the problems of a colonial class system, particularly as it manifests in an urban setting, which involves more layers of social standing. Given Miguel Street's location in Port of Spain, the peculiarities of the characters are part of their lives in the city. The narrator's distinction between his life in Chaguanas and his life in Miguel Street is clear in the sketch "Titus Hoyt, I.A." He is awed by his first ride on a city bus and gets lost without his mother's guidance. Although there is not much money in Miguel Street, there is evidence that it is not the poorest neighborhood in the city. When Laura begins living with Nathaniel, the men of the street look down on Nathaniel because he is from another part of the city. The narrator describes Nathaniel as from "the east end of Port of Spain, which we considered dirtier; and his language was really coarse" (110). So there are other places in urban Trinidad that the people of Miguel Street consider themselves above. Even in Miguel Street itself, however, there are indicators of class. Some of the boys have access to education while others do not. Mary, "the Chinese," can afford better treatment for her children than Laura because Mary's husband is part of the household and owns a shop. Within her own neighborhood, Laura has an example of how she should be treating her children and living her life. This type of pressure about what one should be doing is also a large part of city living and can, as suggested in "Titus Hoyt, I.A.," send city dwellers "off their heads." The opportunities available just beyond those class barriers, and the close contact with people who have achieved relative success, can lead to madness—as Naipaul also indicates in *The Middle Passage*—or to giving up. The latter option is Elias's approach to the obstacles to his ambitions of escaping Miguel Street and becoming a doctor. Elias has test-taking nerves, or perhaps he is just not as smart as the self-educated Titus Hoyt believes he is; in either case, he is incapable of passing an exam. Elias continually lowers his goals from doctor, to sanitary inspector, until he becomes one of the "aristocrats of the street," that is, a cart driver.

The futility of Elias's and other residents' efforts, though always related in the ironic-comedic form of the narrative, reaffirms even as it resists the social order. This results in a mix of humor and pathos (similar to that praised in Naipaul's eminently popular *A House for Mr. Biswas*) that works in *Miguel Street* to underscore the instability and insanity of living in a small place on the edge of nominal independence. In many of his early texts, Naipaul repeatedly returns to this implacable social order, particularly in connection to history. In *Mimic Men*, for example, Ralph considers his father's madness as part of an "eccentric lower-class movement" that was relatively common at that time in the Caribbean. Ralph's reflections on the popularity of his father's movement involve social, historical, and psychological analysis. On the individual and social level, he views "these religious excesses, still an aspect of the tourist quaintness of the islands, as an attempt to deny the general shipwreck."[16] Ralph often resorts to the term *shipwreck* to indicate the external colonial order and the internal psychic disorder that is inevitable given Isabella's colonial history. His use of *shipwreck* is reminiscent of Derek Walcott's own focus on history, literature, and form in his essay "The Muse of History." Walcott writes that "to most writers of the archipelago who contemplate only the shipwreck, the New World offers not elation but cynicism, a despair at the vices of the Old which they feel must be repeated."[17] In both *Mimic Men* and *Miguel Street*, it would seem that Naipaul offers "contemplation" through his narrators and "denial" through characters such as Gurudeva and Man-man. But this is too simple a conclusion. The narrators' own subject positions are questionable; in their narratives (and *by* their narratives) they question the subjectivity of written history. They create their own order, even as they seem to be only relating the chaos of the shipwreck.

The apparent "disorder" of *Miguel Street*, which critics sometimes disdain, results from approaching it as a novel, as, in Naipaul's words, "one particular thing."[18] This tendency to read the collection as a novel springs not only from the popularity of the form but also from the network of obvious and subtle bridges between the sketches in *Miguel Street*. There is a loosely chronologically developing narrative, sometimes flashing back to explain the way things were before the event that the narrator wishes to focus on. The sketches are intricately connected to each other, representing the complex relationships among neighbors and countrymen. As with the place they reflect, the stories seem fragmented but are linked through a common present and a common history. The communal web Naipaul weaves between the sketches in *Miguel Street* recalls the oft-quoted lines from Derek Walcott—"The sea is history"—and Kamau Brathwaite—"The unity is submarine"—that are used to describe the larger web of connections (geographical, social, cultural, historical) between Caribbean islands and people.[19]

The form of *Miguel Street* exemplifies the community it represents. The sketches are individual, with their own titles and miniplots. They could easily be anthologized as stand-alone short stories, but they are clearly related to each other, despite these relationships occurring on different registers. On a simple, surface level, the repeating characters and the narrator who remains the same (though growing into adolescence as the sketches progress) draw the individual stories together. But some connections are less evident during an initial reading. For instance, many of the sketches in *Miguel Street* begin with a statement about something that appears to be eternal. "Bogart," the first sketch of the collection, begins, "Every morning when he got up Hat would sit on the back verandah and shout across, 'What happening there, Bogart?' Bogart would turn in his bed and mumble softly, so that no one heard, 'What happening there, Hat?'" (9). As the rest of the sketch, and the rest of the text, show, such seemingly eternal routines can and do change. When Bogart disappears for the first time, the narrator sadly recognizes that "something which had appeared unalterable was missing" (11). Indeed, each sketch details the ways that these heretofore "unalterable" personalities, relationships, and interactions change over time, sometimes suddenly and without warning. Most of the sketches begin with a similar description of how things have always been, or have been every day for the narrator. Even the beggars are predictable—they appear on specific days with routine requests. From a very sure beginning, however, each story becomes more uncertain: the idle Popo becomes an earnest contributor to his household, the promising student Elias becomes a cart driver, and Laura loses her ever-present smile. The last sketch, of the narrator leaving Trinidad, reads as the culmination of these unexpected changes to the customs of life in Miguel Street. For the most part, such changes are noticeable only to the community and therefore not challenging in any way to the larger social system. Order remains in place, always the preordained result of any seeming alteration, just as the narrator's eventual migration is imperative to his telling any story.

Throughout the sketches, however, the young narrator laments any change because he finds comfort in sameness. When Popo returns to being his old, jovial self after reconciling with his wife, the narrator is happy to see him repeating his daily rum ritual on the sidewalk in the morning: "It was good to ask him again, 'What you making, Mr. Popo?' and to get the old answer, 'Ha, boy! That's the question. I making the thing without a name'" (23). The narrator's comfort resides not so much in the absence of change as in the repetition of old conversations, in knowing the answer before asking the question, in returning to rituals that seem "unalterable." Hat, who functions as a secondary narrator, feels that people must be mad "if they do the same thing so many times" (46). Here Hat describes two citizens who vote for Man-man (an impossible political candidate) in every election, but his diagnosis applies to many of the residents of Miguel Street (including the narrator) who daily repeat actions that seem meaningless. Even Hat relies on this repetition. When Bogart disappears, Hat wakes to repeat the ritual the following morning, but realizes there is no one to answer him. In his disappointment, "he milked the cows earlier than usual that morning and the cows didn't like it" (11). Even as he deems seemingly useless repetition mad, Hat himself is vexed when the choice is taken away from him.

Naipaul writes later in *The Middle Passage* that "neuroses afflict communities as well as individuals," particularly when there is the need for a resistive development of a "psychology of survival."[20] We may read back from this assertion to interpret the communal reliance on repetition in *Miguel Street* as part of a psychology of survival in the face of inscrutable yet pervasive influence of colonialism on the very details of their lives. In *Le discours antillais*, Édouard Glissant connects such repetition and routinism to resistance in a section on madness in the Martinican setting. Glissant's theories of "delirium" as a reaction to the untenable colonial situation help explicate the aptness of the form of *Miguel Street* for the madness of its characters: "The analysis of what I am calling mental anguish shows that its most obvious manifestations are not to be found in the pathological or the delirious, but in the texture of daily existence" (L'analyse de ce que j'appelle misère mentale montre que les manifestations les plus évidentes n'en sont pas données dans le pathologique ni le délirant, mais dans la texture même de l'existence quotidienne). Glissant then introduces the term *delirium*, which I am equating here with *madness* as I use the term. He makes a crucial distinction between "mental anguish" and "delirium": "'Delirium' is a form of resistance to mental anguish" (Le "délire" est une forme de résistance à la misère mentale).[21]

Madness becomes a method of managing the mental anguish that exists at every turn in colonial society. The *Miguel Street* sketches are snapshots of these daily existences, each repeating their own forms of resistance to mental anguish.

As in *Miguel Street*, both the form and the content of *Mimic Men* represent such repetition. In *Mimic Men* the narrative circles and repeats, spiraling toward the end, which is really only a repeated beginning. By the end of the novel, Ralph has, in essence, repeated his father's cycle and now has to decide whether to begin the cycle again or repeat the recluse stage in perpetuity. The text is narrated by one who has returned "from the brink." Ralph has been touched by madness both as the son of a madman and as a mad, frenzied wanderer himself. When describing his own brush with fame through politics, Ralph writes, "It has happened in twenty places, twenty countries, islands, colonies, territories—these words with which we play, thinking they are interchangeable and that the use of a particular one alters the truth. I cannot see our predicament as unique."[22] Ralph's party's socialism is as repetitive as the actions of Miguel Street, albeit on a larger scale. As the title *Mimic Men* indicates, the pattern is that of repetition: the changes that exist are only the mimicry of previous politics, a mimicry repeated throughout various "countries, islands, colonies, territories." The colonial ideology is now represented by brown faces, but beneath the flurries of official change lies the same structural system that Gurudeva railed against. Naipaul does not position change in opposition to repetition. In *Mimic Men*, change is only the return of previous governments in different guise and under different names. But for the characters of *Miguel Street*, the repetition lurks in the daily expectation of yesterday's pattern, in the near-obsessive dependence on a sameness that lacks sense beyond the illusion of autonomy.

The repetition of calypsos throughout *Miguel Street* is another subtle but equally insistent connective thread forming the variety of voices in the stories into a cohesive collection. John Thieme, who counts quotations of at least ten calypsos in *Miguel Street*, finds that the calypsos employed in the text "help to lend unity to what may initially appear to be no more than a number of very loosely related accounts of the lives of the street's inhabitants."[23] The calypsos, as part of the ordered disorder of *Miguel Street*, become part of the innovation of this text that is midway between a collection of short stories and a novel. Both the *Miguel Street* sketches and the quoted calypsos are short commentaries on the state of life for the working class in Trinidad in the 1950s. The two major changes in the island—Americanization and the move toward independence—are evident in both the calypsos of the time and the stories of *Miguel Street.* The characters' desperate attempts to escape these upheavals are often summed up with snatches of calypso lyrics—Mrs. Hereira is subject to "love, love, love alone"; Eddoes's delight at claiming a baby girl as his daughter is ridiculed with the lines, "Chinese children calling me Daddy! / Oh God, somebody putting milk in my coffee" (127); and Edward, Hat's brother, is taunted by the lines, "I was living with my decent and contented wife / Until the soldiers came and broke up my life" (185). Gordon Rohlehr describes the calypso in *Miguel Street* as possibly "a sign of the pathological insensitivity of the Trinidad people," thereby making even the songs part of the madness of the text and its time.[24]

Miguel Street also reflects a schizophrenic tension in its use of the calypso. The narrator's proper English and analytic hindsight seem opposed to the casual and playful lyrics. The calypso functions as a linguistic foil for the narrator; it offers another way of knowing, another way of labeling, and another way of interpreting events and people.[25] This approach is especially helpful in providing different fictional perspectives of madness, with the residents as both agents and observers of the daily insanity. A similar formal fragmentation is also evident in the difference between the dialogue of the characters and the narrative. "B. Wordsworth," the sketch with perhaps the fewest characters, provides the clearest evidence of this disparity. When Wordsworth first shows up at the narrator's house, the narrator's mother grants his request to watch her bees, but as the narrator remembers, "His English was so good it didn't sound natural, and I could see my mother was worried" (57). She instructs the narrator to stay and watch Wordsworth while he watches the bees. This dual watching is mirrored in the dual "good" English. The narrator's own voice, in contrast with the remembered dialogue from his youth, is as "proper" as B. Wordsworth's language. This is the only story in which the boy has so major a part in the events, so readers confront an extended juxtaposition of the boy's past dialogue with the man he has become. The boy has become the poet that Wordsworth predicted. Reading this sketch, Garth St. Omer states, "On the one side, and in the earlier time, there is Wordsworth who, for all his correctness of language, is reduced to panhandling on the island; on the other, the narrative, written at a later time, testifies to the success, in another environment of that boy now grown up and himself a 'poet.'" He concludes that the sketch "makes a comment on the inability of the local environment to allow for literary achievement."[26] But the achievement may not conform to the standards that St. Omer is applying. The lyricism and inventiveness of both the quoted calypsos and the dialogue achieve an effective alternative commentary throughout the sketches. As he writes in *The Middle Passage*, Naipaul considers the calypso as one of the few artistic forms "native" to Trinidad. *Miguel Street*, patterned as it is on the calypso, is not therefore as pessimistic about Caribbean culture as it may seem. Despite remaining unfulfilled, the promise held out by figures such as Man-man and Gurudeva for the possibility of revolt represents an optimistic, albeit incomplete, move on Naipaul's part in his early work.

Glissant's revaluation of madness in *Le discours antillais* also provides a means of viewing madness as creative resistance in the sketches of *Miguel Street*. In both works, generally pathologized disorders, such as compulsive repetition and religious mania, are contextualized as part of a larger system of madness. Naipaul's representation of the "mad" preacher in *Miguel Street*—and similar representations in other works of Caribbean literature, including Naipaul's own return to this figure in *Mimic Men*—troubles the easy separation of Man-man as the madman of the street from the implicit categorization of the other *Miguel Street* characters as sane. The advantages of such literary perspectives are implied in one of Ralph's passages about Gurudeva. In his retrospective on the information available about his father's leadership, Ralph writes, "The monographs tell accurately enough of the rise and withering-away of the movement; they describe its occasionally frightening ritual. But like so many sociological studies, they leave the mystery as mystery; they explain nothing." He also disparages history's treatment of his father's movement; it is inadequate because it recorded the movement as "just another part of a recognizable pattern of events in one region of the world."[27] Thus both the historian and the sociologist are ill equipped to examine the deeper meaning of, or reasons for, his father's movement. They cannot plumb the mysteries of his success. Perhaps only the writer, the creative writer, can successfully address the mystery. Despite the sometimes comedic and ironic results, Naipaul's continuous return to the figure of the Messiah/religious leader/politician in works such as *The Mystic Masseur*, *Miguel Street*, and *Mimic Men* evidences his attempt to fathom the meaning behind this mystery and its implications for those who consider themselves sane.

Man-man: Medium, Messiah, Madman?

In *Miguel Street*, the first-person narrator is made imaginatively omniscient with help from other regular commentators (and, arguably, by the repetitive usage of calypso lyrics). Hat performs one of these running commentator roles. He, alongside the young male narrator and perhaps the boy's mother, is the most frequent character in the sketches. His constant presence has the additional effect of strengthening the connection between the sketches in *Miguel Street*. John Thieme sees Hat as having a "choric role," providing "the voice of experience which frequently acts as a foil to the boy's ingenuous reaction to events."[28] Hat is seemingly the most adjusted "character" on Miguel Street. He knows how to straddle the line between make-believe and the reality of his colonial condition. His sketch is the penultimate story, appearing only before the narrator's own sketch, locating Hat in a place of importance in the text. But, as with the narrator, before we get to Hat's sketch we know a great deal of information about him from the previous stories. In the last sketch, the narrator fast-forwards to his leaving Trinidad, seeming to jump the three years that Hat is in jail; nothing happens if Hat is not there to comment on it.[29] Hat has the power in the narrative to form definitions and declare others mad. He often makes judgments, predictions, and conclusions that are given prominence in the sketches. In the sketch "Man-man," Hat considers Man-man's business practices and pronounces, "Is things like this that make me wonder whether the man really mad" (50). Like the primary narrator, Hat also begins to question Man-man's sanity, or, rather, his insanity.

Miguel Street is a minefield of characters exhibiting a variety of questionably neurotic behaviors; however, Man-man is the only character to be both socially and officially marked as mad in the text. Man-man is labeled the madman of the street. He spends his days writing on the sidewalk, often repeating one letter carefully and lovingly for an entire block. He runs for every election with well-printed posters that contain only his picture and the word "Vote." And he supports himself by buying and selling laundry that his dog has soiled. In the course of the sketch, Man-man discovers religion and begins sidewalk preaching, garnering a substantial following. He then develops a Messiah complex and stages a crucifixion. Tied to the cross, Man-man urges the reluctant audience to stone him, but soon begins cursing them when he realizes they aim to kill him.[30] He is arrested by the police and kept "for observation." But the end of the sketch indicates that he is never released.

Man-man's sketch begins, "Everybody in Miguel Street said that Man-man was mad, and so they left him alone. But I am not so sure now that he was mad, and I can think of many people much madder than Man-man ever was" (46). Thus we begin with the positioning of madness as dependent on what "everybody said" rather than with clear objective criteria for the label. But the narrator immediately questions this type of knowledge, this type of diagnosis. His experience with Man-man does not fall within his current definition of madness. In addition, there are others, whom presumably everybody does not label, that he would describe as mad. And not just mad, but "madder." For the narrator, there are hierarchies of madness. In describing George—another resident of the street, in another sketch—for example, he finds it "strange that no one should have said that George was mad, while everybody said that Man-man, whom I liked, was mad" (26). The narrator's hierarchy of madness is unashamedly based on his affection for the person in question.

The objectivity of what "everybody said" however, is limited to the community. At the beginning of the eighth sketch, titled "The Pyrotechnicist," the narrator reveals: "A stranger could drive through Miguel Street and just say 'Slum!' because he could see no more. But we who lived there saw our street as a world, where everybody was quite different from everybody else. Man-man was mad; George was stupid; Big Foot was a bully; Hat was an adventurer; Popo was a philosopher; and Morgan was our comedian" (79). Miguel Street, therefore, has its own cadre of definitions, which are different from those outside the community. These definitions are created among the residents. "Privacy," for instance, becomes something that can occur among the men gathered on the sidewalk, but not when outsiders are perpetually visiting the street. When American soldiers begin frequenting George's impromptu whorehouse, the street residents feel a shift: "It was as though Miguel Street belonged to these new people. Hat and the rest of the boys were no longer assured of privacy when they sat down to talk things over on the pavement" (32). Residents of the street define their "world" with their own labels and language. Still, the narrator questions his neighbors' labeling of Man-man as mad.

The characters often use the term *mad* in *Miguel Street*, making such a label even more problematic. Apparently, any form of unfamiliar peculiar behavior in Miguel Street generates suspicion of madness. For example, when Bolo first tries to leave the street and gives away his possessions, Eddoes asks, "You think Bolo going mad?" (172). And later, the narrator tells the men of the street, "Bolo mad like hell" (177) when he cannot get Bolo to see his reason. Bolo's belief (or refusal to believe), however, is very reasonable, based on the background information the narrator has provided. Though his suspicions may be extreme, they are not wholly unwarranted. He has believed before: in the newspaper's endorsement of a housing scheme that was fraudulent; in previous contests based on luck; and even in his own people. So although he continues to repeat his ritual of playing the sweepstakes, it is only to assure himself that what he knows is true, that not winning is "just what [he] expect" (176). When the narrator unbalances this ideology by telling him that he has the winning ticket, Bolo draws on another of his longstanding (and proven) principles—that "you mustn't believe anything you read in the papers" (166). When the narrator tries to circumvent this logic by asking the Trinidad Turf Club about the winning ticket, Bolo has a reason to disbelieve them as well—"these Trinidad people does only lie" (177). Thus, although his distrust may seem excessive or "mad," the sketch—aptly titled "Caution"—reveals that on the basis of his personal history Bolo's behavior is reasonable and logical, even as it costs him the very thing he seems to desire.

Miguel Street makes evident the range of linguistic variety in the usage of the term *mad*. In addition to referring to something strange, in Miguel Street *mad* can also signal a potentially dangerous person. When the "big trouble" begins in the Hereira household, Mrs. Hereira describes Toni as mad: "He's going mad! He's going mad, I tell you. He will kill me this time sure" (140). But this madness is not dangerous enough for her to leave. When she does decide to leave, however, she cites her doubt of Toni's sanity again: "I think he is going mad, and if I don't get out I think he will kill me" (143). Toni's employment of the dog in his torture becomes for Mrs. Hereira proof of his madness. The madness here is a dangerous sort, certainly not the same as the one the narrator accuses Bolo of after Bolo refuses to believe he has won a prize in the weekly sweepstakes. Paradoxically, "mad" can also be a compliment. Morgan's deepest wish is to have the men on the street clap him on the back and say, "But this man Morgan really mad, you hear" (86–87). Such a pronouncement would delight Morgan not only because he wants to be the center of attention but because he would be assured of the men's appreciation of his efforts at comedy. He feels this would make him, as Hat pronounces Bogart, "a man among we men" (16).

The community's categorization of Man-man as mad does not, however, have this positive valence. The narrator tries to free Man-man from this stigma by utilizing his own understanding of madness in Trinidad. He considers the way Man-man looks and the expected actions of a madman: "He didn't look mad. He was a man of medium height, thin; and he wasn't bad looking, either. He never stared at you the way I expected a mad man to do; and when you spoke to him you were sure of getting a reasonable reply" (46). The narrator, even in his youth, has developed ideas of the appearance and performance of madness. Man-man challenges these assumptions: he is not ugly and he conducts his conversations in a "reasonable" manner. The narrator allows, however, that Man-man "did have some curious habits" (46), such as his preoccupation with the written word and his participation in every council election. From the descriptions of the other residents of Miguel Street, however, such actions make Man-man fit right in. In Miguel Street, Man-man is not abnormal, not even ex-centric, because everyone has "some curious habits," especially of the repetitive kind.

Even his conversion to sidewalk preacher is common. Man-man's claim that he had seen God does not surprise his neighbors: "Seeing God was quite common in Port of Spain and, indeed, in Trinidad at that time. Ganesh Pundit, the mystic masseur from Fuente Grove, had started it. He had seen God, too, and had published a little booklet called *What God Told Me*. Many rival mystics and not a few masseurs had announced the same thing, and I suppose it was natural that since God was in the area Man-man should see Him" (50–51). Despite this frequency of being chosen by God, when Man-man converts to a religious life, the people of Miguel Street are confused and unsettled. In the narrator's words, they "didn't know what to make of the change": "They tried to comfort themselves by saying that Man-man was really mad, but, like me, I think they weren't sure that Man-man wasn't really right" (52). To categorize Man-man as mad makes the people of Miguel Street comfortable. If they can write off his preaching as the polemics of a madman, then they do not have to pay attention to the meaning behind his words, or, worse, what it is about their society that would produce these imaginings in a man. By deflecting deviance unto Man-man, the "pathological insensitivity," at least in this part of Trinidad, can continue uninterrupted.

In *Mimic Men*, Naipaul similarly recognizes conversions like Man-man's as common, but he situates them as part of the historical moment. His narrator is aware of the ways in which his father's movement fits into its geographical and historical location, especially with the benefit, always available to the survivors, of hindsight: "Today we can see this exodus from our city as a small part of the unrest in the colonies and poorer territories of the Americas just before the war. Each territory produced its own symptoms of disease, its own fantastic growths. We lived with disease; we had ceased to notice. Every day, if you looked, you could find some crazed preacher under a shop awning singing with his little band of the destruction to come."[31] There seems to be a large gap between Ralph's reflective conclusions about the Caribbean region and his (fictional) Isabellan evidence. He shifts from a larger Caribbean "we" to a more particular "you." He expands his observations of the "crazed preacher" often visible in Isabella at the time to the West Indies in general. In this larger region, he includes the "poorer territories of the Americas" as well. Despite the varied outcomes of the "unrest" for the differently colonized nations, Ralph groups them together here as sharing in the same dis-ease. The eruptions of preachers like Man-man and Gurudeva are simply part of—"symptoms of"—this general turmoil in the region.

Glissant also offers self-proclaimed prophets as exemplary forms of Caribbean delirium. He specifies them as exhibiting what he describes as "dramatizing verbal delirium" (le délire de théâtralisation).[32] Glissant privileges dramatizing verbal delirium for its social recuperative, or reappropriative, potential. As Glissant formulates it, dramatizing verbal delirium "has no elite form, it corresponds to an attempt at re-appropriation, it integrates a vision of history, it manifests itself theatrically as a common goal, speaking at the level of spectacle, by an individual or a homogeneous group."[33] Under Glissant's system the sidewalk preacher, determined to save society from itself, exhibits the main characteristics of dramatizing verbal delirium. This figure, as religious performer, dramatizes the dis-ease prevalent in the rest of the society at the time, with his followers as part audience, part cast in his play.[34]

Glissant offers Evrard Suffrin as an example of the "crazed preacher" performing dramatizing verbal delirium. Suffrin was "an agricultural worker from Le Lamentin who from the 1950s through the 1970s produced numerous pamphlets and preached his doctrines to crowds in public places"; Suffrin also founded a religious sect called le Dogme de Cham.[35] But for Suffrin and his movement, as for many of these "sidewalk preachers," little documentation can be found. Despite the prevalence of these religious leaders, men like Evrard Suffrin and Alexander Bedward of Jamaica are special because they became recognizable names in the mass of "crazed preachers." Gurudeva and Man-man represent similar, albeit fictional, successes; but Gurudeva surpasses Man-man to become a recognized political figure: one captured, not in the obscure asylum records, but in the history books—regardless of how misconstrued and misunderstood that written history may be.

Caribbean writers make the danger of such religious leaders visible by imagining their emotional effect on their followers. Even Man-man's audience is uneasily aware of the danger of his preaching, which the narrator describes as oddly frightening. Man-man's sermons are unique in both their content and their delivery. The narrator ascribes some of the power of Man-man's allure to his perfect English accent. In describing Man-man's speech the narrator imagines that "if you shut your eyes while he spoke, you would believe an Englishman—a good-class Englishman who wasn't particular about grammar—was talking to you" (47). When paired with his long beard, black skin, and Trinidadian syntax, his accented preaching alarms and worries his audience. But the more he scares people, the more successful he becomes as a preacher. The impressive performances that transform Man-man from one of the many madmen before him into "a new Messiah" (52) grant him power over his continuously increasing audience. But the very madness that convinces them that Man-man is a Messiah moves him even further away from traditional avenues of political action. This paradox might be explained by one of Ralph's analyses of Gurudeva. He writes, "Movements like my father's—without that purpose which might have turned them into true revolutions—expressed despair but were at the same time positive. They generated anger in people who thought they were too dispirited even for that; they generated comradeship. Above all, they generated disorder where previously everyone had deluded himself there was order."[36] His description could be applied to Man-man in *Miguel Street*, to Moses in *The Hills of Hebron*, and to Makak in *Dream on Monkey Mountain.* All three are rooted in religious responses to their social situation, questioning and refusing the status quo, figuratively breaking down the same barriers as the "tall, handsome Negro" aboard the *Francisco Bobadilla* in the beginning of *The Middle Passage.* As such, these men generate a complicated mix of fear, anger and hope, but without any "purpose" that might be understood within the existing social and political structures.

Like Gurudeva, Man-man has the power to release anger in his followers, but unfortunately he cannot direct it toward changing the oppressive structures that are the root cause of such anger. In the end, his followers' anger and frustration overflow in his direction as they pelt stones at him on the cross.[37] Madness contains this contradictory mix of power and impotence—both in the mad and in those who empathize or sympathize with them. In *Mimic Men*, when Ralph is forced to confront his half-brother, Dalip, in what is meant to become a duel, he feels even more connected to his father. At this moment, when he should feel disdain for his father's weakness—as Dalip does—Ralph instead understands it: "Poor Gurudeva! There on the beach I had felt linked to his power, madness and humiliation." His father's madness combines both power and humiliation. Either may understandably *lead* to madness, but in this case they are both inextricably source and result, as Ralph later realizes: "A man like my father, extravagant as he was, had been a passing disturber of the peace. He fitted into the pattern of dependence, as did those who came after him, taking advantage of the limited constitution we were granted just before the end of the war."[38] There is, in the end, only the repetitive pattern of order and seeming disorder. Such disturbers of the peace operate with a contradictory dependence on the language, systems, and constructions that their actions—indeed, their very existence—struggle against.

These complex characteristics of madness are evident in the success of Man-man's preaching. One element of his newfound power is in forcing people to consider alternatives, not simply because he now has a large audience, but because, having been safely categorized as mad, he has more leeway to speak against any norm. Man-man delivers polemics about the life of poor people and, as no one else is speaking about or *to* them, the poor in his community begin to listen, even if they later decide that Man-man is mad. In yet another move characteristic of the contradictory dependence I mention above, Man-man utilizes the Christian language of suffering and redemption to preach against the current church. Members of his following understand the religious paradigm that he is using, but the message is new. One could view this as repeating the pattern that Naipaul notes, in his essay on Conrad, of "the curious reliance of men on institutions they were yet working to undermine," but Man-man's actions are not as futile as the work Naipaul describes in that essay. Man-man's sermons raise questions about the political system in Trinidad. His previous method of running for office was not nearly as effective as his turn to religion. His preaching garners a much larger audience than his "well printed" posters. So his new form of "madness" has the potential to destabilize established power. When the police (or unnamed "authorities") take Man-man away at the end of the sketch, they are also locking up the possible uproar and change that he could cause among his followers. Like Moses and Makak (and even the barrier-breaking man aboard the *Francisco Bobadilla*), Man-man must be contained before he creates change.

Man-man's earlier involvement in politics connects him to other characters in Naipaul's fiction. Though he does not campaign beyond the unexplained posters, and has little hope of winning, he demonstrates interest in the political process. Like Gurudeva, however, his political aspiration is described in a circular manner. He is mad and his participation in elections is evidence of his madness; but his madness is also grounds for his participation. It is his madness that makes him unsuccessful, but it is also his continuous aim that proves he is mad. Before his religious conversion, Man-man's bids for political office are harmless and comedic. But even then, he has followers "at large" in Port of Spain. Whether these two voters are the same in each election—as the narrator assumes—or new supporters each time, Man-man, even before employing the rhetoric of religion, has succeeded in tapping into a discontent, however minor, with the current political system. His posters are well printed, which evidences a certain investment in the process. Unlike Ralph and Browne in *Mimic Men*, Man-man does not worry about speeches and wordy advertisements. Indeed, even his name is absent from the posters, so his supporters must vote by habit, familiarity, or coincidence; in each case, it reflects the absurdity of the political system in Trinidad at the time. If Man-man can run for office with simply a picture and still consistently receive exactly three votes (one of which the narrator assumes comes from Man-man himself), then what do the elections mean at all? His actions seem to be mostly his criticism of the elections themselves. If that is his aim, then he is, to the degree that the society is self-reflexive, successful even without winning the election. But only the grown-up narrator of *Miguel Street* is close to that type of self-reflexivity, and he leaves this portion of the narrative mostly to the young, naive boy that he was while he knew Man-man. The reflection is left to the readers, particularly the informed reader who has read *The Mystic Masseur* and *The Suffrage of Elvira*, both of which exhibit Naipaul's contempt for the political system in Trinidad.

Movements such as Man-man's and Gurudeva's are dangerous because they disrupt the safety of pretense in colonial relationships. They point out the tenuousness of social consent and the meaninglessness of adhering to the rules when one is the colonial. Man-man and Gurudeva make apparent the insight that Ralph Singh gains while still a young boy at school: "We, here, on our island, handling books printed in this world, and using its goods, had been abandoned and forgotten. We pretended to be real, to be learning, to be preparing ourselves for life, we mimic men of the New World, one unknown corner of it, with all its reminders of the corruption that came so quickly to the new."[39] Societies such as those on Isabella, or in *Miguel Street*, can only copy what they know (or believe they know) of Western society. They can only mimic the culture and values of these places they may never have visited.

Independence, therefore, seems doomed to failure for such mimic societies. A major concern in *Mimic Men*, independence is rarely directly discussed in *Miguel Street*, though Naipaul does raise the question in the only example of Man-man's "odd" sermons. Though timely, Man-man's position on independence is not clear. He warns his audience, "I have been talking to God these few days, and what he tell me about you people wasn't really nice to hear." On the subject of independence, God has shown him "husband eating wife and wife eating husband" as well as "father eating son and mother eating daughter . . . brother eating sister and sister eating brother" (51).[40] But after relating this vision, Man-man only concludes, "This is what these politicians and them mean by saying that the island going to become self-sufficient. But brethren, it not too late now to turn to God" (51). The reasons behind Man-man's urgings to turn to God are ambiguous. In this sermon, Man-man may be criticizing the politicians, the people of Trinidad, the idea of independence, or all three of the above. Given the focus of Naipaul's first two published novels on the corruption of Trinidadian politicians and the gullibility of a constituency new to suffrage, an informed reader may believe Man-man is continuing this Naipaulian trend. But with these problems already explored, Naipaul may be looking forward to the potential problems of full independence, which he explores further in *Mimic Men*. Man-man and later Gurudeva provide an apt and safe medium for this new political commentary. After all, in the anglophone tradition, at least as early as Shakespeare's plays, the truth has often issued from the mouths of fools and madmen.

2 The Necessity for Madness

Negotiating Nation in Sylvia Wynter's *The Hills of Hebron*

In *Miguel Street*, V. S. Naipaul's use of sketches affords him the opportunity to provide a multifaceted view of Trinidad on the brink of independence. Yet while several voices are represented, the use of the unnamed narrator limits access to the thoughts and motivations of the characters. Readers are restricted by the narrator's thoughts and judgments, and although these are mitigated by the addition of hindsight, by Hat's voice, and by the snippets of calypso, the text still provides only the narrator's point of view and what he is privy to through conversations with others. In contrast, Sylvia Wynter employs an omniscient narrator in her novel *The Hills of Hebron*. With a mix of limited third-person and communal narration, this perspective allows for more representation of the interiority of madness and also of a communal consciousness. In the opening scene, for instance, the entire community of Hebron is gathered in church to celebrate the close of the hurricane season. When, during this celebratory mass, Miss Gatha accuses Hebron's leader, Obadiah, and his wife, Rose, of breaking a promise to the community, the narration flows, respectively, through Aunt Kate's, Sue's, Zacky's, Obadiah's, and Sister Gee's perceptions of Miss Gatha's interruption of the mass and finally broadens to encompass the entire congregation's perceptions. This narrative style first provides the thoughts of the individual members of the congregation—Aunt Kate worries that she has missed something important; Sister Gee imagines that God is angry at the events in the church—and then the combined attitude of the Hebronites toward Miss Gatha:

> No one in the congregation quite remembered when she started carrying a stick, crouching over it as if to concentrate the integrity of her purpose. All they knew was that this stern spare woman who hovered behind Prophet Moses had, at some time after his death, emerged from her anonymity,

> stamped herself upon their consciousness. Whilst her husband was alive she had been something of a specter at a feast, someone whose inability to laugh had made them uneasy. But they had taken no more notice of her than a man takes of his shadow. Then all at once she was there, enforcing respect. They were afraid of her; she reminded them of something lacking in themselves.[1]

Here the congregation is represented as thinking, feeling, and remembering as one being. With this continual alternation between singular and plural perspectives throughout the text, both the form and the content of the novel reflect a seamless connection between the individual and the community.

Perhaps this form of narration is left over from the story's beginnings in drama. Wynter originally wrote *The Hills of Hebron* as a play but later rewrote the story as a novel for publication in 1962, the year Jamaica became an independent nation. This moment in Jamaica's history, for Wynter, necessitated this particular generic form. Wynter was conscious of her participation in creating and maintaining the emerging Jamaican identity—"our new self-conception as Jamaicans, our new imaging of ourselves as a nation."[2] A play may perform nationhood as part of a necessarily communal experience—Derek Walcott's *Dream on Monkey Mountain*, for example, has a lot in common with Wynter's figuration of nation in *The Hills of Hebron*—but at this crucial moment in Jamaica's history Wynter chose to reframe the story of the Hebronites as a novel. In a 1992 article on C. L. R. James's reliance on multiple genres, Wynter writes, "The novel, in its true pedagogical function, Pierre Macherey argues, is not the product of a doctrine, not the form-giving mechanism to an already preestablished content. It is rather, the condition of possibility of the emergence of a new doctrine."[3] Accordingly, the novel form provided for Wynter the space to imagine the newly independent Jamaica.

In *The Hills of Hebron*, Wynter employs diverse figurations of madness to map the problematics of an emerging nation. The novel chronicles the genesis, trial, and rebirth of a religious community. This community, Hebron, is created by Moses Barton, who styles himself the son of the true black God. Some years after he leads the New Believers in an exodus from the town of Cockpit Centre into the hills to form Hebron, Moses crucifies himself, leaving Obadiah as his successor. The novel opens during a troubled moment of Obadiah's leadership, approximately fifteen years after Moses's death, then moves backward in parts 2 and 3 to narrate the building of Hebron. The fourth and final section returns to the present, and to the drought that threatens life in Hebron and the available solutions. Although Wynter often provides the communal perspective, much of the narrative is told from the points of view of three key people—Obadiah, Moses, and community member Kate Lansing—all of whom are, at various times and by various factions, marked in the novel as mad.[4]

Through this fictional community, *The Hills of Hebron* creatively examines the anxieties surrounding independence in Jamaica. Though published in 1962, the novel is set in the earlier part of the twentieth century, during the labor strikes of the 1930s. Wynter's turn to a previous revolutionary moment in Jamaica's history becomes the foundation for the national allegory she creates in her novel. I utilize the term *national allegory* with caution—I recognize the weight that it carries after Frederic Jameson's conclusion that "all third-world texts are necessarily . . . allegorical" and Aijaz Ahmad's objection to Jameson's "generality" about both "third world literature" and the concept of allegory.[5] But I find the term useful and applicable here, given the significant timing of the novel's publication and Wynter's own description of her project.[6] In the novel, the developmental stages of Moses Barton's religious followers as they move from cult to community address the avenues through which the new nation could exist and grow. Wynter offers visions of how the new country could proceed under its own steam, under the leadership of black Jamaicans. While the potential leaders in the novel—Moses, Obadiah, and Kate—are marked as mad, the novel situates this insanity as a necessary, and necessarily temporary, stage in the development of successful visionaries. Wynter's novel incorporates myth and allegory in conjunction with madness to portray the forces and constituencies that struggle for power in nascent Jamaica. Wynter's later theoretical writings on Caribbean culture, gender, and the reinvention of humanism help illustrate the tensions evident in her novel between old European paradigms and new Caribbean situations. With these writings as a guide to reading the novel, in this chapter I focus on the various types of madness presented in the text (particularly the gendered aspects of these variations); the utility of madness in the definition of the human; and the ways a community, and by extension a nation, can be realized in the daily intimate connection with madness. In both her choice of genre and her intricate portrayal of her characters' mental fragmentation, Wynter locates madness as a positive space from which to imagine new ways of being in an emergent postcolonial Caribbean society.

Contesting Colonial Conceptions

Part 1 of *The Hills of Hebron*, titled "Saturday," introduces Hebron in its current state, opening with the community's anniversary celebration of Obadiah's vow of celibacy; the vow seems to have helped the community escape any damage during the hurricane season. This section presents the discovery of Rose's pregnancy, the drought that follows Obadiah's fall, and Miss Gatha's rise to power. With the exception of numerous but brief flashbacks, "Saturday" focuses on the current troubles in Hebron. The following section, as its title "Friday" suggests, relates events leading up to the previous section; it focuses on the creation of Hebron. The first chapter in this section details Moses's arrival in Cockpit Centre and the first religious group he forms, the Believers in the Kingdom of Heaven Now. He promises his followers that at the end of the year he will "fly to heaven" and, once there, will "send back golden chariots to take them up so that they [can] lay claim to the kingdom" (120). Wynter's description of Moses's promises to his first congregation recalls the legend of Alexander Bedward, who was a religious leader in Jamaica for three decades, beginning at the end of the nineteenth century. Bedward likened his followers to a "black wall" and would preach, "The time is coming! There will be a white wall and a black wall, but now the black wall is becoming bigger than the white, and we must knock the white wall down. The white wall has oppressed us for years: now we must oppress the white wall."[7] Bedward recognized the racial nature of poverty in Jamaica but still thought in terms of the existing hierarchical structure; he could not envision a solution beyond the parameters of the current class system. The "black wall" would simply replace the white wall and vice versa, leaving the existence of these power structures firmly in place. As Barry Chevannes states, "The Bedwardites, while calling for the black 'followers of Christ' to crush the white 'Pharisees, Scribes and Sadducees,' retained the view that white was superior to black; so that the end of white oppression would at the same time be the transformation of black into the status of white."[8] Similarly, Moses's description of heaven for his first followers parallels the failure of the Bedwardites to escape the colonial mentality. Moses promises the Believers in the Kingdom of Heaven Now that in heaven "the masters [will] be slaves and the slaves, masters. Stars and new continents [will] be theirs to rule over, and their subjects [will] be angels, white angels" (120). During this first attempt at leadership, Moses believes that there will always be masters and slaves but that the races occupying these positions will change; and his message convinces several members of the community to believe in the possibility of such a reversal.

On December 31 of his first year in Cockpit Centre, Moses does climb to the top of a breadfruit tree to fly to heaven but instead ends up with a broken leg. Moses is treated for his injury and is reported to the commissioner of police in Kingston as a "political agitator and a lunatic" (130). But instead of placing his actions officially within a political context, the authorities ostensibly try him only for lunacy. During his trial, however, Moses is variously condemned for insubordination and ignorance. The black jurists are affronted by his actions; both the prosecuting and defending barristers "work[] out their frustrations on the prisoner, attacking him for being black and stupid and not knowing the white man's ways, not talking like him, not hiding his black madness under a wig and gown, as they [have] done." But these men, though privileged in Jamaican society, realize that they are still viewed as "savages" because of the color of their skin. The white judge considers them equals with Moses, viewing them as "all black clowns striking postures in a circus of civilization" (140). Under the definition of civilization imposed by this white judge and by English culture, *black* would always mean "savage." The madness that these barristers feel hidden beneath their "wig and gown" springs from the tension between this white definition of blackness and the seeming universality of the European definition of the human. In this tension lies the propensity for madness. In a lengthy 2003 interview with David Scott, Wynter reveals, "The guiding thread that has lasted all through my work is, How do you deal with the stereotyped view of yourself that you have been socialized to accept? . . . Because the stereotypes are not arbitrary. It's not a matter of someone getting up and suddenly being racist. It is that given the conception of what it is to be human, to be an imperial English man or woman, you had to be seen by them as the negation of what they were. So *you*, too, had to *circumcise* yourself of yourself, in order to be fully human."[9] In *The Hills of Hebron*, the characters who cannot successfully "circumcise themselves of themselves" become alienated. Because they have absorbed these English definitions of what it means to be "human," the lawyers must reject the parts of themselves that do not fit, namely, their blackness, in order to attain any success in the standard colonial hierarchies of power. When Moses's son Isaac is away at teachers' college, he witnesses a similar assimilation among his fellow students. Aloysius, Moses's second-in-command, and Miss Gatha, Moses's wife, also operate under these standard notions of success. For both, their failures in the novel are due to their inability to abandon their traditional definitions of power.

As part of his own traditional definition of power, Moses cannot relinquish his idea of himself as singularly saved rather than an integral part of a community. Moses fails to transition from an individual with a vision to a communal leader. Alexander Bedward similarly failed when he began thinking of himself as singularly crucial to the saving of his people. Shortly before his last "flight," Bedward "announced that he was no longer the 'shepherd,' but Jesus Christ himself, and took on the title of 'Lord.'"[10] Bedward began to reenvision God in the likeness of himself, as Moses later does. Although Chevannes concludes that "regardless of the nuisance Bedward was thought to be to the status quo, he never challenged the identity of the colonial Christian God," Bedward does present this challenge by imagining himself Lord, and it lands him, like his fictive kin Moses, in a mental asylum.[11] In her novel *Free Enterprise*, Michelle Cliff describes Bedward as "a healer, prophet, asylum inmate, early Pan-Africanist, flying African manqué" and links his incarceration in an asylum not to any "clinical" madness but to his efficacy in reaching the poor black people of the island. As the main character tells it, "When Bedward prophesied that the 'black wall shall crush the white wall' in his best Calibanesque voice, the authorities realized this was not a homily of architecture, and its speaker not some country parson who dabbled in community theater, and Bedward was locked away as a madman. . . . He remains in the asylum today. Likewise will happen to Marcus Mosiah Garvey. You mark my words."[12] Excepting the power of his continuing legend, Bedward's influence is effectively ended by his incarceration: he dies in the asylum. Moses, however, survives his years in the asylum, and despite his earlier failed flight he returns with new vigor and inspiration. He formulates a new concept of God, one outside the traditionally white Christian image.

This second return parallels the religious beliefs of Marcus Garvey, whose movement was contemporary with Bedwardism. While Alexander Bedward positioned himself positively as the Aaron to Marcus Garvey's Moses, Garvey had a different vision of God: like Wynter's fictional Moses during his "second coming," Garvey envisioned a black God. Ironically, it is Moses's stay in the mental asylum that enables him to transcend his earlier limitations. His doctor, an alcoholic Irish expatriate, often requests him as an audience for perspectives he would never have dared share with Moses "if he were sane, and white" (150). It is during one of Dr. O'Malley's diatribes on colonialism that Moses deduces the reason for his first failure. In considering how the English were able to become successful at colonization, the doctor tells Moses:

> My God, look what they did to your people, Moses. Sent their missionaries to trade in African souls, to promise them the kingdom of heaven in exchange for a few strings of beads and a paper with a big red seal. Your African chiefs signed away a continent for a Christian conscience, bartered their land, their souls for a slice of the kingdom of heaven. And when the kingdom of heaven didn't materialize, the missionaries, those traders in blood, conjured up a God in the image of an Englishman, a wise and holy father-figure who never existed. They sold this God to the natives as a new kind of fetish. Take my word for it, Moses, Christianity was the greatest fraud ever perpetrated on any peoples. That's why they put you away, my friend. You were dangerous. You challenged this God of theirs, went in search of this heaven that you had been offered in exchange for your malnutrition, disease, ignorance, and poverty. You wanted to feel this Heaven in your hand, see it with your eyes, not later in the good bye and bye, but right here, right now!" (147–48)

Despite the directness of the doctor's searing analysis of the collusion between colonialism and Christianity and despite the explicit relationship to Moses's incarceration, Moses hears nothing but the idea of making God in one's own image. Moses connects this strategy to the reason for his first failure: "The idea of man's being able to conceive of a God of his own provided Moses with the answer to his defeat. He had been stupid enough to accept the white man's God, had worshipped Him and had been betrayed" (149–50). This realization renews his belief in himself as a chosen leader. Moses then begins to apply himself to his tasks at the asylum, learning trades and acquiring the trust of the authorities that allows him to perform odd jobs outside that earn him money. He works toward his new plan of creating God in his own image and of building a second following, a following to be distinguished from the first as the *New* Believers, though many of the same people are involved.

Though still working within a monotheistic model, Moses's "new belief" represents a radical vision for his followers. More than mere racial exchange, the idea of a black God challenges the system that Dr. O'Malley describes during his drunken speech on colonialism in a way that Moses's first attempt at glory did not. The genesis of the new vision is represented here as the result of communion (though not actual understanding) between two minds marked as mad by the colonial authorities. From their marginal positions, the doctor and Moses are able to see—and say—things that accepted members of society cannot. In the article on C. L. R. James mentioned above, Wynter also notes that "James was one of the first to see the significance of the great Orphic heresy of the Rastafarians[,] . . . to understand under the apparent absurdities of their alternative cosmology, a determined refusal of the 'great fictions that pour in upon them from every side.'"[13] For Wynter, James was "among the first to grasp that [Rastafarians] were reinventing the imaginaire social, refusing that of Babylon, and creating a new vision of life for the whole body of people." Like the Rastafarians, the insane constituted a force that Wynter describes as "outside the productive process[,] . . . expelled from it, liminal to its categories."[14] Being similarly situated "outside the productive process," both the Rastafarians and the insane—despite the obvious differences between the two groups—could conceive of and create different social structures. I am not, like V. S. Naipaul in *The Middle Passage*, suggesting here that "Ras Tafarianism is like a mass neurosis."[15] Rather, by reading Wynter's later argument alongside her novel, I am identifying how madness, like Rastafarianism, can allow for a way around (as opposed to through) the sovereignty of colonial representations, particularly of Afro-Caribbeans.

Moses's new vision of God is even more dangerous than the first redefinition of heaven because it challenges a fundamental part of the Christian religion. With this new idea of God, the New Believers can question their position in poverty, because a black God would not let his people suffer so on earth. Unfortunately, like Garvey in his Back to Africa movement and the Rastafarians in their disengagement with society, Moses chooses an exodus rather than the fight that the socialist Bellows wages in Cockpit Centre and other towns or the connection to the rest of Jamaica that Obadiah advocates in the end. For Moses's second "flight," Wynter drew on the myth of Prophet Jordan in Guyana, who also attempted his own crucifixion.[16] Like Obadiah's wooden doll for the German refugee in part 4, legendary men such as Prophet Jordan and Alexander Bedward symbolize for many Caribbean writers the "newer, brighter worlds that could spring from the fusion of men's creative dreams." Through the incorporation of these legends in their work, Caribbean writers such as Wynter, Naipaul, and Cliff, as well as others such as Earl Lovelace and Samuel Selvon, indicate that, as *The Hills of Hebron* states, "man's attempts to create Hebrons would continue forever" (305). Through such figures, these writers provide an artistic version of contesting colonial definitions of madness. Of course, a certain pathos is involved in their use of these figures; but it underlies their recognition of the situation that simultaneously produces such pathos and such extraordinary action.

Collective and Individual Madnesses

It is evident in works like Cliff's *Free Enterprise* and Naipaul's *Miguel Street* that even as characters are designated "mad"—for whatever reason—they are still respected by their communities, often for the very behavior that earns them the title of "mad." In *The Hills of Hebron*, the actions of mad leaders inspire a form of reverence in the New Believers—and, by extension, Jamaicans and West Indians—for insanity. Indeed, there is a certain level of this madness in all the New Believers, in their faithful belief in Moses. Before Moses, this type of fanatical belief was the domain of the pocomania worshippers in Cockpit Centre. The African-inspired pocomania religion combines elements of revivalism and obeah.[17] Its ceremonies consist of elaborate celebrations with drumming, dancing, and spirit possession. In the novel, Obadiah's mother is a leading medium among the Cockpit Centre pocomania sect, and Obadiah is haunted by the memory of her total submission to religion, even as he believes blindly in Moses and Hebron. When Miss Gatha accuses him of breaking his vow of abstinence, Obadiah "searched her face trying to fathom the madness that had taken possession of her. For this could only be pocomania, the little madness which used to seize his mother when the drums beat their frenzies into her limbs and her eyes became fixed and staring and she was lost to him" (26). Obadiah shows himself to be his mother's son not only in his brief madness when he searches for the adulterer but also in his complete belief in Moses. The other New Believers are similarly under the spell of this "little madness" as they continue to believe completely in Moses's resurrection.

Part 3 of the novel, "Night," describes the testing of this faith. It takes readers through the dark times of Hebron—Moses's crucifixion and Isaac's rape of Rose and his betrayal of the community. The section begins with Rose's birth but moves quickly to a scene in which Moses realizes the limits of his own power. In the Cockpit Centre marketplace, Moses witnesses a speech by Bellows, who is encouraging his countrymen to strike against unjust working conditions. When Moses is confronted with Bellows's socialist agenda, he becomes confused and "desolate." He considers Hebron in light of this "new prophet" and concludes, "All that the man said that they would do, he, Moses, had already accomplished. And at one stroke. Up in Hebron they were already free, neither workers nor capitalists, only New Believers owning everything in common, safe from the flood of want on Mount Ararat. And refuged in the arms of God" (227). Indirectly, Bellows challenges Moses's belief in himself and his black God, forcing him to reassert his belief to himself and to others by making the ultimate sacrifice—his life—for his vision. After the encounter with Bellows, Moses decides he must crucify himself for Hebron, partially in response to the goading from the "unbelievers" in Cockpit Centre and partially in response to his own weaknesses.[18]

After leaving Cockpit Centre, Moses goes first to Kate, whom he feels "compelled" to "take" after she requests he grant her Rose to fill her "empty" house. Afterward, however, he feels as though she were "Delilah, come forward from amongst the numberless others, to rob him of the secret of his strength, to draw out of him the substance that had made him inviolable, the Son of God." So he exercises his rage on his wife's body in an effort to "erase the image of the other woman who had diminished him" and to reassert his potency (232). Nine months later, however, Moses is forced to face the results of his inadequacy—his failure to resist Kate and his failure to discredit Bellows's power—in the form of Kate's healthy child and his son's disability: "When the Prophet saw his son's club-foot he took it as a sign. That his seed had been despoiled was a token that he should not live through the descendants of his flesh. His true heirs would be those of his spirit, sealed to him by the blood he would shed on the Cross to confirm eternally that God was black, in the image of His Son" (233). Here Moses avoids his paternity at the exact moment he is faced with two of his "descendants of the flesh." When he finally has a child he can claim legitimately—unlike Kate's daughter, Maverlyn, who will be claimed by Aloysius, and unlike the unnamed children in Cockpit Centre who bear his likeness—he chooses to turn to "heirs . . . of his spirit." Moses clings to his vision of himself as a chosen leader of a chosen people, opting to continue in ignorance, to die rather than change.

In his rationalization of his crucifixion, Moses attempts to confirm not God's greatness but his own. He inverts the common Christian belief that God has made man in the image of himself by remaking God in his (Moses's) own image—"God was black, in the image of His Son." The Son, here, comes first, and God is generated from him. Outside Hebron, this reasoning is deemed madness. Ironically, Bellows's vision of a "raceless world," a vision that Moses is attempting to directly refute with his actions, may similarly be deemed madness. In addition, their followers may be (and are) deemed mad because of their willingness to believe completely in leaders such as Moses and Bellows. If so, then madness, though often characterized as harmless and ineffectual, can have the authority and intelligence to manipulate those who think of themselves as sane. Although the outside world may see Moses as mad, the New Believers accept his visions as part of his ability to lead, as one of the necessary requirements for leadership.

Later, the New Believers at times accord a similar respect to Obadiah. When he enters the church during Miss Gatha's first moments as temporary elder, Obadiah steals some of her glory, taking her authoritative command to the congregation that they remember her instruction and "Do it!" and changing it into a questioning "Do it? Who do it? Who?" (64). Although they have watched him deteriorate into madness, the New Believers are still "mesmerized" by Obadiah's performance. The narrative attempts to explain their fascination:

> They had a respect for madness. It was a private nirvana a man could reach when he was pushed beyond the limits of human endurance, when his spirit was so troubled that his body became a temple of dreams. It was the refuge of those who could not bear the betrayal implied by death; and yet it was the absolute triumph of man over the exigencies of life. In the hearts of the congregation there lurked memories of a time before their exodus, when they too had been pushed near limits. When they, the poor, the shirtless and the unremembered, had walked trails that bordered on heartless rivers of night, had striven to shut out from their ears the shrieks that echoed around them, lest, blinded with fear, they too should drown. As the congregation watched Obadiah, they saw some buried part of themselves, disinterred, laid bare before their eyes. (66–67)

The members of the congregation simultaneously fear insanity as evidence of their own frailty and revere it as evidence of greatness. It is both a "refuge from" and a "triumph over" life. Their attitude—captured in the term *respect*, meaning both special consideration for and deference toward the subject in question—rests on their familiarity with various types of madness. The New Believers make special concessions for both the refugee and the victor in madness, recognizing the variety inherent in types of madness and the constructive elements to be found there. This perspective allows them to view madness as being many things and serving many purposes. The New Believers recognize Moses, Obadiah, and Aunt Kate as having different types of madness, and they each receive different responses from the community. The latter two are treated with a "There but for the grace of God" attitude, but Moses is "There *by* the grace of God." Moses is enabled by his madness. Although it would seem that madness would be a social disadvantage—in the way drunkenness was a disadvantage for Dr. O'Malley, for example—it actually empowers Moses because it allows him to envision a society outside the one currently available to him. For Moses, madness is clearly a condition of possibility, but the advantages are not as clear in Obadiah's and Aunt Kate's situations. Moses has harnessed his madness for potential triumph, but for Obadiah and Aunt Kate it remains a refuge.

This refuge, however, is represented as a catalyst for both Obadiah and Aunt Kate, helping to mold them into better community members and leaders. Significantly, Moses has no past; he simply appears in Cockpit Centre fully formed, already considered mad. Unlike the madness of Obadiah and Aunt Kate, Moses's madness is presented as integral to his personality; the other two characters have histories *sans* madness in the narrative. There are clear boundaries to their madness, a before and an after to their refuge. Obadiah's madness, albeit temporary, periodically has the power of Moses's madness. When Obadiah disrupts Miss Gatha's speech, the congregation wonders at his forcefulness. They are taken by surprise because only the day before, "he had been like Aunt Kate used to be, slyly mad, with a pretense of being sane, going through the motions of praying for rain, thinking that he was fooling them." When he interrupts Miss Gatha, however, "his madness blazoned an authority that was involving them in his blind search, making it seem important to them too" (66). In part, the New Believers' respect for madness grants Obadiah this power. It is short-lived, however, since Obadiah loses what control he has over himself and becomes angry at the congregation. His spell is broken and the congregation's attitude toward him changes. One member, Lazarus, relaxes because he feels "at home with this sort of madness, this uncomplicated one that exploded, spent itself, so that afterwards you could soothe the man, crack a joke or two, get him to laugh with you and forget" (73). The shift in the quality of Obadiah's madness from authority to anger renders him impotent. As the range of responses to Obadiah, Aunt Kate, and Moses indicates, madness is exhibited in different forms, even in the same person, and it demands different responses.

In the fourth section of the novel, when Obadiah reflects on his brush with madness, he thinks of that time as "blind groping days when his body had been muddled, and had become a house of dreams" (286). This echoes the New Believers' conception of madness as turning the body into a "temple of dreams," which in turn echoes the epigraph to part 1 of the novel, quoted from "an Amazulu account of the initiation of a diviner": "At first he is apparently robust, but in the process of time he begins to be delicate, not having any real disease. . . . He tells them that he is being carried away by a river. He dreams of many things and his body is muddled and he becomes a house of dreams" (8). Wynter's use of the same phrasing in describing Obadiah's madness connects his temporary insanity to the positive enterprise of divination. Such madness places him outside even the newly formed structures of Hebron, enabling him to conceive of "a new vision of life for the whole body of people."[19] As part of his "initiation," Obadiah's breakdown serves the entire community because it better prepares him for reassuming the eldership of Hebron. At first, readers may assume the epigraph refers to Moses, but in the end Obadiah shows himself willing, and able, to be a true diviner for Hebron.

Obadiah survives the "blind, groping" period of initiation and emerges less idealistic, but nonetheless optimistic, at the end of the novel. After he abandons his search for the adulterer, Obadiah no longer needs the refuge that madness offers. As he surfaces from his months of madness, he begins to wonder at "the long years of his blindness in which he had slept, and eaten, and made gestures of belief, unthinking, unquestioning" (287). These "long years" include all his time as a New Believer. Obadiah's new clarity is foreshadowed in part 1, when he has a glimpse of this insight at the beginning of his descent into madness. In the church, when Rose's pregnancy is revealed, Obadiah wonders, "What was he doing up here at all, all these years, far away from the safety of Cockpit Centre, with its stinking narrow streets[,] . . . the bunched figures sleeping on the pavement, on benches, in the park but huddled together, secure in their acceptance of the ordinariness of hunger, poverty and defeat. What were they all doing up there, they who called themselves the New Believers, shut in amidst these arid, thorny, almost inaccessible hills, straining for the embrace of God . . . ?" (29). Here there are only questions to which Obadiah does not immediately have the answers; but the questions drive the narrative, which is structured to move between past and present.[20] Readers, like Obadiah here, start with the questions: Who are the New Believers? Why have they chosen to leave the "security" of poverty in Cockpit Centre—the known evil—for the uncertainty of a black man's vision of a black God? What are the individual "limits" they felt themselves approaching before the flight to Hebron?

While the answers to these questions are not conclusive by the end of the novel, it becomes clear that there are no collective answers. While the followers share Obadiah's blind belief in Moses—a belief easily defined as mad both by outsiders and by some Hebronites in moments of doubt—the founding New Believers have various motivations for their beliefs. For example, Hugh chases power and importance, while Kate is motivated by her desire to bear a live, healthy child and hopes that the promised land of plenty will help this occur. Like Hugh, Miss Gatha also seeks status, first in her attachment to Moses, then in her visions for her son Isaac. Although Miss Gatha too begins to identify with Aunt Kate's mad maternal hope when Isaac deceives her, she does not fully succumb to the "frenzy" she feels at the prospect of never seeing Isaac again. Similarly, in an earlier moment when Miss Gatha takes over the eldership, she briefly feels the rush of power that comes with the position: "Standing with her skirt brushing the seat Miss Gatha sensed something of the mad grandeur that must have possessed her husband when he had stood there with the waiting congregation below him." She recognizes that she, like Moses, could become distracted by power and glory. But Miss Gatha resists temptation because she has a different vision for the congregation: "Her way would never be like that of Moses. She would never drug them with dreams of glory. She would spur them to work" (59). Thus Miss Gatha, while not promoting "dreams of glory" like her late husband, does have a vision for Hebron. She views the land as their salvation; the land will provide, provided they work hard for its fruits. Miss Gatha's mad vision is not for herself or for her people but for her son. She tells the congregation, when they offer her the eldership, "I am going to help you not because I want to, but because I have to. I am going to help you so that Hebron can continue and my son Isaac can have the lot of his inheritance" (58). Miss Gatha's mission to save Hebron for her son prompts Janice Lee Liddell to describe her as "singleminded in her traditional motivation as a mother."[21] The loss of this motivation threatens Miss Gatha's sanity, but this proves a temporary threat as (grand)motherhood again rescues her from the lure of "mad grandeur."

Overall, the general respect accorded madness not only makes leaders of individuals but also creates a community of followers. The "mad grandeur" that motivates Moses also motivates his followers and forms them into a community. This type of madness inspires blind belief and loyal faith. Obadiah's madness, however, springing as it does from the grittiness of a real-life disappointment and being uneven in its manifestation, cannot maintain the authority of Moses's madness. Actually, for it to be truly influential, it is imperative that Obadiah's madness not be maintained. He must pass through this delirium to emerge with a new vision for Hebron. The narrative juxtaposition of Moses's and Obadiah's madnesses reveals shades of differentiation between Moses's ultimately futile attempt at triumph and Obadiah's more circuitous route to leadership via mental refuge. The particulars of Aunt Kate's mental decline contribute to this multifaceted view of madness. In the following section, I examine the gendered dimension of her madness and the work it performs in Wynter's narrative shaping of a new nation.

"Mad Hopes" and Gendered Visions of Community

Although at first glance the tale of Hebron might seem to be male centered, the female characters are integral to the narrative. Kate is of particular importance to both the form and the content of the novel.[22] In reading the significance of Kate and the female characters, I rely on Wynter's discussions of gender and of feminism in her critical essays. Wynter's nonfiction has flourished since she wrote *The Hills of Hebron*, but the published response to her as a female intellectual has been much slower. Wynter's work, particularly her later work on humanism, has been difficult for critics of Caribbean literature to classify. She has consistently written from a feminist perspective, although she has not been consistently claimed by the Caribbean feminist community. In "Reluctant Matriarch: Sylvia Wynter and the Problematics of Caribbean Feminism," for example, Natasha Barnes raises the question of Wynter's positioning of race vis-à-vis gender. Wynter's writings, however, resist this form of dissection. Her writing shows a concern with, and consciousness of, being *both* black and female. In her afterword to *Out of the Kumbla*, a critical anthology on writing by Caribbean women, Wynter characterizes this position, that of black women, as both "demonic" and demonized because of race (the "primary code of difference") *and* because of gender ("the secondary—if none the less powerful" signifier).[23] Because of this tendency to read Wynter's writings as, in Natasha Barnes's words, a "repudiation of feminism as a site of emancipatory imagining," I take a slight detour here to emphasize the importance of women in general in *The Hills of Hebron*, before turning to examine Aunt Kate's centrality and the significance of her "mad hope" for the viability of the community.[24]

In her afterword to *Out of the Kumbla*—titled "Beyond Miranda's Meanings: Un/Silencing the 'Demonic Ground' of Caliban's 'Woman'"—Wynter calls for an "unsilencing" of Caliban's woman, represented for her by the other female writers in the *Out of the Kumbla* anthology. In utilizing the term "Caliban's woman," Wynter privileges neither race nor gender; rather, she holds them to be equally important. In a manner similar to Barnes's reading of the afterword, Liddell concludes that "the primary thematic concern of *The Hills of Hebron* is certainly not with women."[25] But the value of the female characters' contributions to the building of Hebron—especially those of Rose and Kate—disputes that assessment. If race, community, religion, and nation are part of the "primary thematic concern" of the novel, then women are more than mere communicators of the theme; they are the ground on which these aspects are built.

Wynter theorizes this idea of women as ground in the afterword to *Out of the Kumbla*. She images this ground as that of the absent female counterpart in Shakespeare's *The Tempest* and finds that Alice Walker's term *womanist* illustrates its function. Wynter envisions Caliban's woman—black and native—who provides unacknowledged ground for even Caliban's dreams. In a complex sentence, exemplary of the connective form of her later essays, Wynter ties the significance of such a space to the creation of new meanings:

> And if we are to understand the necessity for such an *other* term (projected both from the perspective of Black American women (U.S.) and from that of the "native" women intelligentsia of the newly independent Caribbean ex-slave polities) as a term which, whilst developing a fully articulated theoretical/interpretative reading model of its own, nevertheless, serves, diacritically to draw attention to the insufficiency of all existing theoretical interpretative models, both to "voice" the hitherto silenced ground of the experience of "native" Caribbean women and Black American women as the ground of Caliban's woman, and to de-code the system of meanings of that other discourse, beyond Irigaray's patriarchal one, which has imposed this mode of silence for some five centuries, as well as to make thinkable the possibility of a new "model" projected from a new "native" standpoint, we shall need to translate the variable "race," which now functions as the intra-feminist marker of difference, impelling the dually "gender/beyond gender" readings of these essays, out of the epistemic "vrai" of our present order of "positive knowledge," its consolidated field of meanings and order-replicating hermeneutics.[26]

The demonic ground, also the site of womanism (this "other term"), is capable of generating not only new ways of knowing but also new ways of being. This space must be "silenced" because it invalidates dominant discourses about gender, race, and the human. Wynter compares the destabilizing function of "unsilencing" Caliban's woman to the intervention made by European feminist critics of the Enlightenment idea of the human. The model of Caliban's woman, then, serves to (1) provide a methodology for reading texts by Caribbean women writers and characters, (2) decry the absence of and desire for black women in European feminism and male-centered race theory, and (3) indicate and interrogate the continuing insufficiency of "that other discourse" of the human. Almost thirty years before this afterword, *The Hills of Hebron* presents in fiction, in a more concrete form, the theory that Wynter later works out in her critical articles. Women are not lost, forgotten, or ignored in Wynter's work; she reads the nation and race, and later the human, through women, without treating gender as additive.

The novel portrays the silenced ground of Caliban's woman with regard not to Miranda or Prospero but to Caliban himself. Moses in particular becomes a "co-participant" with white men "in the power and privileges generated" by his gender.[27] In a practical manner, women become the means through which Moses can build his following and secure land for Hebron. But women also provide the background that allows other male leaders in Hebron to distinguish themselves in the community; as wives, mothers, and sexual objects, they allow for the "partial liberation" of Obadiah, Hugh, and Isaac. Daryl Cumber Dance views the female characters as primary and the novel as portraying "the strength and endurability of women in relationships with men who attempt to assert their dominance, but who are in actuality weak and impotent."[28] While Dance's assessment may not in the end apply to Obadiah, *The Hills of Hebron* certainly *is* structured around female characters. In particular, Kate's perspective is central in shaping the narrative because the novel opens and closes with her. In fact, Kate appears at the very beginning and end of each of the four parts of the novel, with the exception of the end of part 2, which concludes with Moses's visit to his rival Reverend Brooke; but even then, it is through Aunt Kate's memories that Wynter introduces this scene.

Aunt Kate, though mentally disoriented since her daughter's death, is more important a figure to the flow of the narrative than Moses Barton himself. She is everywhere, often knows more than the other characters, and is crafty even in her madness. At the opening of the novel, Aunt Kate is quite aware that everyone thinks she is mad: "The part of her mind which was secret and cunning accepted that she would have to pretend to practice rites which the others used to assure a reality from which she had escaped. For the others were not without power. If they demanded her involvement in their conspiracy, she needed them in hers" (10). Aunt Kate's strategic escape via madness parallels the communal escape via religion. The system of beliefs, actions, and events that construct the

Hebronites' reality is no more "real" to those outside Hebron than Aunt Kate's reality—that of her daughter, Maverlyn, as merely sleeping rather than dead—is to those within. The inhabitants of Cockpit Centre do not believe in Moses's second coming or in the viability of Hebron. In fact, many have forgotten about it, as evidenced by the policeman's response to Obadiah when he visits the Cockpit Centre marketplace—"Hebron? Where in the hell is that? . . . You don't mean the place where the madman Moses crucify himself?" (300). Hebron is not uppermost in the minds of neighboring residents; and when they do recall it, they remember only "the madman Moses," not the continuance and growth of the community after Moses's death.

Kate's madness, however, is actually vital to this continuance of Hebron; it is a part of the everyday life of Hebron that reassures the New Believers of the existence of their community. When Aunt Kate is sick during the drought, Eufemia and Sister Gee reflect on how strange it is "not to find Aunt Kate waiting by the spring, watching whilst [they] dip up the water, warning [them] to be careful not to wake up Maverlyn!" (49). Not only is there no water for Aunt Kate to watch, although that is an important factor in her absence, but also Hebron itself is ailing; therefore, it is only right that Aunt Kate be ailing as well:

> The old woman's absence emphasized for them the sharp change that had come upon Hebron. . . . Aunt Kate's fantasy that her child was still alive, that she was only sleeping, touched a responsive chord in them. Her mad hope had become theirs. Some mornings, standing around her as she sat and cradled her arms they had almost been persuaded that they could see, glancing on the surface of the water, her child Maverlyn, like some spirit celebrating the eternal life that their youth expected and demanded. And now the spring had dried up. They as well as Aunt Kate had been forced into accepting that Maverlyn was drowned and a long time buried, that Maverlyn was dead. (49–50)

Aunt Kate's "mad hope" is akin to Moses's vision of a black God and Obadiah's search for the adulterer. It is misleading and fruitless. Indeed, all three of these are "mad" hopes, even though they begin in seeming sanity. They lead each of these three characters down into delusion, and only two of them survive the trip. Although they begin at different periods in Hebron's history, these characters' variety of insanities are all influential in the fabric of life in Hebron. Moses's madness is critical for obvious reasons of genesis; Obadiah's, because it marks the change in the community's vision for itself; and Kate's, because it underlies the spirit of life in Hebron, the daily reaffirmed mad hope of its residents in future salvation.

Before her refuge in madness, Kate performs a different but equally crucial role in the creation of Hebron as a community. She convinces Aloysius to follow Moses when she feels that she may have a chance at giving birth to a live, healthy child in new surroundings. Aloysius's membership in the New Believers is so important to the success of Hebron that Moses names him as the second elder. This granting of status is also helpful in convincing Aloysius, but it is Kate's dream of motherhood that drives the couple into the hills. Like the other women of Hebron, Kate leaves the visionary planning of the community to the men; the women pay more attention to the everyday, earthly things of the present. It is from here, however, that the true building of the community springs: from the women's everyday lives. The continuous strength of domesticity and the particularities of women's work are less utopian and glorious than Moses's black God, but rituals such as the bearing and raising of children and the ceremonial preparations for death are crucial to imagining oneself as part of a group. These and other quotidian actions, in their repetition and their prevalence, create community for those continuously performing and observing them.

Hebron is literally founded on one of these actions: Rose's mother's pregnancy. Crucial plot developments rest on Rose's body, although she speaks directly only twice in the novel.[29] Hebron was founded on the secrecy of her birth, and its foundations are threatened by her own pregnancy. In addition, it is with the birth of her son that the semblance of order is restored to Hebron. With the child's birth, the community also experiences a rebirth, symbolized by Aunt Kate's recovery. Kate declines into madness when Maverlyn dies, when she loses her last genetic link to her own future; but she returns when Rose, the daughter she wanted to raise as her own, is about to give birth and needs help. That Kate revives—and survives not only her husband and child but also Moses himself—is symbolic of the community as a whole. When faced with the need to help Rose in childbirth, Aunt Kate eases her hold on the past because "the future now called to her, insisting that her place was with the living" (284). The "future" that calls is inextricable from the present care of the living; the former unequivocally depends on the latter. As Kate notes, there will always be another Moses and other Hebrons, because visions of power and sovereignty are continuous and eternal. She chooses, however, to focus on the present needs of her fellow community members. To return to the metaphor of Wynter's afterword, while Caliban may focus on claiming the island as his own, it cannot be a viable kingdom without his female counterpart.

Although Aunt Kate, in her madness and her recovery, remains fixated on the distinctively female preoccupation of motherhood, she is no less concerned with Hebron's future than is Moses or Obadiah. Her vision for the future is perhaps stereotypically gendered in its focus, but it undergoes a reframing during her period of refuge in madness, resulting in her motherly response to a child not of her own womb and her recognition that her "place" is not dependent on her reproductive capacity. Aunt Kate manages, via Rose's child, to pull Miss Gatha from her own potentially damaging "frenzy" to embrace a similar role in shaping Hebron's future. Thus to read women out of the "primary thematic concern" of the novel is also to read them out of the makings of a new nation. Through the male characters, *The Hills of Hebron* offers theoretical visions of how the country might proceed after independence, but female characters offer the practicality of life beyond colonialism.

The Utility of Madness

Despite the gendered and other differences in foci, however, the male and female main characters of the novel share one evident advantage of psychic alienation: their madness enables them to divest themselves of communal and colonial expectations. Moses, Obadiah, and Kate are able to, respectively, redefine religious leadership, responsibility to/for family and community, and the limits of motherhood. Via these three characters especially, *The Hills of Hebron* demonstrates the extent to which Jamaicans have been mentally molded to accept the status quo, so much so that the ability to envision radical change comes only at the risk of madness. Isaac vaguely recognizes the value of this risk when he is away at teachers' college. Listening to his classmates, he finds that they are operating under European epistemologies of success, vision, and worthiness. Isaac realizes that although they are quite ready to throw out the English, they have no idea what to do after independence. Their visions of postcolonial Jamaica are built on English ideas of leadership:

> For the future road to power lay in politics, man, they assured each other. Once they threw out the British a new day would dawn and the world would be theirs. They never discussed how they would grapple with the problems of the future, how they would feed the hungry, provide jobs for the jobless, wipe out the three hundred years of malnutrition and mental atrophy that was the

> legacy of colonial rule. Instead they argued heatedly over the proper constitutional procedures to be adopted after independence. And always, the high point of their discussion was English constitutional law and practice. (260)

Here Wynter makes an explicit connection between Hebron and the new nation. She gestures toward a shift from anticolonial ideas to postcolonial resistance. In his book *Refashioning Futures: Criticism after Postcoloniality*, David Scott dates this shift as occurring during the 1970s, somewhat later than the publication of Wynter's novel, but his description of the difference between anticoloniality and postcoloniality corresponds with Isaac's criticism of his peers. According to Scott, "the anticolonial project" had been "defined by the demand for political decolonization, the demand for the overthrow of colonial power. Its goal was the achievement of political sovereignty." Scott describes this anticolonial project as ignoring "the whole question of the *decolonization of representation* itself, the decolonization of the conceptual apparatus through which political objectives were thought out."[30] This wholesale acceptance of the English "conceptual apparatus" is evident in Isaac's peers' posturing and their conceptions of the future. They still build their dreams on English ideology, and, as Isaac notes, they "play the game brilliantly without ever questioning the rules" (261). They remain trapped within a framework that defines their black colonial selves as helpless and irrational, capable only of mimicry.

Scott finds that postcoloniality, on the other hand, "turned not so much on the old idea of colonialism as a structure of material exploitation and profit (the question for anticoloniality) as on the idea of colonialism as a structure of organized authoritative knowledge . . . that operated discursively to produce effects of Truth about the colonized."[31] Thus Isaac recognizes the deficiencies of the anticolonial stance, particularly in this group of would-be leaders who can conceive of nation and government only within European parameters. Isaac predicts that his classmates will forever "exchange the substance for the shadow": "They had surrendered even the right to dream their own dreams. Their dreams were second-hand, cut-price, bargain ones. And for the first time Isaac began, dimly, to understand the necessity of his father's madness" (261). Being "outside the productive process" is not merely preferable but *necessary* for conceptions and creations of alternate ways of life. Isaac, however, is not up to the task that he "dimly" comprehends as vital to Hebron's future. Even with his insight, he holds tight to his sanity and rejects responsibility for his legacy, choosing money and flight instead. He will not, or cannot, follow in his father's footsteps.

Like Isaac after him, however, Moses is unable to deal with the practical reality of Hebron. Moses, like Isaac making a futile attempt at fiction, searches for another foundation on which to build primarily his own, and also his people's, self-worth. In envisioning a black God, Moses temporarily "change[s] the hierarchy" for the New Believers: he "made them believe that behind him there was a God, black and made in their image and partial to them, His Chosen People" (72–73). He provides an "escape from the supremacy of the white man's culture" by constructing a different image of God.[32] At the beginning of the last section of the novel, Wynter quotes Dostoevsky's *The Possessed*: "With every people, at every period of its existence, the end of the whole national movement is only the search for God, of a God for it, in whom it may believe as the one true God. God is the synthetic personality of a whole people considered from its origins until its end" (282). For Dostoevsky, the search for nation is simply the search for God, but in *The Hills of Hebron*, the search for a relevant God becomes emblematic of the search for a nation as well.

Reverend Brooke clearly recognizes this relationship between religion and nation. In considering his privileged position, he has a "flash of insight" before his first meeting with Moses: "They were the same questions being asked by the rabble-rousing nationalists who were springing up all over the empire. And concomitant with these queries went the questioning of a God who could so much favor Jacob at the expense of Esau. So one ended up by accepting the way of life in the island as unchanging and unchangeable, since it seemed the lesser evil. For an abyss of change might engulf them all, even reach up to the heavens to threaten God and the Christian religion itself" (200). As with the Dostoevsky epigraph, in Reverend Brooke's logic the state of the nation is dependent on the state of religion and vice versa. The reverend must maintain his, and other whites', "aura of Herrenvolk" through religion; and it is this aura that allows him to maintain his lifestyle and position. Ironically, when he first moved to Cockpit Centre, Reverend Brooke had grand plans for change. Similarly, his wife was excited at the prospect of making change in the Jamaican backwoods. Their transformation emphasizes that although those with privilege within the existing system may begin with intentions to utilize this privilege to effect change, they often end by "accepting the way of life in the island as unchanging and unchangeable." As they become indoctrinated to the colonial hierarchies of the island, they grow less able to conceive of change. Like Isaac's schoolmates, they begin to play the established game, ceasing to question any rules. Reverend Brooke recognizes, however, the role religion plays in this game, authorizing the order of things and placating those who might question it.

Two of the mad visionaries in the text, Bellows and Moses, do attempt to de-establish this order by separating religion from nation; Moses relies on religion without politics and Bellows on politics without religion. While he listens to Bellows in the Cockpit Centre marketplace, Moses thinks, "Not once had the man quoted the Bible, not once mentioned the name of God" (222). This stance presents a "challenge" to Moses because he realizes that Bellows has managed to capture the attention of the "unbelievers" who mocked him. Bellows's politics appeals to a section of the Jamaican population that Moses could not reach with religion. In fact, Bellows advocates against religion; he tells the crowd, "We want nothing to do with churches. Hear what I tell you. In your churches they will deceive you, will tell you it is wrong to strike, will tell you that God won't like it, that it's a sin. Now, when they tell you that, ask them one thing. Ask them to show you this God so that you yourself can ask Him if it's wrong. And if they can't show you Him, tell them that the only religion you believe in is the religion of Man!" (228). In this textual confrontation between the two men, between the two ideals, Moses and Bellows have captured different segments of the population according to their message. They question the rules and suggest a new "game"—Moses Hebron and Bellows socialism—in which each severs the concept of God from that of sovereignty.

Unlike Moses and Bellows, however, Obadiah embraces a connection between religion and nation. He believes that he will need "a new response to a new ritual, a new morality, a new right and wrong, a new God," in order to lead the Hebronites (312). The jacket description of the novel for the Jonathan Cape 1962 edition emphasizes Obadiah's role in this new Hebron: "Out of the crises that ensue, Obadiah emerges with a new self-knowledge and a belief that salvation lies in creative labour rather than the worship of an abstract God." In Obadiah's case, "creative labour" takes the form of religious songs *and* commodified aesthetic production. Although Isaac, with his tortured attempts at writing, seems at first to be the artist in the text, it is Obadiah who saves the community through his art. However, it is not just the art—its production, its beauty, its message—that saves the community, but the *selling* of it, which can be read as a commentary on the value of art in a new nation and on the value of the nation's culture itself. Obadiah discovers (or perhaps recovers) his artistry through his madness. In his "blind, groping," frenzied search for the adulterer, Obadiah finds only himself and his ability to work with his hands. He returns to the carpentry he learned as Aloysius's assistant but also finds himself carving wooden dolls. These he begins selling in Cockpit Centre. Obadiah's madness enables his art, and his art enables him to regain the position of leader of his community.

Obadiah's first plan in the new Hebron is to "build a good road, a broad road out into the world" (310). This comes from his recognition of the New Believers' connection to those outside Hebron. His own resort to the refuge of madness indicates to him that the way forward for the Hebronites does not lie in isolation in the hills. Neither does it lie in their forgetting themselves, in their fledgling history, or in their imagined community; rather, it requires developing communion with others outside Hebron. Obadiah understands, however, that "except they shared his vision, it would be meaningless for him" (312). First and foremost, Obadiah needs the Hebronites to imagine a new community with him—a community that does not rely on seclusion or a self-professed Son of God for sovereignty. Obadiah realizes that to lead them he cannot be like Moses because "to explain it to them he would need the words and the rhythms, not of a sermon, but a song" (310). And in the end, he does have the congregation singing of trial and rebirth, of building Hebron up again "right from the ground." Obadiah helps the Hebronites to believe in a new community, not by preaching it to them, already fully formed in his head, but by having them imagine and create it in song (or art) together.

Having seen Obadiah "pushed past the limits of human endurance" into madness, the community respects the source and direction of his new vision. Hebron, built on one madman's vision and his cunning manipulation of a rejected pregnant girl, is eventually saved by the response to another madness-induced vision and another alienated pregnant girl. The various trials that its members have endured and the mad frenzies that its leaders have survived prepare the community to celebrate this new birth and the future it heralds for Hebron. If we read Hebron as an allegorical nation, then this fictional future depends on cooperating with other countries (Obadiah's new road), appreciating women's contributions to the establishment and maintenance of the new nation, recognizing the significant function of art in engendering and maintaining national culture, and taking the psychic risk of thinking beyond colonialist conceptions and European models of self-rule.[33] In short, it requires a mental as well as political decolonization.

3 "Fighting Mad"

Between Sides and Stories in *Wide Sargasso Sea*

In a 1958 letter to actress and friend Selma Vaz Dias, Jean Rhys detailed her desire to rewrite the story of the "Creole lunatic" in *Jane Eyre*. Despite the challenge, she delared herself firm in rectifying what she saw as the unfairness of Charlotte Brontë's representation of the first Mrs. Rochester and related the difficulties of working with the original text. Although Rhys had described the project to Vaz Dias in previous letters—Vaz Dias expected a script form of the novel for performance—this letter provides more details about Rhys's experimentation with various methods of representing her heroine's story. Rhys informed Vaz Dias that she had decided to begin with Antoinette's youth, with Antoinette telling her own story. In a postscript to the letter, Rhys urged, "I will not disappoint you. Come with me and you will see. Take a look at Jane Eyre. That unfortunate death of a Creole! I'm fighting mad to write *her* story."[1] In an earlier letter to Vaz Dias, Rhys attributed "Come with me and you will see" to St. Teresa of Aquila, with the invitation emphasized as religious ecstasy.[2] Her use of this phrase further evidences Rhys's dedication to the project of reclaiming Bertha. She wrote in another letter that on rereading *Jane Eyre* after beginning to rewrite Bertha, she "was a bit taken aback" to discover "what a *fat* (an improbable) monster she was," yet she would tell her story, "though not without pain struggle curses and lamentation." Whether she had "any *right*" to rewrite Bertha, Rhys noted, was a separate question for a later time.[3]

Rhys's letters expose her investment in what would be her last novel, which she had been contemplating in different forms since as early as 1945. Her phrasing of her commitment—"fighting mad"—resembles Erna Brodber's description of "ancestral anger." Although Brodber utilizes Afro-Caribbean examples to illustrate ancestral anger, Brontë's Bertha, represented as merely an impediment in *Jane Eyre*—"necessary to the plot, but always," Rhys emphasizes, "*off stage*"—evokes a similar anger in Rhys.[4] Rhys's emphasis on claiming Bertha ("*her*") expresses how imperative it is for her to rescue this "poor ghost." "Fighting mad" also reveals Rhys's position vis-à-vis *Jane Eyre* and its century of readership. In writing *Wide Sargasso Sea*, Rhys had to contend with the established reading of Rochester's mad wife and her legacy of lunacy. It is therefore understandable why it took Rhys twenty years to publish the novel, as she struggled with the literary method of "fighting" the earlier established representation of Bertha's madness.

Wide Sargasso Sea, published in 1966, is Rhys's last novel, finished considerably later than her first four novels, which were all published between 1928 and 1939. And while *Wide Sargasso Sea* shows similarities in style to the previous novels, the differences are significant, with the most significant, perhaps, being Rhys's turn to the Caribbean as the primary setting; although she mentioned the Caribbean in previous novels, it was never her focus. Of her earlier heroines, Anna Morgan of *Voyage in the Dark* has the strongest relationship to the Caribbean: throughout the novel Anna experiences flashbacks to her youth in Dominica. In *Wide Sargasso Sea*, however, Rhys is wholly concerned with the West Indies; even the last section, set in England, focuses on the lost Caribbean space. Locked in the attic at Thornfield Hall, Antoinette (as Rhys renames Brontë's Bertha) wraps herself in memories of Jamaica in an effort to keep warm. In Rhys's previous novels, England is similarly cold and unkind to women, but for Antoinette it is particularly harsh. In the last section of the novel, Grace Poole tells Leah that Thornfield Hall is "big and safe, a shelter from the world outside which, say what you like, can be a black and cruel world to a woman."[5] In her other novels, Rhys's protagonists find the world as Grace Poole describes it, but they seem to be searching for their own Thornfield Hall. Those women wander around Europe ostensibly searching for, yet never finding, a rich husband or protector like Rochester to prevent their wasting away from misunderstanding, loneliness, and poverty. In *Wide Sargasso Sea*, Antoinette achieves the permanent privileged situation they seek but finds that the loneliness and cruelty do not end outside the walls of Thornfield Hall. Rhys's other protagonists show symptoms of depression and, as Elizabeth Abel diagnoses, "ambulatory schizophrenia,"[6] but Antoinette is the only one that becomes incapacitated by her fragmentation. As Antoinette and her mother, Annette, indicate, the financially fortuitous connection that the earlier heroines seek could offer the very opposite of salvation.

The publication of *Wide Sargasso Sea* was followed by a revival of interest in Rhys and her work. Her earlier novels were republished, and she was once again part of the literary world, at least, part of the British literary world. While Wally Look Lai's 1968 article "The Road to Thornfield Hall" began the Caribbean's claiming of Rhys, this process was slow and debated.[7] As late as 1974, A. Alvarez, in the *New York Times Book Review*, could uncomplicatedly claim Rhys as "The Best Living English Novelist."[8] The explicitly Caribbean subject of *Wide Sargasso Sea* and some of Rhys's later short stories, however, eventually shifted attention to her own Caribbeanness. Just as it compelled a new vision of *Jane Eyre*, *Wide Sargasso Sea* compelled readers to look at Rhys's earlier work through new eyes. These earlier writings had received some attention as modernist stories of lost women, but after Rhys's literary revival they also became important reflections of a Caribbean exile's perception of Europe. The later reception of *Wide Sargasso Sea* made Rhys a canonical figure in European, feminist, and Caribbean literary studies.

Rhys's work, then, was in effect retrospectively drawn into the conversation on Caribbean literature, but its inclusion in the canon is now generally accepted. However, its relationship to the other texts in this project, texts that are more directly concerned with the politics of decolonization, may still seem questionable given that (1) the novel is set in a period during which there is no inkling of independence, and (2) there is no clear-cut connection in the text or in any of Rhys's other writings to the question of independence. Despite these differences, the novel is relevant to my larger argument because it utilizes the representation of madness to directly confront European conceptions of the Caribbean and Caribbean peoples. This type of challenge, though directed outward, is as necessary in this period of decolonization as the visualizations of a new nation to be found in, for example, Sylvia Wynter's *The Hills of Hebron* or Derek Walcott's *Dream on Monkey Mountain*. More important for this project, the figuration of madness in *Wide Sargasso Sea* is fraught with questions of colonial identity, place, and order. Via representations of Antoinette's, her mother's, and her husband's madness, the novel determinedly resists the categories and hierarchies that colonialism depends on for power and perpetuation. In insisting on "other sides" and third spaces, *Wide Sargasso Sea* complicates the fixity and dualism—black/white, European/native, mad/sane—that those in power are invested in maintaining, especially during periods of social upheaval, such as during abolition (the setting of the novel) and decolonization (the period of its creation and publication).

Righting a Creole Story

The general impulse in reading revisions is via a comparison to the texts they revise to determine, for instance, how "true" the revision is to the original, how plausible the later version is, given the parameters of the first. But Rhys's revision asks readers to do the reverse. Michael Thorpe finds that rereading *Jane Eyre* in light of *Wide Sargasso Sea* highlights the earlier text's "coarse assumptions about madness, mingled with the racial prejudice inherent in the insistent suggestion that 'the fiery West Indian' place of Bertha's upbringing (Ch. XXVII) and her Creole blood are the essence of her lunacy."[9] Although Antoinette was fragile before marriage, her narrative offers the possibility that it is her husband's inability and cruel refusal to understand her Caribbeanness that pushes her "over the edge" of Thornfield Hall. Rochester's treatment of Bertha in *Jane Eyre* is undoubtedly cruel, but it is acceptable in the romance plot of Brontë's novel because Bertha is described as mad. *Wide Sargasso Sea* questions this cause-and-effect sequence by providing readers with possible and plausible answers to questions such as "Who was Bertha?" and "Why was she mad?"

In the process, Rhys offers an inside perspective not only of Bertha Mason but also of financial privilege. The other texts in this book focus on Caliban, "Caliban's woman," or even Caliban's imagined privileged progeny (Erna Brodber's *Jane and Louisa Will Soon Come Home*), but, to use Kamau Brathwaite's formulation, *Wide Sargasso Sea* focuses on Miranda. In her semiprivileged status, Miranda interrupts the Prospero-Caliban dyad. As a result, Miranda-centered texts may, as Evelyn O'Callaghan states in connection to Creole women writers, "bring to West Indian literature an obsessive attention to complexities, and a suspicion of fixed categories."[10] As a white female in colonial Jamaica, Antoinette occupies this Miranda space. Although her psychic and physical alienation is most apparently linked to her gender and Creole identity (or lack thereof), class does not fall out of the equation; its very nonissue makes it significant. She has little access to her own money; but after her mother's remarriage she is never again in dire financial need. Antoinette's situation provides a different view of madness by removing the financial duress cited by both Derek Walcott and V. S. Naipaul as one of the roots of madness. Her character complicates these writers' connection between madness and poverty because even in the midst of material surplus she too falls victim to the delusions and mental damage associated with less privileged members of colonial societies. Her financial and cultural privilege war with her financial and cultural reality, resulting in social and psychic fragmentation.

Rhys carefully delineates the effect of this indeterminate social position on Antoinette's mental decline. Although Antoinette alternately embraces and laments her placelessness, her repeated failure to find a sure social space for herself takes its toll on her, eventually breaking her sanity, depriving her of the ability to tell dream from reality. As a white Jamaican, Antoinette is what Helen Tiffin identifies as a "double outsider," with "the double problem of rejecting former affiliations and power structures and of being accepted into a community from which she seems irretrievably excluded by the hostilities of a history which is, and yet is not, her own."[11] In Tiffin's construction, the white Creole struggles with marginality even as she is seemingly accepted on racial and national characteristics. But for Carine Mardorossian it is the black Caribbean population that is "doubly silenced, doubly marginalized" by the portrayal of the white Creole in the novel.[12] Rather than merely reacting against a marginality foisted on her, the white Creole has the opportunity to create herself against the black community while rejecting the appearance of collaboration with the "real whites." *Wide Sargasso Sea* provides the space for both these approaches and more. Antoinette can be read as victim, with both the white English and the black Caribbean communities represented in the novel defining their boundaries against her. But just as the truth is "never one sided" for Rhys, neither are these boundaries.[13] White Creoles also have more agency than the victim position would afford them; they frequently cross sides, slipping in and out of identification as easily as they slip in and out of patois. This interstitial space may be dangerous for Antoinette because it deprives her of dependable social support, but it is also dangerous for the two groups she exists between because it deconstructs the boundaries they are invested in upholding.

Born into this intermediate social status, Antoinette opens her narrative by informing the reader of how she "ranks" in the social order: "They say when trouble comes close ranks, and so the white people did. But we were not in their ranks" (9). Though she does not indicate it here, she is also outside the "ranks" of the black population. When she faces trouble, she cannot count on support from the black Jamaicans. Even Christophine, the closest she comes to having a caring guardian, retreats when she senses trouble at Granbois. Although Christophine continues to oppose Amelie in defense of Antoinette, she leaves Granbois soon afterward, announcing: "I see enough trouble. . . . I have right to my rest" (60). Antoinette is left to attempt happiness with a husband who does not understand her connection to the newly freed black population. She finds herself in the same position as her mother many years earlier of fighting both the lies told about her by neighbors and her husband's prejudices about colonial life. She ends up caught between the English she should be and the Jamaican she has become. Annette tried to convince Mr. Mason of "the other side" as Antoinette later tries to convince her own English husband that "there is always the other side" (19, 77). Mason's money, although it saves them from sure death, also reestablishes Annette and Antoinette's position outside the ranks of the black population. Although Antoinette feels fleetingly safe after Mr. Mason marries her mother, she realizes that "in some ways it was better before he came" because the black Jamaicans "did not hate us quite so much when we were poor" (20). Antoinette's position, more a cultural "inbetweenity" than marginality, is clear from her use of pronouns. When Mr. Mason criticizes her aunt Cora for not helping when Antoinette and her mother were near destitution, Antoinette thinks, "None of you understand about us" (18). She firmly places Mr. Mason, with his English food, English ways, and English ideas, in the "you" group. Antoinette attempts to "close ranks" against Englishness by identifying herself in the oppositional "us."

Fifteen years later, Michelle Cliff would include herself in this "us," expanding on the tenuousness and psychic danger of the white Creole's social position in her poetry, prose, and fiction. Cliff, who identifies as "white cockroach" herself, explores many of the same issues as Rhys does in *Wide Sargasso Sea*.[14] In Cliff's second novel, *No Telephone to Heaven*, the protagonist Clare reflects on the irony of her academic success in England, where they "admired her mind and implied her good fortune in escaping the brain damage common to Creoles."[15] It was this stereotypical conception of Caribbean Creoles that motivated Rhys to write *Wide Sargasso Sea* decades earlier. In acknowledging her indebtedness to the work begun by Rhys, Cliff writes in 1993 that the particularities of the Caribbean and its histories color the character of its fictions. For her, the region's "customs and travails, its dangers and its gifts, forge extraordinary creatures."[16] Cliff extends the line of these "extraordinary creatures" in her first book, *Claiming an Identity They Taught Me to Despise*, a collection of what can best be characterized as "proems," in both the intuitive and the official meanings of the word. Cliff describes the title piece as "about being a Creole and about being neither one nor the other,"[17] and in it she unmistakably calls on Antoinette Cosway and

Bertha Mason as inspirations, with quotations from both *Wide Sargasso Sea* and *Jane Eyre*.

Cliff continues to build on this kinship with Antoinette/Bertha in her later works. In her essay "Clare Savage as a Crossroads Character," Cliff states that Clare is descended from Bertha Rochester, "wild and raving . . . as Charlotte Brontë describes her, cursing and railing, more beast than human. It takes a West Indian writer, Jean Rhys, to describe Bertha from the inside."[18] For both Cliff and Rhys, however, this "inside" reflects the conflicting loyalties of privileged colonial subjects. In a section of *Claiming an Identity* imagining Bertha's attempt at escape, Cliff considers this aspect of mixture and complicity. First through Grace Poole, the "alcoholic female keeper" who, like Rhys's Grace Poole, must have felt something at having to keep another woman captive; then through Bertha's actions, "Setting fire to the great house / the masters / sometimes ourselves."[19] The spacing of these lines indicates the collusion between "the masters" and "ourselves." It implies that sometimes "the masters" *are* "ourselves." Cliff identifies the confusion inherent in the white Creole position. Regardless of what action they take, they are forced to choose between two sides, with each option involving opposing a group to which they feel some connection.

Antoinette herself practices this complicity when she rejects the group identifications available to her. For example, at first she aligns herself with her fellow convent residents, black and white, but when trouble comes she finds she must reject this alignment and "close ranks" against the other girls. When her stepfather hints at her upcoming engagement she refuses to believe it will happen, resenting his reintrusion into her life. She turns this resentment on the entire convent: "They are safe. How can they know what it can be like outside?" She closes them out and sees herself once again set adrift alone. Later, when she flees to Christophine to request help with making her husband love her again, she performs a similar rejection. Christophine suggests that she leave her husband, but Antoinette thinks, "How can she know the best thing for me to do, this ignorant, obstinate old negro woman, who is not certain if there is such a place as England?" (67). Here she dismisses Christophine when she offers help; Antoinette can envision salvation only as her husband's return to her, not as a result of the independence that Christophine suggests. She can also conceive of Christophine's help in only one way, the obeah potion. She bows to Christophine's knowledge there, but otherwise Christophine is simply an "ignorant" old negro.

It is impossible, however, for Antoinette to continuously reject group inclusion without incurring psychic damage. Only in true exile, the mental and physical exile of the infamous attic, does she attempt to join a culture completely. At the end of the novel, she dreams of rejoining Tia, her childhood friend, turning her back on her English husband and England itself. Before this moment, however, Antoinette is paralyzed by the fear of cultural rejection. She articulates this fear in her explanation of Amelie's song of insult: "It was a song about a white cockroach. That's me. That's what they call all of us who were here before their own people in Africa sold them to the slave traders. And I've heard English women call us white niggers. So between you I often wonder who I am and where is my country and where do I belong and why was I ever born at all" (61). Although she herself cannot make this choice until the end—and even then, only driven by lunacy and dreams—the text often aligns Antoinette with the Caribbean. Antoinette knows the land and the people—she can tell her husband about the pond, what time is the best part of the day, what type of rain is falling and when it will end. She knows the proper protocols for visiting neighbors and the significance of Christophine's mode of dress. She exhibits an expertise that she cannot claim even about herself. She is often unsure about other things, but not about the land, climate, or culture.

Even in her madness, in the cold English attic, Antoinette still exhibits intimate knowledge of the Caribbean. She knows the smells of trees and the names of flowers. She know that "if you are buried under a flamboyant tree . . . your soul is lifted up when it flowers" (109). But by then her mental state makes her final alignment with the Caribbean—symbolized by her dream jump toward Tia at the end—questionable as a conscious choice. Critics alternately read Antoinette's dream jump as fulfilling her wish to be part of the black Caribbean community of her youth or as yet another deferment of this wish, mirroring Tia's rejection of her earlier in the novel. As with the various readings of Antoinette's agency (and, by extension, that of white Creoles) vis-à-vis the black and European communities, I read *Wide Sargasso Sea* as offering these possibilities, and more, as valid. With this ambiguity, Rhys claims a different identity than does Cliff after her. Cliff, immediately after describing the Creole as being "neither one nor the other," adds, "Basically, the identity is Jamaican and black."[20] In *No Telephone to Heaven*, the protagonist, Clare, tries passing in London, tries invisibility but finds that she cannot erase the longing within herself to connect to the colored immigrants from various parts of the empire. Days before she begins hallucinating and hearing an imaginary visitor calling her name, Clare reads *Jane Eyre* and finds that "the fiction had tricked her. Drawn her in so that she became Jane." Clare considers: "Yes, the parallels were there. Was she not heroic Jane? Betrayed. Left to wander. Solitary. Motherless. . . . No, she could not be Jane. Small and pale. English. No, she paused. No, my girl, try Bertha. Wild-maned Bertha. . . . Yes, Bertha was closer to the mark. Captive. Ragout. Mixture. Confused. Jamaican. Caliban. Carib. Cannibal. Cimarron. All Bertha. All Clare."[21] Clare begins to choose her alliances—"Jamaican. Caliban. Carib. Cannibal. . ."—Rhys, however, does not choose Caliban over Miranda. Instead, she problematizes the choice by focusing on the common ground between the two. In this "confused" space, madness resides, threatening, then eventually overtaking Antoinette as it did Bertha before her. In its representation of the indeterminacy of both creoleness and madness, *Wide Sargasso Sea* confirms only the impossibility (and improbability) of confirmation.

Revising *Jane Eyre*

M. M. Adjarian suggests that making Bertha "the narrative subject implicitly sets Jean Rhys and her text in opposition to her nineteenth-century literary predecessor."[22] But the reception of *Wide Sargasso Sea* has not always placed it in opposition to *Jane Eyre*. At first, many critics saw parallels between Jane and Antoinette as the primary point of interest. In their seminal text *Madwoman in the Attic*—a title that elevates Bertha's influence above Jane's—Sandra Gilbert and Susan Gubar describe Brontë's Bertha as an "avatar of Jane," and much of the early scholarship on *Wide Sargasso Sea* read the connection between Jane and Antoinette in a similar manner.[23] In 1978, Helen Tiffin identified clear differences between the two heroines and the two texts, differences rooted in colonialism; and in 1985, Gayatri Spivak refigured these differences into a groundbreaking critique of Euro-feminism's narrow focus on patriarchal relationships in both *Jane Eyre* and *Wide Sargasso Sea*.[24] After Tiffin's and Spivak's critiques, *Wide Sargasso Sea* could no longer be read as simply a Caribbean version of *Jane Eyre*. But the newly apparent opposition between the texts began to influence the reading of *Wide Sargasso Sea* itself, with binaries becoming the rule of thumb. Tiffin, for example, finds that the "parallel between destructive male/female relationships and between imperial nation and colonial underdog is obvious."[25] But the imposition of inter- and intranovel binary oppositions ignores the complexities of Rhys's novel. The intranovel relationships I will explore in the following section of this chapter, but here I turn to the internovel relationships—the revisions Rhys made in focusing on the madwoman in Charlotte Brontë's text. These revisions reflect not only Rhys's interest in fighting Bertha's madness by representing white Creoles from another perspective but also her attention to the histories of slavery, emancipation, and colonialism in the Caribbean.

The opening lines of *Wide Sargasso Sea* indicate not only Antoinette's social position but also the new time period that Rhys has chosen. The "trouble" that Jamaican whites respond to by closing ranks is emancipation in the Caribbean. Rhys shifts the story to later in the nineteenth century to accommodate this time period. *Jane Eyre* was set at approximately the turn of the nineteenth century, so *Wide Sargasso Sea*, as a "pre-story," should occur in the late 1700s; but Rhys rewrites the story to include the social upheaval incited by abolition. Sandra Drake describes this move as emphasizing "the abolition of European plantation slavery and the transition—or failed transition—to some other set of social relations that would constitute a viable Caribbean identity."[26] This is an especially fitting backdrop for the story of a Creole woman who is already unable to access a "viable Caribbean identity." At no time is the "placelessness" of the white Creole more apparent than at emancipation, when the most clear-cut legal difference between blacks and whites is demolished. The redefinition of society requires outsiders, and Creoles are expected to align themselves with white European society. White Creoles like Annette and Antoinette, who resist such an alliance, are categorized as mad in order to maintain the hierarchies that are at risk with emancipation.

Rhys's choice of shifting the story to the emancipation era, then, does more than simply distinguish her heroine from Brontë's madwoman. It manages to question Charlotte Brontë's mid-nineteenth-century ideas of the Caribbean as well as those of the earlier, fictional world of *Jane Eyre*. In addition to highlighting the confusion of emancipation, *Wide Sargasso Sea*, twenty years in the making, highlights the confusion of the period leading up to its publication in 1966. What is the Creole's place after abolition? Or during decolonization? Does she have the *right* to a place, to creating a place, in either historical moment? Arguing for an interpretation of the novel sensitive to Rhys's "insight into the workings of imperial and patriarchal ideologies," Mardorossian writes, "Both contexts (of and in the novel) are often referred to as 'the best and worst of times' since they represented liberation, hope, cultural and intellectual regeneration as well as continued political and economic independence."[27] In the midst of these major social and political revolutions, the

Creole figure presents a gray area in the black-and-white of slavery and freedom, colonization, and independence. Rhys questions the Creole's place in building both the newly emancipated nineteenth-century society and the newly independent twentieth-century nation.

The difficulty of *Wide Sargasso Sea* lies in its being simultaneously a repetition (Naipaul's mimicking) and a criticism of an earlier story. Thus I read Rhys's stylistic choices in the novel as a commentary on her relationship to, and distancing from, Brontë's text. How she writes her revision is important in her representation (re-representation?) of madness. Rhys, of course, rewrites not only a Creole story but a mad Creole's story. As such, Antoinette is more alienated than Rhys's previous heroines. Caribbean writers often focus on those on the periphery, and mad figures are even more marginal, often signifying ignored or overlooked problems in the center. Evelyn O'Callaghan finds that like Brodber's *Jane and Louisa Will Soon Come Home*, Rhys's *Wide Sargasso Sea* "represents the complex demands of gender roles/options, racial stratification and colonial double loyalties that combine to fragment both individuals and societies. Here, one can see West Indian women writers reinterpreting the 'quest for identity' theme pervasive in regional literature, using the 'madwoman' as metonymic of the debilitating 'illness' of the self which still haunts Caribbean societies in the wake of the colonial encounter."[28] O'Callaghan's conclusion that Caribbean writers utilize mad figures in a "metonymic" sense to illustrate the ways the self can be split under (and after) colonialism undercuts the very complexity she argued for earlier in *Woman Version*.[29] It reduces the madwoman to mere sign, having no meaning without the more important concept she signifies. Perhaps a better word would be *representative*, with its dual meanings of both "example" and "delegate." The mad become dangerously both constituted by and exemplary of "their" society. Pushed to the edges, they define the center by exclusion but not expulsion. In England, for example, Antoinette's attic prison "holds her fast" to her husband, who needs her to suffer to validate his ideology. If *she* is the lunatic, as even he doubts during his confused moments before leaving Granbois, then *he* is sane, logical, blameless. But with Rhys's attention to "sides" and stories, Antoinette can also be read as freer than her husband, formed by the events narrated but not reliant on either them or her husband for meaning or agency.

Antoinette, then, becomes (a) representative of and for the friction of "the colonial encounter." She was by no means a unique creation of the Brontë/Rhys imagination. Rhys wrote in 1964, "I think there were several Antoinettes and Mr. Rochesters. Indeed I am sure. Mine is *not*

Miss Brontë's, though much suggested by 'Jane Eyre.'"[30] The plurality of these figures simultaneously refers to the results of the social treatment of white Creoles and the misapprehension of cultural ambiguity. Antoinette's husband also positions Antoinette as representative of many others like her when he begins contemplating locking her away:

> Very soon she'll join all the others who know the secret and will not tell it. Or cannot. Or try and fail because they do not know enough. They can be recognized. White faces, dazed eyes, aimless gestures, high-pitched laughter. The way they walk and talk and scream or try to kill (themselves or you) if you laugh back at them. Yes, they've got to be watched. For the time comes when they try to kill, then disappear. But others are waiting to take their places, it's a long, long line. She's one of them. I too can wait—for the day when she is only a memory to be avoided, locked away, and like all memories, a legend. Or a lie . . . (103; ellipses in original)

Although Rhys differentiates her white Creole from Brontë's, she works with the same legend of mad Creoles in England. She shows how close the legend is to the lie by questioning Brontë's easy dismissal of Bertha as a lunatic. Rhys admits in an earlier correspondence with Diana Athill, "I borrowed the name Antoinette—(I carefully haven't named the man at all) and the idea of her seeming a bit mad—to an Englishman."[31] Rhys was conscious of the differences in madness between the two cultures. Antoinette's cultural inbetweenity was incomprehensible to an Englishman, secure in his national and racial identity. The only way that someone with such stability could understand her inability, and refusal, to choose sides would be to see her as "a bit mad."

The letter to Athill also raises Rhys's attention to naming in the novel. Rhys has "carefully" chosen (and avoided choosing) names for her characters. Antoinette and Christophine voice the reasons for this in the novel. Antoinette rejects her husband's renaming of her, telling him, "Bertha is not my name. You are trying to make me into someone else, calling me by another name. I know. That's obeah too" (88). He tries to make her into her mother, into Brontë's madwoman, but she resists. He also tries to make her into a doll that he can manipulate—"Marionette, Antoinette, Marionetta, Antoinetta"—and Christophine identifies this renaming as his wish for power over Antoinette. Christophine tells him, "That word mean doll, eh? Because she don't speak. You want to force her to cry and to speak" (93). Antoinette thinks, in her confusion in part 3, "Names matter" (106); and so they do for Rhys. She muses in a letter to Francis Wyndham that "Mr. R's name ought to be changed,"[32] and she considers the name Raworth, but in the end she chooses to not name Antoinette's husband. Rhys works her own authorial obeah on Brontë's Rochester to make him one of many nameless Englishmen who came to the Caribbean to secure their financial future. Nameless as he is, his narrative of Antoinette's madness slides dangerously close to stereotype.

Antoinette's familiarity with obeah is another major Rhys revision to Brontë's madwoman. This too is part of the "other side of the story" of Antoinette's madness. It is part of the secret that remains untold—glimpsed, yet ignored. The "ambiguity" surrounding obeah "persists throughout the narrative and reflects the two narrators' inability to grasp a Caribbean experience whose opaqueness cannot be reconciled with their interpretive frameworks."[33] They try to cross the boundaries and end up alienated even from themselves. Her husband recognizes this and rights himself, but Antoinette, who was never sure of her place, has no way of reclaiming steady mental ground. Although she is disoriented and desperate beforehand, she truly deteriorates after using Christophine's potion. Her husband also becomes mentally disoriented in connection with obeah. The shift to Antoinette's narration in part 2 occurs after her husband is drawn into the magic of the forest. He begins to research obeah, and while he is reading, Antoinette goes to Christophine to request a love potion. Under the spell of this "other side" that the servant Baptiste refuses to acknowledge to him, Antoinette's husband loses the power of narration that Rhys grants him in this section of the novel. This alternation in narrators is perhaps the clearest indication that *Wide Sargasso Sea* is not an "anti-*Jane Eyre*" text. If indeed the novels were opposed, *Wide Sargasso Sea* would not present the ambivalence toward England evident in the novel. Rhys does not, as Caliban does in Aimé Césaire's *A Tempest*, use her text to curse the colonizers. Instead, she writes from a space outside this binary, the Miranda-space that challenges both Prospero-inclined and Caliban-inspired renderings of race, class, and madness. In the following section I examine Rhys's method of challenging such binaries in the formal choices she makes in representing Antoinette's madness.

Method and Madness

Rhys's letters reveal how much she struggled with the question of form. How to tell the other side of the story? Especially when the side you might claim allegiance to is already marked as mad? Rhys's eventual choice of two first-person narrators provides access to the ambiguity and complexity of the white Creole in a manner impossible in *Jane Eyre*. In her 1958 letter to Vaz Dias, Rhys wrote that to avoid a one-dimensional picture of Antoinette, the very thing she objected to in Brontë's rendition of the mad Creole, she needed to have another narrator: "Another 'I' must talk, two others perhaps. Then the Creole's 'I' will come to life."[34] Rhys needed a narrative that respected the Brontë text but did not commit the same error she noted in *Jane Eyre*—she wanted to provide more than just one side of the story. As Antoinette tells her husband, "There is always the other side, always" (77). Accordingly, the husband speaks in part 2 of the novel. This helps with filling out Antoinette's character and with avoiding naming the male narrator. He becomes "I" rather than a third-person Rochester (or Raworth). Rhys's deviations from a linear narrative, with a singular narrator, are not always easy to follow. The novel does not clearly differentiate characters' thoughts from their dialogue, and it switches between Antoinette's and her husband's narratives without a visual signal; there are no italics, font modifications, or changes in perspective (from first to third person).[35] Mary Lou Emery describes Rhys's narrative strategies as indicative of her own and her characters' outsiderness: "The alterations of conventional narrative that we find in Rhys's early novels may appear as silences, inactions, or even formal flaws; however, they record a double displacement, colonial and sexual, that the conventional narrative and even European modernist narratives, with their presumption of a self to be displaced, divided or lost, cannot adequately express. Rhys's narrative strategies and the masquerade that in her novels *is* character, expose the limits of novelistic convention and give us glimpses of other possibilities."[36] In *Wide Sargasso Sea*, Rhys takes more liberties with convention than in her earlier novels. She made attempts with *Voyage in the Dark*, which is commonly referred to as the other West Indian novel, but she had to change the ending to suit her publisher's (and his idea of her audience's) needs. She also demonstrates a preference for first-person narration in her later novels. With *Wide Sargasso Sea*, Rhys intensifies the first-person perspective by doubling the "I's" that speak in the text. While *Jane Eyre* was very much told from the point of view of Jane, *Wide Sargasso Sea* presents a multifaceted view of Antoinette, of her husband, of the Caribbean, and of madness. Joya Uraizee writes that the novel "must be viewed as an example of literary symbiosis (a combination of voices at once powerful and silent), and not as an attempt to replace the master-narrative of *Jane Eyre* with an 'alternative history.'"[37] There are several voices because the novel differentiates between members of each group. Although she follows in her mother's footsteps to a certain degree, Antoinette is different in various ways from Annette, just as, despite similarities based on race, class, and/or nationality, Amelie is different from Christophine and Baptiste, and Mr. Mason is different from Antoinette's husband. To varying degrees, each of these segments of the population is allowed to speak within the narrative. These voices, though they can perhaps be generally categorized as white, Creole, and black, multiply the platforms in the novel.

The different voices also present different dimensions to the representations of madness. Part 1, with Antoinette's "I," provides more access to who she becomes in the attic at Thornfield Hall. As a child, Antoinette is afraid of people, specifically of strangers. She explains this phobia when she describes her early life with her mother to her husband: "She [Annette] was so lonely that she grew away from other people. That happens. It happened to me too but it was easier for me because I hardly remembered anything else" (78). The younger Antoinette often ran from people or expressed fear of them. Animals, snakes, everything was "better, better than people" (16). She equates safety with peacefulness, solitude, and quiet. Her social anxiety is manageable at Coulibri and the convent, but it resurges when her mother marries Mr. Mason and later when Antoinette herself is married.

The Rochester figure narrates the beginnings of this marriage in part 2. His perspective provides the disorientation of the English subject as he tries to place his own interpretation on a land and a people foreign to him. This foreignness, though tinged with familiarity because of the rhetoric of imperialism, may seem "a bit mad—to an Englishman." Toward the end of part 2, Antoinette's husband, in his own semimadness, admits that "suddenly, bewilderingly, I was certain that everything I had imagined to be truth was false. False. Only the magic and the dream are true—all the rest's a lie" (100–101). But the feeling is fleeting and easily forgotten as he reminds himself that, unlike Antoinette, he "knew that [his] dreams were dreams" (100). Afterward, he describes his state as "exhausted," because "the mad conflicting emotions had gone and left [him] wearied and empty. Sane" (103). Like Rochester in *Jane Eyre*, Antoinette's husband goes temporarily mad from his interactions with his wife and "the tropics." He rids himself of these strong emotions, however, and resorts to the coldness that used to be Antoinette's armor. If Antoinette were to return to the safety of indifference that she practiced at the convent, if she were to empty herself of the passions stirred by her marriage and her attachment to the people and places that her husband found strange, she too could appear sane. But she refuses to reject these attachments only to gain her husband's favor; she attempts, instead, to embrace the increasingly fragmented and contradictory parts of herself until she becomes more than "a bit mad."

In the early stages of their marriage, before she mentally "gives up" like her mother before her, Antoinette tries to inspire similar passions and attachments in her husband by telling him stories of her island and herself. But, sure of his place outside of and in opposition to these things, he purposefully ignores her. He admits to the reader, though not to Antoinette, "I won't tell you that I scarcely listened to your stories. I was longing for night and darkness and the time when the moonflowers open" (102). He displays a similarly self-interested disregard when Christophine tries to explain Antoinette to him after the love potion debacle. Mardorossian writes that in this discussion with Christophine, "Rochester . . . seems to act as an obstructing surface from which Christophine's words bounce back unheeded."[38] But the parenthetical lines that alternate with Christophine's statements transform her diatribe into a dialogue. Although the narrator claims that "every word she said was echoed, echoed loudly in [his] head" (92), the echoes are not merely a repetition of Christophine's words. Rather, there seems to be a chorus of voices moving through him, breaking Christophine's monologue and sometimes giving different meanings to her statements. The italicized parenthetical lines approximate an interlocutor:

> "But all you want is to break her up"
> *(Not the way you mean, I thought)*
> "But she hold out eh? She hold out."
> *(Yes, she held out. A pity)*
> . . .
> "Not telling her why."
> *(Why?)*
> "No more love, eh?"
> *(No more love)*
> (92)

Rhys's narrative choices in this scene result in a "conversation" that becomes an onslaught on the narrator from outside and inside. The various voices include his own attempt at defense, worn down by Christophine's words and a choruslike emphasis on her argument. As in the parenthetical descriptions of her convent life, Antoinette may also be interjecting a later commentary in this story, perhaps from the attic at Thornfield Hall. Just before the Rochester figure resumes the conversation, the last parenthetical is clearly in Antoinette's voice: "(*I lay awake all night long after they were asleep, and as soon as it was light I got up and dressed and saddled Preston. And I came to you. Oh Christophine. O Pheena, Pheena, help me*)" (93).[39] This cry for help, especially if read as Antoinette speaking from Thornfield Hall, once again defies any argument that her madness robs her of the ability (or the power) to coherently interject her perspective. Such interjections ensure that although the unnamed man narrates most of the book, Antoinette's story does not get lost in his account of events. Not only is Christophine there to offer her own view of Antoinette, but the eruption of Antoinette's voice into the narrative at moments in part 2 also serves to contribute a different side of the story.

Although the novel has two official narrators, Christophine has quite a lot of dialogue in parts 1 and 2, avoiding a simplistic opposition between the European man and his white Creole wife by inserting a third powerful perspective. Christophine places Antoinette in a comparative middle position when she tells Antoinette's husband, "She is not *béké* like you, but she is *béké*, and not like us either" (93). Although she cannot name this third space, and can only refer to it in terms of the dominant binary of "you" and "us," Christophine recognizes Antoinette's place between the two.[40] As with the narrative and these categories, the novel itself is structured in threes, which supports Rhys's objective of providing a fuller story. The three-part structure of the novel forecloses an either/or imperative. Antoinette employs this antiduality logic when she corrects her husband's opinion that Granbois is his enemy and on her side: "It is not for you and not for me. It has nothing to do with either of us. That is why you are afraid of it, because it is something else" (78). Rhys avoids simple Manichaeanism (it is either "for you" or "for me") in her revision. In utilizing a three-part structure and multiple voices, the novel provides that "something else" missing in *Jane Eyre*. It is in this third space that Bertha, previously an "improbable monster," can become Antoinette, still troubled, vulnerable, and mentally suspect but not as easily dismissed as insane and unreliable.

Although this three-part structure seems to progress forward chronologically, the novel actually resists a narrative of progress. Rhys often hints at the novel's position as prestory to an already written narrative. Therefore, it is sometimes difficult to determine the temporal space that either narrator occupies. In a first-person narrative told in the past tense, the distance between the speaking self and the acting self is usually clarified by the narrator. In V. S. Naipaul's *Miguel Street*, for example, the narrator is obviously older and "wiser." Similarly, in Naipaul's *Mimic Men*, Ralph tells his readers that he is writing from England, years after the events he describes. But in *Wide Sargasso Sea*, there are only a few hints by the narrators, and these are ambiguous. Mardorossian's application of the term *focalization* to the novel is useful in distinguishing between these differently located narrators. She writes that "one of the most distinct narrative patterns in *Wide Sargasso Sea* consists of an oscillation between the internal perceptual focalizer (the experiencing child) and the external focalizer (the older, narrating Antoinette)."[41] Focalization, then, occurs within narration and shifts on the basis of time. In Antoinette's husband's narration, both internal and external focalizations remain rigid, despite the disorientation during and after his conversation with Christophine. His reference to sacrificing his "eyes never to have seen this abominable place" and his drawing of an English house may be recognizable to a *Jane Eyre* reader, but they are inaccessible to him as foretelling the future (96, 98).

However, even a reader unfamiliar with *Jane Eyre* would recognize the shifts in Antoinette's focalization. During her last conversation with Christophine, Antoinette has a premonition that jettisons her into Brontë's text. She thinks, "I must know more than I know already. For I know that house where I will be cold and not belonging, the bed I shall lie in has red curtains and I have slept there many times before, long ago. How long ago?" (67). Antoinette's vision, portrayed as a memory, epitomizes the text's overall disregard for chronological order. Antoinette's narrative in particular, in her adolescent years, gives the feeling that time is irrelevant. She shifts from past to present tense easily, without explanation. After she begins living at the convent, Antoinette tells the reader, "Quickly, while I can, I must remember the hot classroom," and she proceeds to describe a moment in sewing class at the convent in the present tense (31). The effect is to make the portrait more immediate for the reader, but this portrait is interrupted by Antoinette's later self. She parenthetically questions Mother St. Justine's readings of the lives of the saints, first with her own "Oh, but where? Where?" and then with Helene de Plana's assertion that Mother St. Justine is menopausal and therefore cannot be blamed for a disconnected narrative (32). It is not clear who this "remembering" Antoinette is and from which temporal space she remembers.

In an effort to *fix* this temporal ambiguity, Kathy Mezei writes that part 1 of the novel is told from the convent, that the interval in part 2 is written from the attic of Thornfield Hall, and that both are Antoinette's attempt to hold on to sanity because her "very sanity is tied to her ability to narrate." Mezei, however, applies the European standard of order to Antoinette: "To prevent a false telling of her story by others—the lie—Antoinette must tell herself in the first person following the conventions of narrative order. When the narrative disintegrates, as it does in Part Three, so does Antoinette. When the narrative stops, Antoinette dies. By her act of narration, she retains her tenuous fragile hold on sanity, on life itself, since to narrate is to live, to order a life, to 'make sense' out of it."[42] What if, however, we read part 3 of the novel not as a "disintegration" of the narrative but rather as a skillful handling by Rhys of the representation of madness from the sufferer's perspective? Antoinette *can* still tell her own story, and she insists on telling it even as her mental faculties decline. Even in madness, Antoinette controls the narrative, and rather than indicating her death, the end of the narrative indicates her having accomplished her objective ("What I have to do" [112]) of telling of "the other side."

In telling her story, Antoinette does not display any need to "make sense" of her life; at least, she does not, and cannot, approximate the "sense" that her husband values. His narration follows the accepted "conventions of narrative order," which Mezei lists as "linear chronology, sequence, narratorial lucidity, distance."[43] Time, order, sanity, objectivity—these qualities are prized by her husband's European standards but are less meaningful in Antoinette's Caribbean world. "Linear chronology," in particular, is disregarded in the novel as a whole as Rhys works to interleave her story with Brontë's original. In a 1934 letter to Evelyn Scott, Rhys writes that in *Voyage in the Dark* she was concerned "with time being an illusion": "I mean that the past exists—side by side—with the present, not behind it, that what was—is."[44] Rhys structures the narratives in *Wide Sargasso Sea* around the meshing of time she tried to capture in *Voyage in the Dark*. The distortion of narrative time is not necessarily a *disintegration*, or a losing of control, but instead may be related to an acceptance of, or a desire for, a different form of "time-telling," such as the one Emile utilizes at the beginning of part 2. When the Rochester figure asks Emile, one of the helpers on his honeymoon journey, his age, the old man replies, "Fourteen? Yes I have fourteen years master." Antoinette's husband expresses disbelief and Emile replies, "Fifty-six years perhaps," and indicates that his mother would know the truth, but she is dead and he has no reason to be concerned with his age. But as the editors of the Norton edition indicate, Emile could have been born on the 29th of February, which would make both his answers correct (40). The Englishman and the

Eurocentric Young Bull, however, cannot consider Emile as anything but a foolish old man. Emile points to another center, one that, like Antoinette's narrative, is not necessarily ruled by European ideas of time and order.

This is not to impose yet another binary—European versus native time and order. *Wide Sargasso Sea* maintains past, present, and future simultaneously. To add that third space to Rhys's conception of time, one could say that in the novel "the past exists—side by side—with the present *and the future*, . . . that what was *and what will be*—is."[45] While seeming to disregard it, Antoinette is hyperaware of time even in her madness; she is particularly sensitive to the "time" she has to tell her side of the story. Her "Quickly, while I can, I must remember the hot classroom" interjection in her description of the convent indicates that the future heavily influences her narration. I read these interjections as made by the fragmented Antoinette of Thornfield Hall's attic. Therefore her "Quickly, while I can" may refer to her limited time alone, before Grace Poole returns and presumably prevents her writing in some way, or before her literarily ordained death. In any case, Antoinette cannot be concerned with rigid delineations of time in telling her story.

Indeed, this breaks down altogether when she narrates part 3 of the novel, in which she struggles to cope with her present by remembering the past and dreaming of an already-occurred future. Antoinette's dreams, paradoxically, *remind* her of something that has not yet happened in her narrative; they become alternative passages to access knowledge that she already possesses. In the novel Antoinette relates three dreams in detail. The dreams have similar characteristics, and Antoinette refers to all three as "my dream," indicating that for her they form one continuous narrative. During her final dream she connects all three: "That was the third time I had my dream, and it ended" (111). The dream ends because it has succeeded in getting Antoinette to stop running from her literary fate. In the dream, Antoinette's life, her imprisonment, and her madness end; in waking, her denial ends. At the end of her third dream, she thinks, "Now at last I know why I was brought here and what I have to do" (112). Past, present, and future coexist in her statement. She has been brought to England by Rhys to rejoin her previous story. She must there rewrite Bertha's end in *Jane Eyre*, claiming her power to narrate her own delirious dreams and potential death.

Delirious Desires and Dreams of Death

Dream endings are at best difficult to read, as is also evident in Derek Walcott's *Dream on Monkey Mountain.* When dreams are mixed with madness, the text is especially ambiguous, because both narrator and narrative become even more untrustworthy. Part 3 of *Wide Sargasso Sea* begins with Grace Poole's words and thoughts on the mad woman she has been hired to "care" for in Thornfield Hall. The novel seems, then, to have brought Brontë's and Rhys's stories together; but Rhys's ending for Antoinette is still not Brontë's ending for Bertha. Of her ending, Rhys writes: "I want it in a way triumphant!"[46] Bertha must be recuperated as more than a unidimensional lunatic figure, a plot device necessary merely for the maturation of Jane Eyre. Engaging fully with Bertha's madness now that she has brought her tale to Thornfield Hall's attic, Rhys turns to dreams to map potential routes of triumphant escapes for Bertha and Antoinette.

Although she had "never read a long novel about a mad mind or an unusual mind or anybody's mind at all," Rhys felt that the mental world of the character was "the only thing that matter[ed]." She tried at first to write the entire story from Antoinette's point of view, presenting a monologue of madness beginning and ending with dreams. She had successfully blended dream and reality, time and place in the original ending of *Voyage in the Dark*, but she found the process too difficult to maintain for the length of *Wide Sargasso Sea.* In addition, she imagined that after the "fuss" that led to her changing the end of *Voyage in the Dark* for publication, the response to her vision for *Wide Sargasso Sea* would be "A mad girl speaking all the time is too much!" She decided, therefore, "to tell the story straight—more or less—and keep the madness for the last act." The rest of the text, however, does not escape the madness; it is not all contained in "the last act." The madness also manages to seep into Antoinette's husband's narration.

Rhys writes that even after she decided to "tell the story straight" rather than start with dreams and have a mad narrator, she still worked on "keeping the dream feeling and working up to the madness."[47] The "dream feeling" of the text is accomplished in several ways. The dialogue, for instance, is often mixed into the narrative with no quotation marks to indicate its beginning and end. And there are, of course, the vivid repetitions of Antoinette's dream. After each of these dreams, Antoinette still wakes to a nightmare: she wakes to various levels of indifference from the women "caring" for her. When she wakes from her first dream her mother covers her but does not comfort her. Annette immediately rejects Antoinette's possible need in order to care for her brother Pierre. Antoinette is left to comfort herself. After her second dream, Antoinette wakes to a nun at the convent, who provides more physical comfort than Annette but similarly dismisses Antoinette's fear. By the time she wakes from her third dream, Antoinette no longer looks for comfort. She pretends to be still asleep, leaving Grace Poole to wonder if perhaps she was the one dreaming.

Each dream marks a transition in Antoinette's life. These three transitions are connected to England's interruption of Antoinette's search for safety. After her first dream—which occurs after the Luttrells, newly arrived from England, visit Coulibri—Antoinette wakes "the next morning knowing that nothing would be the same. It would change and go on changing" (16). This is true for her other dreams as well. After her second dream Antoinette leaves the security of the convent to marry her newly arrived English husband. After her third dream, having lost her last hope to English marital law, she appears ready to retaliate by burning Thornfield Hall, but her narrative ends before she achieves this goal. Though it repeats the imagery of the first two dreams, Antoinette's third dream ends her flight. The first two dreams express her fear of the immediate future, while the last one shows that she has come to accept what she "must do." She dreams of setting fire to Englishness, represented by Thornfield Hall and her husband, and aligns herself with the Caribbean, represented by Christophine, Tia, and Coulibri. At this point, however, the text rejects her effort—"[She] jumped and woke" (112)—deferring her death and her escape from England.

When Antoinette wakes, her thoughts are lucid and determined; she is not the confused lunatic of Brontë's novel. Her final dream, with its fatal "choice" of Tia and Coulibri, restores her to some semblance of sanity. This of course is if we read her waking as "real" rather than more delirium. It is difficult to trust the narration of a madwoman relating dreams. Without the pre-text of *Jane Eyre*, readers could not even be sure that Antoinette had arrived in England. Throughout the novel, she questions the reality of England and therefore her refusal to believe Grace Poole about her location may simply be a logical continuation of her earlier attitude. During the "honeymoon phase," for instance, Antoinette asks her husband, "Is it true . . . that England is like a dream? Because one of my friends who married an Englishman wrote and told me so. She said this place London is like a cold dark dream sometimes. I want to wake up." Her husband counters: "That is precisely how your beautiful island seems to me, quite unreal and like a dream." But Antoinette continues to believe that it is England that "must be like a dream" (47–48). Intimate knowledge of their respective "place" makes Granbois more real to Antoinette and England more real to her husband. At the beginning of *Voyage in the Dark*, Anna Morgan, also a transplanted white Creole, thinks, "Sometimes it was as if I were back there [Dominica] and as if England were a dream. At other times England was the real thing and out there was the dream, but I could never fit them together."[48] Anna's inner conflict becomes this difference of perspective between Antoinette and her husband in the later novel.

Anna exhibits other connections to Antoinette, particularly in terms of her questionable sanity: she has the same phobia of people—when she has an abortion, she thinks, "I'm glad it happened when nobody was here because I hate people"[49]—and in the original unpublished ending she also suffers from madness. In the revised ending, despite some complications from the abortion, Anna lives. In part 4, she is in and out of consciousness, with memories of Dominica interwoven with the conversation around her. The doctor pronounces her "all right" and "ready to start all over again." Anna, however, does not receive this diagnosis positively. As the doctor leaves, Anna thinks about "starting all over again. And about being new and fresh and about mornings and misty days, when anything might happen, and about starting all over again, all over again."[50] Given Anna's memories of Dominica and her life in England so far, "starting all over again" is not a bright prospect. Though Rhys has changed the words, she has kept some of the debilitating despair of the original ending. Read against Anna's second chance, Antoinette's dream flight from the roof is an exhilarating leap toward freedom.

Antoinette's waking is therefore anticlimactic. She too receives a second chance, and though she seems destined to fulfill her dream, the end remains ambiguous. Though we may not be sure of Antoinette's fate, *Wide Sargasso Sea* exists as proof that Bertha's leap was "in a way triumphant!" She escapes her literary confines to reappear in Rhys's novel and in later texts where her story may be told from a Caribbean perspective. For example, in a short story titled "Contagious Melancholia," Michelle Cliff describes a family that has dwindled to two elderly unmarried women. The narrator ends by asking, "Who were the Misses Small? For these are real women I have been talking about. Down to their names. They are long gone. Girlhood chums of my great-grandmother, they cluster together in my mind with all the other mad, crazy, eccentric, disappointed, demented, neurasthenic women of my childhood, where Bertha Mason grew on trees. Every family of our ilk, every single one, had such a member. And she was always hidden, and she was always a shame, and she was always the bearer of that which lay behind us."[51] Here Cliff intersects several histories: the history of families of a certain "ilk"—read, privileged "Jamaica White" or Creole—who are revered on the island even after their finances have been decimated, as have the Misses Small's holdings; the history of the variously alienated women in Jamaica—the spinster, the lesbian, the "disappointed"—who are grouped under the heading of mad or crazy; and the history of Bertha Mason, who "grew on trees," or, to be more specific, who grew on Caribbean family trees. Bertha has escaped the pages of *Jane Eyre* to become the "bearer" of her own literary history.

In an interview, Rhys tells Elizabeth Vreeland that Bertha "seemed such a poor ghost. I thought I'd try to write her a life."[52] Consequently, *Wide Sargasso Sea* is a rendering of one possible life, not (as Cliff's different renditions of her later indicate) *the* life of Bertha. Without changing the plot of *Jane Eyre*, Rhys revolutionizes the reception of the earlier novel. Other postcolonial revisions—J. M. Coetzee's *Foe* or Césaire's *A Tempest*, for example—succeed in changing the reception of the texts they revise, but most also change the parameters of the original text. As a prestory that leaves *Jane Eyre* intact (albeit temporally displaced), *Wide Sargasso Sea* has a stronger impact than a more intrusive revision. Antoinette may still die, but Rhys gives her death intent. Whenever readers of *Wide Sargasso Sea* return to *Jane Eyre*, then, they can no longer passively accept European definitions of the first Mrs. Rochester as "intemperate and unchaste" or her "seeming a bit mad—to an Englishman" as the only cause of her imprisonment and death. They *cannot* accept only one side of the story.

4 Shared Dreams and Collective Delirium in Derek Walcott's *Dream on Monkey Mountain*

In 1967, just prior to the play's first production, Derek Walcott described *Dream on Monkey Mountain* as "an attempt to cohere various elements in West Indian folklore, but . . . also a fantasy based on the hallucination of an old woodcutter who has a vision of returning to Africa."[1] This first production occurred in Canada, but Walcott's utilization of folklore grounds the play in the Caribbean without limiting it to stereotype; he avoids fruitless nostalgia by layering the "various elements" of folklore within the experimental dreamwork of the play. If, as Édouard Glissant writes, "experimentation is for us [in the Caribbean] the only alternative: the organization of a process of representation that allows the community to reflect, to criticize, and to take shape," then in *Dream on Monkey Mountain* Walcott's mosaic of folklore connected by fantasy creates space for the newness that will allow for the psychological and material "shaping" of a Caribbean community.[2] Walcott organizes the folkloric elements within the hallucinations of the play's protagonist, Makak, allowing dreams and madness to create the glue that produces a cohesive Caribbeanness within the play.[3]

Dream on Monkey Mountain is uniquely situated for an examination of the "West Indian discourse" within which Walcott situates himself. In this play, and in most of his work, Walcott positions himself as participating in a Caribbean aesthetic, as building *in* the Caribbean, not in a larger diasporic tradition. He describes himself as "primarily, absolutely a Caribbean writer,"[4] and he is one of the few West Indian writers of stature who continues to live in the Caribbean.[5] Regarding the Caribbean people and landscape as vital to his writing, he not only considers his muse Caribbean but also situates his primary audience in the region. In a 1994 collection of written comments in the *Caribbean Writer*, Walcott states, "I don't care if people don't understand what I write in England or in Paris as long as West Indians appreciate what I'm trying to do; that's all I care about."[6] He envisions his work as speaking not only about but *to* a West Indian community. Although the majority of his publications are of poetry, Walcott has expressed an equal commitment to both art forms, seeing his plays as "large poems that are performed before an audience."[7] His desire for an immediate "roar of response" from the audience, however, highlights the major difference between his connections to his readers and to his theatrical audiences.[8] It is this latter connection that I examine in my reading of Walcott's exploration of mental decolonization through the staging of dreams and delirium in *Dream on Monkey Mountain*. What is it that Walcott communicates about and to West Indians during these independence years? He designates the setting of the play as "a West Indian Island," which is simultaneously general and concrete. While not anchored to a particular nation, *Dream on Monkey Mountain* is specific to the nation-building process in the Caribbean, a process that lends itself to drama, dreams, and delirium. In *Caribbean Discourse*, Glissant asserts, "When a nation is taking shape, it develops a theatrical form that 'duplicates' its history (gives it significance) and provides an inventory."[9] In producing one vision of a balance between change and tradition during this "taking shape" period, *Dream on Monkey Mountain* "inventories" the problems and opportunities involved in building a new Caribbean nation, any new Caribbean nation.

Walcott maintains the balance between specificity and universality in *Dream on Monkey Mountain* by staging these issues in a dream. In his "Note on Production," which precedes the 1970 printed version of the play, he advises: "The play is a dream, one that exists as much in the given minds of its principal characters as in that of its writer, and as such, it is illogical, derivative, contradictory. Its source is metaphor and it is best treated as a physical poem with all the subconscious and deliberate borrowings of poetry."[10] This gives the reader, if not the past and potential audiences of the play, an insight into Walcott's vision for Makak and his other "principal characters." But Walcott's wording also emphasizes the ambiguity inherent in the dream format of the play. By ascribing the dream to the "principal characters," Walcott obscures the status of the remaining cast members. Are Makak and Corporal Lestrade dreaming but not the vendors in Quatre Chemin Market or the sisters who surround the dying Josephus? Do the members of the supporting cast exist outside the dream, and have they decided for the moment to, in Tigre's words, "dissolve in [the] dream" (289)? Is it the same dream in the "given minds" of Walcott and his main characters? That is, is Moustique's dream the same as Makak's, and are they both sharing Walcott's dream? John Thieme, on the basis of Walcott's "Note on Production," views the play as "a product of the collective consciousness of all the characters . . . a collective fantasy."[11] But *fantasy*, with its connotations of coherence and logic, does not cover Walcott's broader use of the term *dream*.[12] In accepting the playwright's directives in his "Note on Production," one would also have to accept that Makak's hallucinations spawn various "illogical, derivative, contradictory" visions for the future in the play's cast, theatrical audiences, *and* readers. Indeed, these visions would necessarily be different with each performance or reading, creating a collective consciousness that relies on differing combinations of images from individual and communal dreams, given and lost minds.

Dramatizing Dreams

Dream on Monkey Mountain is staged in two parts of three scenes each, with a prologue and an epilogue. Part 1 opens with the prologue, set in a jail cell where Corporal Lestrade harangues Makak and his two cell mates, Souris and Tigre. Makak, in an effort to defend himself, begins to describe his vision of a white woman on Monkey Mountain. The next three scenes of part 1 follow Makak and his companion, Moustique, from Monkey Mountain to Quatre Chemin Market as Makak pursues his dream of kingship in Africa. Moustique first derides, then takes advantage of Makak's dreams and ostensible healing powers, eventually dying at the end of part 1. Part 2 returns to the jail cell, where Makak and his cell mates escape to Monkey Mountain and are followed by the Corporal. The Corporal and Souris become Makak's apostles, and in scene 3—an extravagant court scene—Makak is glorified as king. The epilogue returns again to the jail cell: it is the following morning and Makak is released from jail. In *Nobody's Nation*, Paul Breslin asserts that at the end of the prologue, "Makak enters the dream world that rules the play until its epilogue."[13] Breslin also speaks of Makak "waking" from his dream at the end of the play. But Walcott does not separate the six scenes of parts 1 and 2 as the dream; he designates the entire play as a dream. So although Breslin argues that we should take Walcott at his word in the "Note on Production" and accept the play as "illogical, derivative, contradictory," he falls prey to the attempt at ordering that he warns against.[14]

Breslin also highlights the beginning of scene 3 (in part 1) as evidence of the nonlinearity of the play because it returns briefly to the jail cell setting; but he does not acknowledge that in incorporating the staging of the prologue and epilogue within this "dream," Walcott signals that nothing should be taken for reality. To accept the whole play as a dream, without the prologue and epilogue as waking framing devices, sets the audience on shaky ground. With only the six scenes as the dream spaces, the prologue and epilogue provide a form of rootedness: somewhere to anchor the chain, tangled though it may be, of events that occur in the play. The audience could, following this line of reasoning, accept the opening and closing of the play as linear and "real" in the fiction of the theater. But Walcott refuses to provide that type of security. If we accept the middle of the story as a dream, then we must accept the entirety as a dream. And we cannot ascribe this dream only to Makak, because the playwright has mandated that it be a dream in the minds of all his "principal characters." If Makak's falling into a fit signals the beginning of a dream state, then we should see similar moments for Moustique and the Corporal. Similar waking moments should also exist at the end of the play.

In the last scene of part 2, Lestrade announces the dream as communal; at the very least, he indicates that it belongs not only to Makak.[15] When he accuses the resurrected Moustique of betrayal, Lestrade says, "You have betrayed our dream" (314). His choice of the first-person plural claims the dream for the other characters *and* the audience. Lestrade makes it clear that although it may have begun with Makak's hallucinations, the dream no longer resides solely in Makak's mind. Like Moustique, however, some critics ignore the Corporal and the implications of his charge and refocus their attention on Makak. Although the Corporal resists Makak's dream in part 1, and Moustique continues to resist it throughout the play, they are also participants in the dream. To assign the dream only to Makak denies their parts as principal characters in shaping the action of the play.

The audience for *Dream on Monkey Mountain* also becomes a part of this army of dreamers. As Lloyd Brown notes: "Walcott does not allow us the luxury of viewing Makak's dream as an isolated, individual fantasy. For we are a part of his dream. And *our* implication is dramatized by the manner in which the 'spectators' *within* the play/dream are incorporated into Makak's visionary world; his cell-mates, Tigre and

Souris, the jailor Corporal Lestrade, and Makak's partner, Moustique—they are all principal actors in Makak's fantasies because, although they see him as a weak-headed old man, the dream also exists in *their* minds, and, implicitly in the minds of the play's Black (theater) audience."[16] For the audience, there are physical bodies on the stage, but, if the producer has heeded Walcott's note, the play is dreamlike. Both the cast of Walcott's play and the play's audience are constantly aware of their precarious position between dream and reality. Even the "apotheosis" of the dream—as Walcott designates scene 3 of part 2—maintains this tension between reality and fantasy. When Moustique returns to face Makak and his court, the audience is forced to consider the contradiction of a dead man's reappearance on the stage. The charge the Corporal lays against him—"You have betrayed our dream"—may refer to Moustique's impersonation of Makak in the marketplace or to Moustique's callous attitude toward the dream as a whole and his refusal to believe in and support it. Another possibility, however, is that by returning from the dead Moustique has betrayed the entire play as a dream. Makak and Corporal Lestrade, the principal characters in this scene, accept Moustique's presence easily, but this is their dream. To the audience and perhaps to the other characters who appear to be "dissolving" into this dream, Moustique's reappearance rends the fabric of the dream, reinforcing the play's status as a dream narrative.

Moustique is a key character, not merely for his betrayal of Makak's dream in Quatre Chemin Market and his return from the dead, but also for his practical rebuttal of Makak's madness, a madness that others in the play accept without question. When Makak tells him in early in the play that he is going mad, Moustique promptly refuses to accept it. He tells him, "Go mad tomorrow, today is market day" (232). Indeed, Moustique's very body reminds him of the impotence of dreams and the meaninglessness of madness. Walcott describes "someone with an incurable wound" as representative of "some containment of human agony."[17] For readers of the play, Moustique's "twist foot" is not as memorable, but for audiences, his limp is a constant reminder of the material effects of poverty. Moustique's pain, however, is not enough for him to believe in Makak's dream; he has a different, more practical response to his misery. When Makak tells him of his dream, Moustique responds by reminding Makak that he has seen him thus before: "You remember one morning I come up and from the time I break the bush, I see you by the side of the hut, trembling and talking, your eyes like you crazy, and was I had to gather bush, light a fire and make you sweat out that madness?"

(237). For Moustique, this new vision is no different from that earlier feverish madness, even to the extent that it affects their ability to earn money. He does not believe in Makak's sudden royalty. Despite the obvious evocative imagery when they leave Monkey Mountain at the end of scene 1, with Makak riding his donkey Berthilia, Moustique is not the credulous Sancho Panza to Makak's Quixote.

Sancho Panza, though misguided, had his own form of practicality: he expected to gain an island, prestige, wages at the very least. Similarly, Moustique believes in benefiting from Makak's visions of glory. Instead of endorsing Makak's dream, as Souris and eventually Lestrade do, Moustique continuously rebuts Makak's dream with capitalism. At every turn, he reminds Makak that the market is waiting and they have money to make and debts to repay. Later he tells Makak not only that nothing is free but that conversely, everything is for sale, even dreams. After Makak's messianic performance at the crossroads, Moustique reveals his plans to capitalize on Makak's healing powers. Makak refuses to sell his "power," but Moustique responds, "Look, I tired telling you that nothing is for free. That some day, Makak, swing high, swing low, you will have to sell your dream, your soul, your power" (254). Negative, but practical, Moustique convinces Makak that they will need money to fulfill his dream of going to Africa.

Later, Moustique's materialism prompts him to impersonate Makak in Quatre Chemin Market, but it leads only to the fulfillment of the spider's prophecy (in scene 1) of his death. Even as he dies, however, Moustique can speak only in economic terms. He tells Makak, "Yes, I will die. I take what you had, I take the dream you have and I come and try to sell it" (273). This serves somewhat as an apology, but it is mixed with Moustique's condemnation of Makak for being willfully ignorant of the ways of "the marketplace." He refuses to excuse Makak's protestations of innocence and lack of concern with money: "No. You didn't know. You would never know. It was always me, since the first time in the road, where . . . always me who did have to beg . . . to do . . ." (273; ellipses in original). Though it appears to be at odds with Makak's new status as prophet, Moustique's careful attention to the practical details of their lives and livelihood complements and enables Makak's behavior. Moustique's own attempts at prophecy are also included in his dying declarations. He warns Makak that he must return to Monkey Mountain or he will suffer a similar fate. But Moustique's practical rebuttals, his deception, and his prophecy of death are not enough to deter Makak's delirious belief in his African dream. In the end, Moustique is too tired to fight and gives in to the fate twice decreed by the spider. After all, as he notes each time the spider crosses his hand, "Every man have to die" (239, 274). And, in Moustique's case, given his resurrection and sentencing to death in the penultimate scene, every man "have to die" twice.

While on Monkey Mountain with Souris and Tigre in part 2, Makak foreshadows Moustique's resurrection. In a short speech that encapsulates the many threads of the play, Makak responds to Souris: "What power can crawl on the bottom of the sea, or swim in the ocean of air above us? The mind, the mind. Now, come with me, the mind can bring the dead to life, it can go back, back, back, deep into time. It can make a man a king, it can make him a beast. Can you hear the sea now, can you hear the sound of suffering, we are moving back now" (291).[18] Thus the mind is powerful, man's real power in essence, but, like all power, it can destroy those who try to use it. The psyche becomes the connection between dreams and madness because it can envision change (in dreams) but can also distort visions (in madness). The mind serves simultaneously as source and destructive force for both. It is the reasonable mind that is pitted against the madman, and the reasonable mind that defines an acceptable reality. The power of the mind that Makak refers to, therefore, is this twofold power that opposes itself. If Makak believes his kingly dream and not the reality of his poverty, he can continue to live quixotically in the dreamworld; and if he releases the dream of the moon woman for a darker reality, he can function in the "real world." He can function logically in either realm, but he cannot straddle both.

Staging Madness

The advantage of the theater is that performance *can* straddle opposing worlds. In performance, *Dream on Monkey Mountain* bridges the spaces between fantasy and reality, madness and sanity. With this negotiation of dreams and madness, the play can, and should, be different with each performance. Even the printed play slips easily out of grasp, particularly with instructions from the playwright that suggest continuous change. The different responses to *Dream on Monkey Mountain* signal this ambiguity: for the critics, the language and characters symbolize different concepts. Walcott's own "Note on Production" cautions that the play's source is metaphor. And metaphors are often open to various readings. Walcott began with the image of Makak ("the man, the moon, and the mountaintop") as the "dominant metaphor," but as he wrote the play, this dominant metaphor spawned others, which then, in the cultural and critical marketplace, became "subject to all kinds of true and perhaps contradictory interpretations."[19] Thus Walcott leaves space within the play for the varied and various critical approaches.

The very creation of the play is based on the flexibility and changeability of the genre. Walcott worked on the play for ten years before its production, but after he had what he describes as a "prepared text," he found that production of the play could greatly influence its form. In a 1970 essay, he describes adding the part of Basil after the first draft of the play: "I had a prepared text, but there was one figure at the back of my mind, a death figure from Haitian mythology, that wasn't written in. There was an actor . . . but there was no part in it for him. So I worked in the figure from the center of the play's design, and the part radiated through the whole text—the part of Basil. I think that this figure tightened and webbed its structure."[20] Basil's character is at the center of both part 1 and part 2 of the play. In the first he warns of, and exposes, Moustique's treachery in the marketplace, while in the second he has a revealing dialogue with Corporal Lestrade:

CORPORAL. Who are you? I'm going mad, goddammit. Stiff upper lip . . .

BASIL. I am Basil, the carpenter, the charcoal seller. I do not exist. A figment of the imagination, a banana of the mind . . .

CORPORAL. Banana of the mind, figment of the . . . ho! That's pretty good. Goodbye. . . .

BASIL. You have one minute to repent. To recant. To renounce.

CORPORAL. Repent? Renounce what?

BASIL. You know, Lestrade. You know. . . .

CORPORAL. My mind, my mind. What's happened to my mind?

BASIL. It was never yours, Lestrade.

CORPORAL. Then if it's not mine, then I'm not mad.

BASIL. And if you are not mad, then all this is real.

CORPORAL. Impossible! There is Monkey Mountain. Here is the earth. Banana of the mind . . . ha . . . ha . . . ha . . . (297; ellipses in original)

If Lestrade is not in control of his mind, then he cannot be mad. This model of insanity is first expressed in Moustique's directive to Makak, "Go mad tomorrow, today is market day" (232), indicating that Makak can control his fits of madness. In this paradigm, madness is a conscious choice, making control a requirement for madness. If Lestrade is not in "possession" of his mind and never was, he cannot be responsible for what it does; therefore, he cannot "choose" to be mad. With the shifting meanings of the play, however, Lestrade's emphasis could be on "I" rather than "not," in the sense that whoever or whatever possesses Lestrade's mind is infected with madness. Is Walcott, here, suggesting that the playwright functions as the mind giver, the controller of his characters' consciousness? Basil's statement that Lestrade's mind was never his own reflects simultaneously on the power of the playwright and on the power of colonialism. It implicates both the immediate creator/giver of minds in the play and the systematic control of minds under colonialism. When one considers that the playwright himself is a product of the British colonial educational system and is writing the play during a decade of political decolonization, all "minds" involved are suspect. In any case, if the madness is outside Lestrade, then his vision of Basil is both reasonable and real.

In the interchange between Basil and the Corporal, the dichotomy between *mad* and *sane*, *dream* and *real,* is clear. There is an added relationship between these terms as Walcott aligns them analogically: *mad* is to *sane* as *dream* is to *real.* While the characters apply the usual values to these terms—it is better to be sane than mad, real than illusory—the play on the whole does not create a similar hierarchy. Though he claims to be "going mad" when confronting Basil, Corporal Lestrade's "sanity" in part 1 is no less mad than his strange rebirth in part 2. Walcott questions each of these terms throughout the play, each becoming relative for the characters and the audience on the basis of their relationship to power. As Walcott notes, "Every question, eventually, even with literature, is a question of power. . . . It's simply a matter of who's in charge really."[21] We can read the play, then, as representing definitions of madness and dream, sanity and reality, as entangled in struggles for power. In *The Wretched of the Earth*, Frantz Fanon states, "Because it is a systematic negation of the other person and a furious determination to deny the other person all attributes of humanity, colonialism forces the people it dominates to ask themselves the question constantly: 'In reality, who am I?'"[22] But *Dream on Monkey Mountain* forces its audience to consider *whose* reality. The reality of the colonized differs greatly from that of the colonizer's, and that is, in large part, the cause of the mental disorder and dissociation often attributed to many natives. Middlemen like Corporal Lestrade have different conceptions of reality from both groups. As an officer of the crown, the Corporal sees Makak as a drunk and possibly insane old man. After literally stripping himself of his office, however, Lestrade can envision Makak as a leader, if only a hollow one. He can begin to believe—if not so much in Makak's dream, then in the validity of him as sane and gifted. When the Corporal, in his Corporal's uniform, asks, "In reality, who am I?" he relies on a very different reality for his answer than the naked Corporal in part 2 would for the same question. In the former he is an officer of the crown and largely interchangeable with others of his class; in the latter, he becomes an integral part of a resurgence of black power. Although he questions his sanity at times, it is his reality that truly shifts during the play.

The Corporal's shift in part 2 signals an overall shift in the focus of the play. In a short 1971 interview for the *New Yorker*, after having received the Obie Award for *Dream on Monkey Mountain*, Walcott describes his vision for the play's structure: "In the first half of the play, the concept of the beginning of the world and the evolution of man is—shall we say?—basically white. Then, when Corporal Lestrade, the brainwashed colonial servant, retrogresses to become an ape and emerges as a man to walk through the primeval forest, the play swings over to a black Adamic concept of evolution."[23] In partitioning the play in this manner, Walcott explores two of the three perils that Fanon predicts for members of a newly decolonized nation. Jean-Paul Sartre's preface to *The Wretched of the Earth* summarizes these "dangerous will o' the wisps" as "the cult of the leader and of personalities, Western culture, and what is equally to be feared, the withdrawal into the twilight of past African culture."[24] I will return to the problematics of leadership below, but the attractions of the two cultures—Western and African—are evident in parts 1 and 2 of the play respectively. These ideas are not locked in to their respective parts, however, as Makak dreams of Africa in part 1 and Lestrade continues to valorize European culture for the first half of part 2.

The allure and disadvantages of European and African cultures are not the only connections to Fanon's writings and theory in *Dream on Monkey Mountain*. Although Moustique makes passing reference to Fanon's *Black Skin, White Masks*, Walcott relies most heavily on *The Wretched of the Earth* as an intertext for his play. Although *Dream on Monkey Mountain* was first published in 1970, it was first performed in 1967, and Walcott had worked on the play for several years before then. *The Wretched of the Earth* was published in 1961 (the English translation in 1963), making the two nearly contemporary. Walcott translates several of Fanon's themes in his last reflections on colonialism into theatrical form and quotes Sartre's preface at the beginning of both part 1 and part 2. The first of these quotations reads: "Thus in certain psychoses the hallucinated person, tired of always being insulted by his demon, one fine day starts hearing the voice of an angel who pays him compliments; but the jeers don't stop for all that; only, from then on, they alternate with congratulations. This is a defence, but it is also the end of the story. The self is disassociated, and the patient heads for madness."[25] Although clearly relevant to the happenings in part 1, the epigraph is ironic because Sartre's ending becomes Walcott's beginning. For this is how he begins his play, with Makak's declaration of his madness: "I am an old man. Send me home, Corporal. I suffer from madness. I does see things. Spirits does talk to me. All I have is my dreams and they don't trouble your soul" (225). For Walcott, insanity spells not the end but the beginning of creative possibilities. He describes both part 1 and part 2 as explorations of two opposing "insanities," and the play begins with Makak's dream journey through this madness.[26]

Later, however, when Makak is relating his dream/vision to Moustique, he tells him, "Listen to me. I not mad. Listen!" (236), and shortly afterward—"Is not a dream. . . . I tell you is no dream" (237). Makak's denials reverse the tenuous privilege Walcott accords to madness and dreams—hallucinations—in his "Note on Production" and prologue. Moustique does not believe either of Makak's protestations, for after all, can a mad man tell you he is sane? Can a dreamer recognize reality? As Shoshana Felman writes: "To say 'I am mad' is already a contradiction in terms: either the speaker is 'mad' and what he says . . . is non-sense, or else he is saying something meaningful, and is therefore sane (at least at the moment he says it). The act of enunciation contradicts and problematizes the statement it issues."[27] Similarly, a dreamer, caught in the dreamworld, cannot say with certainty that he is or is not dreaming. Even upon waking, he cannot be sure that he has awakened to reality or to another level of his dream. From the uncertain dreamworld of the play, Makak's "I not mad" and "Is not a dream" contain an inherent contradiction that parallels that recognized by Felman in "I am mad."

In a related manner, Lestrade also does not recognize his own madness in either part 1 or part 2 of the play, though they mirror each other in his zeal and his language. In the mock court of the play's prologue, Lestrade presents Makak to the "lords" as "a being without a mind, a will, a name, a tribe of its own." He does not allow Makak to speak, in order to "spare [the court] the sound of that voice, which have come from a cave of darkness" and continues to describe Makak's person: "These hands are the hands of Esau, the fingers are like roots, the arteries as hard as twine, and the palms are seamed with coal. But the animal, you observe, is tamed and obedient" (222). This profile resembles Lestrade's future portrayal of himself in the forests of Monkey Mountain. When he confronts Basil, Lestrade finds that he too has no mind, no race, no voice. After divesting himself of his colonial uniform and presumably his colonial post, he announces: "Now I see a new light. I sing the glories of Makak! The glories of my race! What race? I have no race! Come! Come all you splendours of imagination. Let me sing of darkness now! My hands. My hands are heavy. My feet . . . *[he rises, crouched]* my feet grip like roots. The arteries are like rope. *[He howls]* Was that my voice? My voice. O god, I have become what I mocked. I always was. I always was. Makak! Makak! forgive me old father" (299–300; ellipsis, brackets, and italics in original). Here Lestrade "retrogresses to become an ape," very much like the monkey he makes of Makak earlier. And at the close of this later scene, he further identifies himself with his previous description of Makak when he realizes, "I have no ambition of my own. I have no animal's name. I simply work" (307). Thus Lestrade, in the end, has no mind, no will, no name, and no tribe to lay claim to.

When Makak has made his biggest conquest, Corporal Lestrade, he loses his belief in his vision. Walcott marks the fight between Souris and Tigre as a dream-breaking occasion for Makak, but Makak continues to pursue his dream even after this moment in the play.[28] Or rather, Makak is propelled through his dream by Corporal Lestrade. Once he has won the support of the Corporal and Souris, Makak becomes a "shadow," a front for the movement, but one who does not know where to go or what to do next. In this last scene, Makak resembles the men Fanon describes, "who have sung the praises of their race" but who, once they are recognized as leaders, "act as a braking-power on the awakening consciousness of the people."[29] Walcott furthers Fanon's denigration of leaders by making Makak a powerless figurehead and his "team of [bourgeois-minded] administrators" visible and potent in the form of Lestrade. When Makak hesitates, Lestrade announces: "Put him in front. He's a shadow now. Let him face the moon and move towards it. Let him go forward. I'll take over. Come on. Go" (306–7). Ironically, Lestrade believes in the dream and falls victim to the romanticization of blackness, but not in the manner of a withdrawal into the past. He finishes with "Now, where to old father? No. We cannot go back. History is in motion. The law is in motion. Forward, forward."[30] Although he recognizes the pitfalls of trying to move backwards into history, Lestrade repeats the same silencing of

Makak—in fact, silencing of any form of dissent—as he enforced earlier when he opposed Makak's dream. He places Makak as a silent, ignorant leader who is effective only insofar as he is recognizable to his followers. Makak does not and cannot make any decisions; Lestrade is there to "take over" that function.

Lestrade is fully cognizant of Makak's and his own roles. At the end of his monologue he commands, "Now, let splendour, barbarism, majesty, noise, slogans, parades, drown out that truth. Plaster the walls with pictures of the leader, magnify our shadows, moon, if only for a moment. Gongs, warriors, bronzes! Statues, clap your hands you forests. Makak will be enthroned!" (307). The "truth" is that Lestrade's cooperation is as detrimental to Makak's dream as his opposition, perhaps more so. In choosing to do the "black man work" instead of the "white man work," Lestrade still relies on the law as a color-blind tool. But his statement—"I breathe over the shoulder of your leaders, I hang back always at a decent distance, but I am there to observe that the law is upheld, that those who break it, president or prince, will also be broken" (307)—is ambiguous. To whom does Lestrade's "your" refer? White or black? Colonizer or colonized? With the presence of Makak, a reader or audience member might connect "leaders" to black leaders; but the rest of the sentence, and the rest of the speech, implies that he refers to white presidents or princes. Lestrade, who now dubs himself "Bastard, hatchet-man, opportunist, executioner," is once again relying on the law to decide right from wrong. Although he seems willing to break the law in order to "break" other lawbreakers, he still relies on the justice system as impartial and unbiased, true and just. As he states in the court scene of Makak's apotheosis, he still believes that the "law takes no sides, it changes the complexion of things" (311). He recognizes that there are different laws (Roman law, tribal law), but he does not acknowledge that the very existence of different forms of law—incompatible forms of law—indicates the fragility and inadequacy of the law as a judge of human action.

With this emphasis on the law, the "apotheosis" becomes a court scene in the dual sense, with Makak as king and his followers judging Western civilization. This scene also becomes the apotheosis of the play's bridging of the space between hallucinations and reality/sanity. The experience in the theater becomes surreal; with everyone on stage believing in and exalting Makak, the audience is compelled to believe in his royalty as well. Makak is no longer the "weak-headed old man" of the prologue. When the action returns to the jail cell in the epilogue, the euphoria of the previous scene is not altogether shattered. Souris and the Corporal treat Makak more kindly than in the prologue, Makak rejects the white mask, and Moustique is resurrected yet again. With self-reflexive references to dreams and madness, the play incorporates the epilogue in the ongoing collective hallucination.

Scripting Schizophrenia

The 1970 publication of *Dream on Monkey Mountain* is part of a collection of four of Walcott's plays—including *The Sea at Dauphin*, *Ti-Jean and His Brothers*, and *Malachon, or Six in the Rain*. The preface to the collection, an essay by Walcott entitled "What the Twilight Says: An Overture," provides information about his goals and inspirations when writing and producing theater in and for the Caribbean. Like his "Note on Production," it gives the reader, but not the audience, some insight into the plays themselves. With the "Note on Production" and the quotations from Sartre at the beginning of parts 1 and 2, *Dream on Monkey Mountain* is the most textual of the plays in the collection. The other plays do not have notes on production or epigraphs, although *The Sea at Dauphin* and *Malachon*, like *Dream on Monkey Mountain*, do have quotations on their title pages.[31] With these additions, reading *Dream on Monkey Mountain*, more so than the other three plays, produces a different experience than watching it in performance. The difference lies not just in the individual reader's abstract visualization of the characters versus the availability of a concrete picture during performance but also in the privacy of reading versus the experience of sharing the play with other audience members. In part 2, for example, the Corporal removes his clothes to signal his conversion. The brief stage directions—"He removes his clothes"—are easily read without pause. In contrast, the staged removal of his uniform is a highlight of the Corporal's role. The visceral experience of his nakedness in performance cannot be ignored and underscores the momentousness of his new belief in Makak. Also, the collective audience's response to Lestrade's nakedness will affect an individual audience member's response; the collective's disbelief, embarrassment, excitement becomes a part of the experience of the play for the individual.

For all four plays in the collection, the reading experience is enhanced by the addition of the prefatory essay. Walcott's "What the Twilight Says" has been reprinted in anthologies away from this setting next to the plays, but the juxtaposition in the 1970 publication reveals interesting connections between the preface and the plays, opening meanings in both the drama and the essay.[32] For *Dream on Monkey Mountain*, in particular, reading the essay yields information on Walcott's representation of insanity. One of the most striking pictures Walcott draws in this essay is that of hunger as the muse for Caribbean playwrights: not their own hunger, but that of the West Indian poor.[33] This hunger is not the major theme of Walcott's plays (or his poetry) because he believes it cannot be reproduced, but it does erupt in the parts of "rogues, drunkards, madmen, outcasts" (19). Makak is strangely an example of, and an exemption from, this cycle of repression and eruption. On the one hand, his poverty is not at the center of the play; *Dream on Monkey Mountain* is not a play about poverty, or even the direct effects of poverty in the West Indies. On the other hand, Makak's poverty does drive the action of the play in a manner reminiscent of Bertha Mason in *Jane Eyre*, who resides behind every plot movement from Jane's arrival at Thornfield Hall until "Reader, I married him." Makak is driven to and through his dream by his poverty and need; and his followers are similarly caught up in his promise of an alternative reality because of their own situation. Even Moustique and Tigre, who refuse the dream, do so on the basis of need; neither of these disbelievers has time for a dream that cannot produce material benefits. Walcott continues in his preface: "Hunger induces its delirium, and it is this fever for heroic examples that can produce the glorification of revenge" (19). His description resembles Lestrade's condemnation of Makak to Pamphilion in Quatre Chemin Market and Sartre's "hallucinated person," in the epigraph to part 1 of the play. Such moments indicate that poverty, hunger, and perhaps even boredom can lead to delusion and madness. In *Dream on Monkey Mountain*, Walcott provides examples of this happening on both the individual and the communal level.

Like the prefatory essay, the Sartre quotations guide the reader through the play, providing interpretive access routes unavailable to the theatergoer who has not read the play beforehand.[34] The use of Sartre's summarizing of Fanon's ideas rather than the direct quotation of Fanon may be read as problematic, but it represents the split between worlds that the colonial feels. The juxtaposition of the European speaking for the colonial with Makak attempting to speak for himself exemplifies the split that Walcott describes in the play itself. Walcott notes Lestrade's conversion as evidence of the split personality of the play itself—beginning with the white conception of "the evolution of man" and switching to "the black Adamic concept of evolution."[35] The play is split between Sartre's "two worlds" of the second epigraph, quoted at the beginning of part 2:

> Let us add, for certain other carefully selected unfortunates that other witchery of which I have already spoken: Western culture. If I were them, you may say, I'd prefer my mumbo-jumbo to their Acropolis. Very good: you've grasped the situation. But not altogether, because you *aren't* them—or not yet. Otherwise you would know that they can't choose; they must have both. Two worlds: that makes two bewitchings; they dance all night and at dawn they crowd into the churches to hear mass; each day the split widens. Our enemy betrays his brothers and becomes our accomplice; his brothers do the same thing. The status of the "native" is a nervous condition introduced and maintained by the settler among the colonized people *with their consent.*[36]

Although he uses religious examples, there are many other facets to the "Western culture" that Sartre positions on one side of this divide. Makak, Lestrade, Moustique—all the "principal characters"—define success, respect, desire by Western standards. These characters exhibit the nervous condition of Sartre's "natives."

Sartre's words have been quoted in various colonial, anticolonial, and postcolonial contexts. But the seeming contradiction of the ending of the last sentence is often overlooked or simply cut out, as in Tsitsi Dangarembga's epigraph to her novel *Nervous Conditions.* Sartre himself italicizes the words "with their consent," flourishing them at the end much like a trump card. His observations are based on Fanon's own comments on the mental disorders prevalent in colonized countries, particularly where there is no opposition to colonization. According to Fanon, "In the period of colonization when it is not contested by armed resistance, when the sum total of harmful nervous stimuli overstep a certain threshold, the defensive attitudes of the natives give way and they then find themselves crowding the mental hospitals. There is thus during this calm period of successful colonization a regular and important mental pathology which is the direct product of oppression" (250–51). Thus "with their consent" does not refer to overt agreement with the colonizer's practices, although there sometimes is this type of assent, especially in the privileged classes. The consent grows from lack of dissent, particularly, for Fanon, lack of armed dissent. Passivity in the face of colonization breeds mental dis-ease, the nervous conditions that Fanon describes. Ironically, the case studies at the end of *The Wretched of the Earth* spring from the revolution, so mental illness surrounds the entire project. Many of the case studies Fanon presents seem to describe the madnesses of war, not of colonialism. But Fanon collates the two at the beginning of this last chapter—"Colonial War and

Mental Disorders"—when he writes, "But the war goes on; and we will have to bind up for years to come the many, sometimes ineffaceable, wounds that the colonialist onslaught has inflicted on our people."[37] As Fanon suggests throughout this section, these "wounds" can manifest themselves in various mental disorders. This conflict of existing between two worlds is continuously demanded of the colonized. Walcott's inclusion of this epigraph, with its italicized ending, emphasizes for the reader the complicity of West Indians at all levels—from Makak to the Corporal—in the schizophrenic quality of their existence.

These epigraphs, then, imply for the reader that in this split, this crack between two worlds, madness flourishes. The colonized exist in the juncture of these worlds, part of neither but enchanted by both. Makak's followers attempt to avoid this split by vengefully rejecting Western culture. In the preface, Walcott dubs such revenge "a kind of vision" (20), and in the play, visions become a kind of revenge for the characters. In their collective dream, the wives, warriors, and chiefs of Makak's court can praise "the glories of Makak" and judge white history, culture, and politics with a "unanimous negative." They condemn the cultural products of Western civilization and wish to banish any "drop of milk" from their past, present, and future. For Walcott, this form of revenge is particular to the Caribbean mentality, which, "historically hung-over, exhausted, prefers to take its revenge in nostalgia, to narrow its eyelids in a schizophrenic daydream of an Eden that existed before its exile" (20). The members of Makak's court attempt to reach past the "colonialist onslaught," to disentangle themselves from the dual bewitching. In this vision, they have the power to withdraw their consent and thereby to avoid this nervous condition. Walcott's description of this vision of revenge as a "schizophrenic daydream" is especially applicable to *Dream on Monkey Mountain.* The phrase encompasses the tense, unstable relationship between madness and dream throughout the play. Because it occurs while awake, a daydream is simultaneously dream and not-dream, both a conscious reverie and an uncontrolled trance. And to describe a daydream as schizophrenic emphasizes the madness inherent in this cleavage of dream and reality.

When asked in an interview about "the 'schizophrenia' of [his] Caribbean inheritance," Walcott admits, "Schizophrenia—I use that word too casually."[38] Walcott is not alone in this "casual" use of the term; to contextualize his usage, I take a closer look at the term in the next few paragraphs. Even within its home field of psychology, the meaning and validity of schizophrenia are debated. A relatively recent addition to the official psychological diagnoses, the term *schizophrenia* was first coined in 1911 by Eugen Bleuler to better describe what had previously been known as "dementia praecox" (early dementia).[39] Bleuler believed the new designation, derived from the Greek for "split" and "mind," more accurately corresponded to the group of behaviors that Emil Kraepelin is credited with having "discovered" toward the end of the nineteenth century. There is, however, some controversy regarding Kraepelin's research methods and whether schizophrenia (dementia praecox) exists as a scientific construct. Such disagreement is reflected in the popular understanding of schizophrenia, which Kraepelin defined as a "loss of the inner unity of the activities of the intellect, emotion and volition in themselves and among one another."[40] Both within and outside the psychological community, the term *schizophrenia* is fraught with confusion and misuse. Understandably, it is especially subject to misdiagnosis in cases that involve cultural differences between the practitioner and patient.

Although Kraepelin and Bleuler are hailed as the fathers of schizophrenia, it has taken on a life of its own, separate from its beginnings. Mary Boyle finds that the term as it has developed and is currently used "represents simply an amalgam of the personal beliefs of prominent users of the concept of schizophrenia" and thus has become "a social and professional stereotype."[41] Despite, or perhaps because of, its vagueness, schizophrenia has become attractive to cultural and literary artists. Its appeal is evident not only in the psychological and psychiatric fields but also in cultural production—film, literature, television, and theory. The utilization of schizophrenia as a metaphor for social conditions has become very attractive to writers as a metaphor for various social processes: it is common, for example, to find theoretical and critical texts linking schizophrenia to such paradigms as modernism, civilization, and capitalism.

Schizophrenia, because of its relatively recent development in the field and its late onset in the subject, is often compared to the adult negotiation of the modern world. Not only is there a chronological association between the advent of modernism and that of schizophrenia, but, as Louis A. Sass convincingly argues in *Madness and Modernism*, modernist art displays characteristics similar to those of schizophrenia. Sass draws parallels between the two, but as he states in his prologue, he is concerned with describing schizophrenia so that in his text "the arrow of interpretation goes from modernism to madness" rather than from schizophrenia to modernism.[42] Walcott, on the other, hand, seems to take the latter, opposite direction; he moves from schizophrenia to Caribbean society and literature. He uses the term *schizophrenia* in a complex yet idiosyncratic way, referring to the split that is defined by schizophrenia but not to the paralysis and unproductivity that could result from full-blown psychosis. Similarly, Deleuze and Guattari draw on the early stages of the disorder for their comparison between schizophrenia and capitalism in *Anti-Oedipus: Capitalism and Schizophrenia.* They refer to the active schizophrenic—"out for a walk"—but not to the incarcerated and incomprehensible psychotic in an asylum.[43] In their opposition of neurosis and psychosis, they find schizophrenia, or schizoid tendencies, to be more descriptive of capitalist societies because they envision a functional mental illness. The lack of definitive boundaries for the collection of behaviors included under the schizophrenia umbrella allows for creative applications but also abuse and misuse of the term. *Schizophrenia*, then, can mean everything and nothing at the same time. It is sometimes synonymous with madness itself, acting as an official-sounding term for all forms of bizarre behavior. Thus the egotistical theatrics of Moses Barton in *The Hills of Hebron*, the silent retreat of Nellie in *Jane and Louisa Will Soon Come Home*, and Makak's dreams of sovereignty could all be described as symptoms of schizophrenia.

Rachel Manley qualifies the term by referring to West Indian authors' ingestion of Western literature while their active lives revolved around Caribbean activities. She refers to this split as "literary schizophrenia."[44] But from her description it is apparent that this type of split occurs not only in writers but in educated Caribbean subjects generally. In *The Divided Self*, his seminal text on schizophrenia, R. D. Laing describes the schizoid person as "an individual whose being is split in two main ways: in the relationship to external reality and in the relationship to the self."[45] For several Caribbean writers, schizophrenia is a powerful metaphor for the artistic and lived Caribbean experience. The split subject is prevalent in the Caribbean existence, whether the split occurs along gender lines, racial lines, linguistic capabilities, or conceptions of reality. Madness studies have often concentrated on the madness of the writer, but that avenue is rarely available, and I would argue not desirable, in Caribbean literary studies. Walcott, however, like Manley, does hint at the madness of the artist: "His defiance now a mania driven to the pitch where only vision was real, the leader would pray: Let me help others and be merciless to myself. But the torment of all self-appointed schizoid saints is that they enact their opposite. . . . He had been warned of this madness, and true enough, paranoia progressed with every inch of slope cleared" (32–33). Walcott gestures beyond the internal struggle that Manley describes; the artist who would speak to his people is subject to madness in taking on this role of service. But as there are very few records of Caribbean writers being incarcerated in an asylum or going mad as "spectacularly" as Nietzsche or Artaud, it is fascinating that there is so much reference to madness in their works.[46]

As the examples here indicate, one of the most attractive metaphors of madness is that of schizophrenia because of the split between self and situation that is common in schizoid and schizophrenic people. In this situation, the subject feels as though he is merely imitating the person he should be, or mimicking a role. There are strong similarities between this symptom of schizophrenia and the Caribbean colonial situation for Caribbean writers. Walcott also invokes the term when he is speaking of the divide between educated Caribbean intellectuals and the less privileged West Indians who are often considered examples of authentic Caribbeanness or of the roots from which the intellectual and/or artist sprouts. The social division is yet another reason that schizophrenia is an attractive metaphor for artists such as Walcott and Manley who wish to indicate the complexities of the colonial situation. As Walcott notes, this nervous condition exists at all levels of colonized society, but particularly for those who would increase their social status: "This society is still patterned on the stratification between rich and poor black. He who has acquired education finds himself on the thin line of the split in society. The artist instinctively moves towards his people on that root level, and yet, at the same time, he must survive. This split is equivalent to a state of schizophrenia."[47] For Walcott, the "more sophisticated [the Caribbean intellectual] becomes, the more alienated is his mental state."[48] The alienation that Walcott refers to here occurs along class lines, but this schizophrenic quality affects many facets of colonial and postcolonial life. As he later clarifies, Walcott uses *schizophrenia* as a means of signifying that "the idea of division is permanent in all countries that have been colonial. It is a shadow, a kind of meridian, a crossing that has to be examined."[49] Although these examinations vary in intensity, many Caribbean texts and texts from other regions with colonial histories represent the psychological effects of this "crossing."

Unfortunately, the criticism of this literature has not kept pace with its production. Patrick Hogan, in his article on *Dream on Monkey Mountain*, finds that "postcolonization literature treating the disintegration of personal identity in the face of oppression has tended to focus on women. Even the male authors who have addressed this issue have often dealt with female insanity."[50] Hogan refers to postcolonial literature in general, but even in the Caribbean field alone there are several examples of male insanity. It is understandable that a critic wishing to focus on sustained madness in principal characters can overlook such texts as *A House for Mr. Biswas* or *The Wine of Astonishment*, where the main (male) characters have only moments of madness. But well-known texts such as *The Hills of Hebron* and *The Lunatic* explore male insanity at length. By ignoring such texts and assuming that a focus on female insanity occludes a focus on race, Hogan can conclude:

> One result of this is that the disintegrating effects of colonialism and racism have been less fully explored in postcolonization literature than one would expect. While a number of writers besides Walcott have dealt with racial or colonial issues along with patriarchy—Head has done this particularly effectively—the feminist concerns of their works, and the feminist focus of much of the criticism on these works has tended to limit the literary study of racism and psychopathology. . . . Walcott is one of the few Anglophone postcolonial writers to have take up the problem of racism, identity and madness, developing and extending Fanon's observations through a literary medium.[51]

I would argue that writers such as Wynter, Rhys, and Brodber, all of whom published well before Hogan's article, were just as concerned about the effects of race and colonization on their fragmented subjects as Walcott in *Dream on Monkey Mountain*. There has certainly not been enough criticism on the connection between the two in the scholarship on these writers, but the criticism on *Dream on Monkey Mountain* is similarly deficient. As I indicate in chapters 2, 3, and 5, these writers' texts make the connections explicit. To position Walcott as "one of the few" is to ignore the prevalence of madness in Caribbean literature *and* in the larger category of postcolonial literature.

Fortunately, with the various textual accoutrements, Walcott makes clear the importance of madness in his creation of *Dream on Monkey Mountain*. The hypertextuality of the play emphasizes the schizophrenic split between language and action. The intricacies of language and perception that accompany schizophrenia make it particularly fascinating to colonial and postcolonial writers. Sass reports that "it is quite common for schizophrenics to complain of the inadequacy of language." He provides an example of a patient who "was preoccupied with the insufficiency of words. . . . 'Words have textures and so do objects,' he said, 'but sometimes the words don't have the same texture as what they refer to.'"[52] Caribbean writers have a similar "preoccupation with the insufficiency of words." Walcott's choice of the theater as the vehicle for his particular message in *Dream on Monkey Mountain* may be related to this disconnection between words and their object. He writes in "What the Twilight Says": "Colonials, we began with this malarial enervation: that nothing could ever be built among these rotting shacks, barefooted backyards and moulting shingles; that being poor, we already had the theatre of our lives. So the self-inflicted role of martyr came naturally, the melodramatic belief that one was message-bearer for the millennium, that the inflamed ego was enacting their will. In that simple schizophrenic boyhood one could lead two lives: the interior life of poetry, the outward life of action and dialect" (4). In a play, particularly *Dream on Monkey Mountain*, which he has described as a "physical poem," Walcott can bridge the "schizophrenic" split he experiences between poetry and dialect, writing and action, private and public life.

Bridging Worlds: Theater and Text

Like other texts that explore the interiority of madness, *Dream on Monkey Mountain* can be frustrating with its lack of narrative linearity and its contradictory images and characters. Part of the above-mentioned drive to separate the prologue and epilogue from the body of the play springs from the need to order the play. Walcott has referred to the nonlinearity of the play as similar to that of a poem. He wanted in the play to "let the action come out of successive detonations of images not dominated by a narrative logic, as occurs in the creative process of a poem, or in the integrity without logic of a dream."[53] Thus, when Walcott asks that producers treat the play as a "physical poem," he refers not only to the performative demands of the theater but also to the play's nonlinear poetic structure. Walcott, in an interview with Denis Scott, addresses the idea of his plays as a "dramatic poem": "I think that any play that works completely is a poem; and the components of that particular poem are physical: there is an actor saying certain things, lights all the rest . . . and once you have a complete concept of any play . . . it is a poem in the sense that it is conceived as a structure and it works metrically as finely as a poem does. And if you happen to write in verse then that's all the better."[54] Walcott views his plays as a form of enacted verse, encompassing the metaphoricity and rhythm of poetry and the materiality of the theater.[55] While the poetics of Walcott's plays have received considerable attention, his "Note on Production" places heavy emphasis on the "physical" aspect of his designation of *Dream on Monkey Mountain* as a physical poem, as does his utilization of the dramatic genre for portraying the shifting realities present in madness. In this play, dramatic poetics serve as the linguistic and experiential route to access and describe madness. In both content and form, the play represents and recreates the characters' hallucinations for the audience at all times.

Although Walcott continues in his "Note on Production" to state that *Dream on Monkey Mountain* "should be spare, essential as the details of a dream," he also emphasizes the importance of the songs and dances: "The producer can amplify it with spectacle as he chooses, or, as in the original production, switch roles and limit his cast to a dozen or so. He will need dancers, actors, and singers, the same precision and vitality that one has read of in the Kabuki. He may add songs more recognizable to his audience once he can keep the raw folk content in them" (208). The songs and dances are part of the connection to the audience, overriding the "integrity" of the "original" written text. Although Walcott recognizes the importance of the playwright to the performance (particularly if the playwright is "established worldwide"), he also considers the play's relevance to, and contemporaneity with, the audience as crucial in its production.[56] For him, "the ritualistic elements of the dance and the chants are not literary because these things existed or still exist with [his] own environment."[57] The play must be not only flexible but accessible on some physical level by the audience. And the former characteristic helps to ensure the latter. Later performances of the play are separated from its publication by time, but a producer may make it seem more current by changing the chants and dances to ones "more recognizable to his [or her] audience" while keeping the "raw folk content" of the play intact.[58]

Unlike the static textuality of the Sartre epigraphs, Walcott's "Note on Production" simultaneously situates the play as performance and text, suspending it between stage and page. Theodore Colson describes the plays in *Dream on Monkey Mountain and Other Plays* as "from the twilight area of poetry and drama."[59] But Walcott relies on the theater, not poetry, to convey the hallucinatory and communal qualities of decolonization. Poetry is often an individual experience, but theater is necessarily shared—not only with the characters onstage but also with fellow audience members. Onstage, *Dream on Monkey Mountain* can represent the drama of madness for, and recreate it within, the audience. Performance, therefore, can create community in the theater and shape responses in a different manner than poetry can. Glissant finds that community theater, in particular, "diverts energy from the individual manifestation of delirium or from the collective tendency to the theatrical, so as to orient it towards the shaping of a popular consciousness."[60] Rather than reduce the importance of the "individual manifestation of delirium," however, theater increases its effectiveness. Glissant perceives individual madness as a prior step: "Individual delirium and collective theatralization, as forms of cultural resistance, are the first 'catalysts' of this consciousness."[61] Thus Makak's madness and the spectacle of his healing Josephus at the crossroads in part 1 pave the way for the expectant consciousness that he—and hopefully the audience—come to at the end of the play.[62]

Although they produce new awareness at the ending of the play, individual delirium and "the collective tendency toward the theatrical" exist within their own right as levels of meaning and resistance within *Dream on Monkey Mountain*.[63] On the individual level, Makak's delirious perception of himself as a king defies the sadness of his situation as a poor coal seller with no future and no power. As the Corporal (mouthing Sartre's summary of Fanon) predicts, one day, inspired by deprivation and hopelessness, a man like Makak might decide to imagine himself as powerful. In the marketplace, the Corporal tells Inspector Pamphilion: "Some ignorant, illiterate lunatic who know two or three lines from the Bible by heart, well one day he get tired of being poor and sitting on his arse so he make up his mind to see a vision, and once he make up his mind, the constipated, stupid bastard bound to see it" (261). The Corporal's next words indicate the second way in which the play performs resistance through delirium: on the communal level. The Corporal continues: "So he come down off his mountain, as if he is God self, and walk amongst the people, who too glad that he will think for them. He give them hope, miracle, vision, paradise on earth, and is then blood start to bleed and stone start to fly" (261–62). Even as it remains individual, Makak's madness becomes a shared refusal and resistance as others in his situation choose to believe in his power, in the possibility of such uniqueness among themselves. But Makak's dream still exists as his own. His resistance maintains its discreteness even as it multiplies. The third level of resistance is evident in the format of the play. It is not only a dream but also a play, with an audience that participates in the dreaming. Makak's hallucinations, which become his people's hallucinations, also become shared with the audience. The audience members complete the play as they participate in the collective delirium, collective dream, and potentially collective resistance.

In an interview with Walcott two decades after the play first opened, J. P. White pronounced that in America the play "was heralded as a call to Black power" with noticeable "political ramifications of the new African king killing his white goddess."[64] Walcott responded that the ending of scene 3 (in part 2)—"Apotheosis"—had been "hysterically judged" by both white and black America because Makak "achieves nothing, but he completes something. What he does is he sheds an image of himself that has been degraded. When he thought he was white, he did what the white man did. When he thought he was Black, he did what he thought the Black man should do. Both errors. So that moment of cutting off the head is not a moment of beheading a white woman. It is a matter of saying there is some act, some final illusion to be shed. And it is only metaphorical anyway—it's only a dream."[65] Various critics, and various audiences, have interpreted this scene in different ways.[66] The seesaw movement between recognizable dream and ambiguous reality leaves room for Makak's killing of the moon woman to be simply symbolic or more complexly allegorical. With Walcott's "Note on Production," readers at least have been forewarned that they will enter worlds built upon dreams and metaphors, illogic, and contradictions. Despite the climactic and symbolic appeal of Makak's decapitation of the moon woman, this moment is not the "ending" of the dream; both readers and audiences must contend with the epilogue's reminder that the play, the entire play, is "only a dream." While it offers definite commentaries on black consciousness and Eurocentrism, the play, with its source in the multiplicity and contradictions of metaphor and its reliance on dreams and madness, resists stable meanings. Critics, and even Walcott himself in later interviews, attempt to impose a recognizable order on the play but often end in contradiction. The "principal characters" could very well lay the claim "You have betrayed our dream" on those wishing to fit the play into a coherent, cohesive, consistent narrative about politics, blackness, or poverty.

Despite this absence of order, however, the opposition between sanity and insanity remains rigid. The play combines real and fantasy worlds when in "Apotheosis" the moon woman becomes visible to everyone; but a similar bridging is not possible across the boundaries of sanity and insanity. With the moon woman visible to the other characters, they accept her as real and Makak as sane. In gaining this dubious qualification for sanity, however, Makak loses his status as a prophet. He becomes a hollow figurehead no more gifted than his followers. When he could see something that was not visible to others, when he was at risk of being insane, he was also most respected for his exceptionality. However, when he loses this power, which was merely faith based in the beginning, he becomes a shadow leader, only following Lestrade's orders. Previously, his dreams provided a way of rebelling against Lestrade's authority, but when Makak loses his visions, his moonlit fever, he also loses any pretense at resistance. In a manner even more pernicious than the farce of the courtroom in part 1, Makak truly becomes Lestrade's monkey at the end of the apotheosis. He no longer "sees things" and is no longer a crazy dreamer. As Moustique predicted, he has sold "his dream, his soul, his power," not for money, but for false respect. With the epilogue, the play positions Makak's "return to sanity" as more problematic than his killing of his white female muse. Instead of having his own dream for his people, he becomes merely a character in the "dream of his people." Even in questioning the valorization of reality and sanity, the play, in the end, cannot escape these divisions between sanity and madness, reality and dream.

5 "Claims to Social Identity"

Madness and Subject Formation in *Jane and Louisa Will Soon Come Home*

In a manner similar to Jean Rhys's brief last section of *Wide Sargasso Sea*, Erna Brodber's *Jane and Louisa Will Soon Come Home* represents madness from a tangled first-person perspective. It seeks to speak from the inside, rather than to merely represent from a distance, the madness of a dissociated Jamaican woman. The resulting text is a densely layered account of the colonial mentality still evident in Jamaican society at least up to 1980, when *Jane and Louisa* was published. Brodber's text also emphasizes the difficulty of representing madness within standard generic divisions—as manifested in Rhys's novel and Derek Walcott's *Dream on Monkey Mountain*. Unlike the previous writers, Brodber bypasses the difficulty of speaking *about* the alienation of the colonial subject; instead, she directly tackles the project of speaking from and through this space of alienation. In interviews, Brodber refers to her main character as an example of a "dissociated identity," but she never utilizes such diagnostic terms in her text. The protagonist, Nellie, narrates her own story and does not mark herself as mad in her narrative. Indeed, aside from her own imagination of her neighbors' thoughts, she is also not marked as mad by others. Relying on symbols such as the *kumbla*, the "spying glass," and the kaleidoscope to convey Nellie's spiraling thoughts, Brodber explores the problematics of social mobility and role expectations predicated on colonial values. In this chapter, I examine how Brodber grapples with the effects of these expectations on mental health as well as how she imaginatively tackles the difficulty of describing madness with the "language of reason" within commonly recognized generic literary boundaries and from a first-person perspective.

"Go eena kumbla": The Dangers of Security

Jane and Louisa Will Soon Come Home presents verbal snapshots of Nellie Richmond's life, including information about her family members and ancestors. Although these snapshots are not in chronological order, most of the major events in Nellie's life are detailed—at least, she details the events she considers important. Nothing generally related in autobiographical narratives is included: no individual accounts of Nellie's birth, graduations, migration, or return to Jamaica, although her narrative indicates that these events have occurred. At best, tracking time in *Jane and Louisa* is difficult, both in the protagonist's life and in periods of Jamaican history. Within Nellie's fragmented and jumbled narrative, there are few historical signposts. Her description of past generations of her family, for example, includes the information that her maternal grandfather was in the Boer War and that her paternal great grandfather was born soon after the crowning of Queen Victoria and the end of slavery in the West Indies. But even with these very specific historical indications for her ancestors' lives, Nellie's own birth remains unremarked and her siblings are merely names in a repeated list. Nellie describes significant moments in her life, indicating her age at the time—eight, eleven, sixteen—but she does not connect these ages to dates or historically specific events, such as Jamaican independence. In fact, that momentous event goes unnoticed in her narrative, even though it occurs during her late teenage years.[1] There are rarely straightforward statements in the text about temporality; the reader has to piece this information together from various clues.

Even determining which pieces of the narrative are part of the "current moment" and which are part of Nellie's memories is difficult. Ironically, the only sustained narrative section of *Jane and Louisa* is Nellie's recounting of the events immediately before and during her mental breakdown. It is the least "loopy" section of the text, the only section that does not double back on itself in the spiral that Brodber's words create. At this point, Nellie seems to be thirty-six years old and has accomplished advanced schooling both in Jamaica and abroad. Earlier, one of the "Still Life" word portraits in section 1 indicates that she achieved the title of doctor, practicing at an American institution. The linear narrative style of this "To Waltz with You" section (notable given the disjointed sequences in other chapters), along with Nellie's description of her bizarre behavior as having "put on a show," calls the appropriateness of the term *madness* into question.[2] In a text that actively demands at least two readings by obscuring time and by juxtaposing fairy tales, ring games, dreams, Anancy stories, and memories, in no apparent order, such use of conventional storytelling seems aberrant. While acknowledging the risk of privileging this discourse of beginnings and endings that Brodber resists, I propose that this chapter describes Nellie's present and is the space from which she narrates the remainder of the text.

With this space as the primary location, the government yard becomes Nellie's final attempt at creating a kumbla before her breakdown. Therefore, Nellie's fellow government yard inhabitants become central as an audience because their judgment causes Nellie to "go off her head" (65). Even before her retreat to the government yard, Nellie is acutely aware of opinions of her fellow Jamaicans. Her description of the discomfort she experiences with each shift in identity is based on her awareness of their attention, particularly the attention paid to the role she is expected by others to play. Nellie has a hard time readjusting to the new roles she has to take on as she moves first to town, then abroad, and then back to Jamaica, and this contributes to her mental breakdown. A major part of this difficulty she experiences stems from the shame she feels in connection to her class, color, and gender. All three easily place her in an object position—as an object of scrutiny for those around her to judge on how well she is "living up to" the standards of these roles. As she emerges from the "mossy covert" of her parents' land, where she knows "the warmth and security of those eggs in the dark of [a mother fowl's] bottom," Nellie finds that she needs to create spaces within herself to find that warmth and security again (9).

Feeling continuously watched by others, Nellie mentally disintegrates as she internalizes their imagined judgment. For instance, in the section titled "The Tale of the Snail in the Kumbla," which presents four scenes of shame connected with sexuality, Nellie rambles, "The walls are moving in and somebody is holding my throat. Good. That will help. So nobody will know she can't hold a man. Let go my throat" (19). The pressure for silence and conformity comes from outside Nellie, but she begins to align herself with these outside forces. She easily moves outside herself to the third person and back again, later thinking,

> That's what he has to give and he wants me to call him father. Holy Father! You are mad. Walking up and down the asphalt road in your high-heeled shoes. You are mad. Stay off the compound. They will say you are mad and cannot hold a man. The sun will melt the brick that is in your brain and return it to normal functioning. "A bunch of red roses please." Walking down the

> road with a bunch of red roses in my high-heeled shoes. The prickles will jab your fingers: and the running blood will make you normal. Walking down the asphalt road in my high-heeled shoes and the hot sun with a bunch of red roses. People will say you are mad, like Miss Mal. (19–20)

The shifting perspectives are not signaled for the reader. At first, it seems Nellie is accusing the unnamed man of being mad, but then it becomes apparent that she is merely voicing the criticism that she imagines others will level against her. The result is what one imagines a schizophrenic break would feel like to the sufferer. Unlike Derek Walcott's metaphorical references to schizophrenia in essays and interviews, Brodber's approach is more concrete. As a social worker she encountered cases of mental illness, and she patterned *Jane and Louisa* on her experiences with dissociation.[3] The passage quoted above typifies symptoms of schizophrenia.[4] At any moment, the "I" has to contend with an outside power that changes the "I" into a "you," even for the subject herself. This break occurs later in Nellie's life, when she is living in the government yard and has lost her boyfriend, Cock Robin. Here she has become so aware of what others may think of her that she cannot separate it from what she thinks of herself. The voices of the "people" whom she imagines will liken her to Miss Mal become louder than her own; they become the arbiters of "normal."

Even in her kumbla, which should be protective, these voices are audible and powerful. There seems to be as many definitions for Brodber's kumbla as there are writings that try to define it. Often the term/concept is used without formal definition, as though it were transparent and self-explanatory. Brodber introduces the term *kumbla* early in the text, in the section "Voices," in part 1; but she does not fully address the concept until part 4, in a section aptly titled "The Kumbla." In this latter section, Brodber weaves an Anancy story into her various descriptions of the kumbla.[5] Among other things, the kumbla is a beach ball, an August worm egg shell, a parachute, "a helicopter, a transparent umbrella, a glassy marble, a comic strip space ship," and a "safe, protective time capsule" that "usually come in white" (123). Perhaps an integral characteristic of the kumbla is the very difficulty of defining it. Brodber—and her critics—offer so many different metaphors and analogies because the kumbla is different for each person.[6] To be effective, it must resist definition, resist any form of pinning down. Furthermore, it shields its inhabitant from the mental effects, beneficial and detrimental, of communal living. Although they cover a wide range of objects, one constant in the kumbla images Brodber utilizes is that they are all enclosures offering some protection from the outside. Inside the kumbla, Nellie does not have to face any role expectations. In the "soft carpeted foam, like the womb and with an oxygen tent" (123), she is not the privileged, brown intellectual who has to negotiate the various and varied strictures on female sexual behavior. In this space, she can also escape the responsibilities of educated intellectuals in Caribbean society.

In its fluidity and security, the kumbla is similar to Farah Jasmine Griffin's conception of safe spaces in African American migration narratives. Although Griffin concedes that safe spaces can be found "in song, oral culture, memory, dreams, and spirituality," she generally configures safe spaces as part of the urban landscape.[7] As such, they indicate more literal community spaces rather than the metaphorical, or symbolic, personal space of the kumbla. In addition, safe spaces are typically gendered: there is the "domestic 'homespace' of women and the street culture space of men." But Griffin's notation that in some circumstances "safe spaces play an important role in assisting migrants to resist dominant constructions of them" is compatible with Brodber's use of the kumbla throughout *Jane and Louisa*.[8] In both cases, the need for protection arises from resistance to the dominant gaze, construed as white American in Griffin's study and layered in Brodber's text as Jamaican informed by British colonialism. This difference in the power of the people holding the gaze is important to note in conjunction with the first section of *Jane and Louisa*, where, in contrast to Griffin's immigrants, Nellie feels freer under the white gaze. She remembers this freedom during her time as a student abroad: "I am in a foreign country. . . . It is the liberty of foreign students to be strange" (27). In her sociological study *Perceptions of Caribbean Women*, Brodber discusses the power of others to engender shame: "Whether this happens at all depends in the first place upon the position of the image-holders within the polity and on whether their opinions and attitudes support each other to form logical, if untrue statements. It depends, too, on the relationship between the image-holders and the perceived and performing women within the communication system."[9] In this "foreign country," Nellie does not feel the weight of Jamaican social and sexual mores. Not only is she free of the Jamaican "image-holders" with whom she has a stronger relationship, but she also cares less about the white "image-holders" who already codify foreign students as "strange." Thus she has a very low standard to achieve and is free to "act out," or not, as she pleases. Like many of Griffin's African American migrants who "can use the very structures and ideologies that repress them as means of enabling their agency," Nellie utilizes these foreigners' low opinion of her to undercut the power of their judgment.[10] It is her return home, not her migration, that threatens her finely built kumbla and her sanity.

Griffin cautions, however, that sometimes these safe spaces "serve only to create a sense of complacency."[11] Similarly, Brodber notes that "the trouble with the kumbla is the getting out of the kumbla. It is a protective device. If you dwell too long in it, it makes you delicate. Makes you an albino: skin white but not by genes. Vision extra-sensitive to the sun and blurred without spectacles" (130). Just as safe spaces range from the positive locations of "nurturing, healing, and resisting" to "provincial sites which discourage resistance and bind the protagonist to an oppressive past," so too kumblas can protect or paralyze.[12] The kumbla, then, can be "a pit or a shelter" (13). It can rehabilitate or strengthen its occupant; conversely, it can lull her into a deep sense of security, robbing her of the will to reenter the world and rebel against the status quo. This prevents her from tackling the communal constructions of roles and possibly changing the harmful "views" that caused her to "spin" the kumbla in the first place. The origins of this deleterious aspect of the kumbla are analogous to those of Griffin's safe space. For Griffin "these spaces are created by the power which migrants seek to resist" and are therefore "sometimes complicit in oppressing them."[13] Similarly, the kumblas in *Jane and Louisa* are often created from such noxious and repressive sources as sexual respectability and color privilege. Nellie's great-grandmother "built a fine and effective kumbla out of [her white husband's] skin" (142), and Aunt Becca's security lies in the distance she creates between the respectable town woman she is now and the abortion she left behind. The kumbla, though it may shield one from communal criticism, can also be created from the very things underlying that criticism.

Thus the act of going into the kumbla can be seen as both helpful and harmful; it can be both a form of surrender to and a resistance against the outside world. Like Griffin's migrants, Nellie may be escaping societal pressures or refusing to accept the societal values that create these pressures. Evelyn O'Callaghan finds it "possible to view the madwoman's strategy of 'opting out' of *all* role models/images/stereotypes as a refusal, if not a deconstruction, of the arbitrary boundaries of a divided patriarchal colonial society."[14] Initially, Nellie's strategy was to act out against such boundaries, particularly those that stipulated "respectable" sexual conduct, but such resistance led to her "walking up and down the asphalt road in [her] high-heeled shoes," a downward spiral into madness and full withdrawal into her kumbla. Whether Nellie is "acting out" or "opting out," her mental disintegration and her retreat into the kumbla indicate that she has accepted that her neighbors are entitled to use these "arbitrary boundaries" of gendered social expectations to judge her.

The Native "Intellectual Worker"

Reviews and criticism on *Jane and Louisa Will Soon Come Home* have focused on the symbol of the kumbla because it is central to the content of the text. But the implications of the kumbla for the form of *Jane and Louisa* require more attention, especially given the timing of its publication. The question "What is the kumbla?" is as important as "Why the kumbla?" And why now? In "Fiction in the Scientific Procedure," an essay in which Brodber details the process behind *Jane and Louisa*, she provides some explanation of her project. She positions the text as her attempt at providing the students in her abnormal psychology course with a "fictional case study" of the dissociative personality. In addition to wanting to "ease [herself] away from tables and who had said what when," Brodber also needed to provide her students with a case that "contributed to the sociology of blacks of the diaspora."[15] She writes that she wanted to bring the social periphery into the center of the text because she wanted her students to be able to recognize themselves and their patients: "It had to incorporate my 'I' and to be presented in such a way that the social workers I was training saw their own 'I' in the work." In *Jane and Louisa* Brodber's "I" may include autobiographical elements but refers more generally to the positioning of a black Jamaican female at the center of the text. Thus both Brodber and her students may recognize their "I's" in the same work, "I's" absent from their foreign-produced textbooks. Although Brodber feels that with the literary community's embracing of *Jane and Louisa* the text "has failed to inform sociology students," she has created a text that mirrors in form the boundary blurring that it addresses in content.[16] Her representation of a dissociative subject calls on not only the creative aspects of fiction writing but also her research in sociology and psychology. And while this combination of approaches may have failed to make the academic intervention she desired, Brodber's innovation in literary form—itself informed by her "sociology of blacks in the diaspora"—has certainly made an influential contribution to Caribbean literature. However, Brodber's reliance on an interdisciplinary approach to represent a mentally fragmented protagonist has resulted in a formally fragmented text, complicating generic categorization. Is *Jane and Louisa* a novel? As a lengthy fictional work, it is often referred to as such, but it is difficult to determine a plot in the assembly of Nellie's memories. The jacket description is as confusing as the text. It states that the text "is an extraordinary prose/poem. It is, like most first novels, autobiographical."[17] In this short description, there is a conflation of genres. The text is prose, poetry, and autobiographical novel, all at once. In addition, Brodber's statement that the text was meant to be a "fictional case study" places it in the category of instructional text. Indeed, at times it seems a didactic example of Brodber's conception of schizophrenia, with moments of explanatory prose (the description of the kumbla, for instance) that move outside what Nellie, in a schizoid break, would be capable of narrating in her alienated state. Though challenging to readers, this mosaic of fragments—poetry, fiction, autobiography, case study—is integral to Brodber's construction of Nellie's madness.

Part of the difficulty of comprehending and categorizing *Jane and Louisa* develops from the language of the text. Brodber's use of fiction to create a case study circumvents the heavy reliance on "scientific" language to describe madness. Shoshana Felman describes this problem in *Writing and Madness*, in relation to the difficulties historians face, but the problem exists for all disciplines with madness as a subject or subfield. The issue rests on being able to use "a language other than that of reason, which masters and represses madness, and other than that of science, which transforms it into an object with which no dialogue can be engaged, about which monologues are vacantly expounded—without ever disclosing the experience and the voice of madness in itself and for itself."[18] Even in fiction, however, Brodber is still limited by the "language of reason" in her portrayal of Nellie's point of view; language that, if Nellie is schizophrenic, is definitively not reasonable. Along with puzzling chronology and references, Nellie's narrative includes incomplete sentences, missing transitions, and connections based simply on the resonance of a word, phrase, or idea. Brodber challenges commonly accepted linguistic rules by approximating the "word salad" associations of schizophrenics and interspersing Jamaican patois and idioms with "formal" English.

At best, the form of *Jane and Louisa* can be described as a spiral without uniform coils. This is useful for approximating madness because spirals, unlike circles, do not offer completion. The coils turn and return "so as to miss anew [the spiral's] point of departure, to miss the closing point. . . . What the spiral actually repeats is a missed meeting with itself." Drawing on Foucault, Felman finds that madness is the "active incompletion of a meaning which ceaselessly transforms itself, offers itself but to be misunderstood, misapprehended."[19] Nellie's narrative revolves around several events in her life, repeating her descriptions, but never in such a way as to allow for comprehension of them or of their effect on her life. The social worker's—and the reader's—job is never completed because it requires and produces constant misapprehension of the subject/text. In the text, this occurs at the level of both form and content. In "Miniatures," Nellie describes several misapprehensions after she "came home." The fourth miniature is a transcript of her difficulty understanding Ida Jenkins, one of her cases in what appears to be a social work agency. Even before the interview, Nellie—and others at her "agency"—doubt Ida's reasons for sending her daughter overseas. Nellie continues making assumptions during the interview about Ida's life until Ida informs her that she has "accepted the Lord as [her] personal saviour" (45). Nellie deems Ida's faith crazy—"This woman mad, Lord"—but her response shows that because of her own anxieties she has "missed the point" in the spiraling words of their disjointed conversation and her own thoughts about Ida's spiritual dedication. After the conversation, Nellie thinks, "Yes, Lord that's faith . . . So where please is my faith, my God, my man?" and the following miniature raises implicit questions about her boyfriend, Robin, and their relationship (45–46). In reading her subject Ida through her own limited and confused ideas of home, family, and intimacy, Nellie herself effects the misapprehension that the text continuously performs. The spiral that forms *Jane and Louisa* ignores traditional expectations of prose, poetry, and autobiography in the same way that Ida Jenkins unconcernedly ignores Nellie's expectations of her conduct, expectations based on rigid patriarchal conceptions of sexuality and motherhood.

The ease with which Nellie switches from considering Ida's situation to questioning her own faith and sexuality indicates that Nellie cannot separate herself from her cases—yet more evidence of the necessity for the type of text Brodber aimed to create in writing *Jane and Louisa*, a text that would incorporate the social work students' "I's" in a case study, especially in definitions of madness. Brodber states that for field researchers in the social sciences, "accountability has not been to the people researched but to fellow academics." This route, however, is dangerous for "the native social scientist" because she is also a member of the community under examination. Accordingly, in writing her first full-length creative work, Brodber "felt that [her] examination of Jamaican society could not be written from the standpoint of the objective outside observer communicating to disinterested scholars."[20] Although she indirectly attacks the idea of *any* objectivity on the part of the observer, Brodber finds that the tension lies in making a distinction between the insider's and the outsider's perspective of abnormal psychology. In making this distinction, she simultaneously makes a case for the validity of the native perspective and the native social scientist's definition of what may be considered "mad" within the context of his or her culture.

Brodber also positions the native researcher as part of her or his own research subject, thereby further reducing the idea of objectivity "in the scientific procedure." For Brodber, the native researcher "is part of the polity examined, and the conceptual framework within which she/he works as well as the way the data are presented have to take this into consideration."[21] Thus, although the social sciences may claim to work with "facts," the gathering, interpretation, and presentation of these facts are heavily influenced by the researcher's background. The researcher constitutes these facts for her or his reader. While it would be an oversimplification to discuss *Jane and Louisa* as merely a different conceptual framework for thinking about schizophrenia, Brodber does imply that the text accomplishes this shift in perspective for her students. More than simply bringing fiction into the classroom to examine the possibilities of schizophrenia, she has created a "case study"—usually supposed to be a factual example—to be used in her course. As such, *Jane and Louisa* questions the factuality of case studies, and the text itself becomes a case study of the impossibility of removing the researcher's biases from her work.

Almost four decades earlier, Frantz Fanon, also a Caribbean social scientist writing on the psychic alienation of the colonial subject, similarly problematized the distance required between the scientist and his object. In chapter 4 of *Black Skin, White Masks*, Fanon directly addresses the difficulty of objectivity:

> I sincerely believe that a subjective experience can be understood by others; and it would give me no pleasure to announce that the black problem is my problem and mine alone and that it is up to me to study it. But it does seem to me that M. Mannoni has not tried to feel himself into the despair of the man of color confronting the white man. In this work I have made it a point to convey the misery of the black man. Physically and affectively. I have not wished to be objective. Besides, that would be dishonest: It is not possible for me to be objective.[22]

Here Fanon recognizes himself as intimately connected to his subject and banishes any notion of objectivity, including any desire for it. Near the end of the text he also admits, "Scientific objectivity was barred to me, for the alienated, the neurotic, was my brother, my sister, my father." Fanon acknowledges that his writing and his practice are informed by his blackness and that his subjects are undeniably close to him. This is a large step for a social scientist who must validate the reliability of his work. Fanon does not, however, directly declare himself similar to his subject. Fanon, like his subject, has moved outside his own culture, and the resulting hybrid is hyperaware of others' assessments of him. For Fanon, cultural miscegenation is necessary for this awareness because "as long as the black man is among his own, he will have no occasion, except in minor internal conflicts, to experience his being through others."[23] Only when he steps outside "his own" community can "the black man" begin to look at himself critically.

However, Brodber problematizes this homogeneous group. In *Jane and Louisa*, the gaze is neither *of* nor *on* the white world. The text explores the effects of colonization in the relationships between the colonized. Brodber shifts the focus from the tension between black/Jamaican and white/American/British to that between Jamaicans themselves (who are primarily black, in Brodber's formulation). She considers the alienating effect of "those in the yard" on the female subject, particularly the westernized female subject who returns home and cannot find her place. Although *Jane and Louisa* is primarily narrated by Nellie, who because of her foreign education could be described as similarly situated in comparison to Brodber and Fanon, the voices and visions of Jamaicans "seasoned" at home on the island are loud and clear. Under their eyes, Nellie becomes hyperaware of the ways her schooling abroad places her in the precarious position of being both inside and outside Jamaican culture, which becomes for her a maddening mix of liminality and inclusion. In "Not You/Like You: Postcolonial Women and the Interlocking Questions of Identity and Difference," Trinh Minh-ha gives name to women caught in this space:

> The moment the insider steps out from the inside she's no longer a mere insider. She necessarily looks in from the outside while also looking out from the inside. Not quite the same, not quite the other, she stands in that undetermined threshold place where she constantly drifts in and out. Undercutting the inside/outside opposition, her intervention is necessarily that of both not quite an insider and not quite an outsider. She is, in other words,

> this inappropriate other or same who moves about with always at least two gestures: that of affirming "I am like you" while persisting in her difference and that of reminding "I am different" while unsettling every definition of otherness arrived at.[24]

This "inappropriate other," the westernized female subject, consistently moves between difference (outsider) and sameness (insider). She subverts classification. She is Brodber's "native social scientist" as well as Fanon's alienated subject. This inappropriate other frequently has some form of social power based on her border position. She is often what Brodber (borrowing Trinidadian Lloyd Best's term) refers to as an "intellectual worker," placed in a position of creating work about her culture, whether fiction, fact, or, as is the case with *Jane and Louisa*, something in between.[25]

Book Learning and Social Control: Education and/as Class Status

Minh-ha's conception of an inappropriate other breaks the mind/body, self/other, insider/outsider barriers. As a result, the inappropriate other experiences a form of dissociation. She begins to look at herself, becoming both subject and object. In addition, she begins to see others seeing her. This happens to Nellie as she progresses in her education and distances herself from the "mossy coverts" of her childhood. As the African Americans' treatment of her in the unnamed foreign institution indicates, though she may still be claimed by "her people," she also now occupies an enviable social position because of her educational achievement. In a study contemporary with Brodber's writing of *Jane and Louisa*, Nancy Foner found that education in rural Jamaica was "the established route to occupational advancement and the acquisition of desirable cultural characteristics"; it therefore "came to have its own symbolic significance and to be a basis for prestige in itself."[26] With her advanced education, Nellie recognizes herself as an object of both her own and others' scrutiny; as such, she is forced to recognize her greater social position, greater social prestige, and greater social responsibility to these "image-holders."

"Image-holders" use several characteristics to judge acceptable role behavior. Three of these characteristics are prominent in *Jane and Louisa* and appear inextricably bound together in Nellie's character: education level/class status, race/color, and gender. Although these are not the only roles that Nellie occupies in her narrative, these receive the most attention and cause her the most anxiety, especially when her life is in flux. In the text, Nellie experiences three shifts in her class identity. Although she views it as punishment, her migration to "town" to live with Aunt Becca makes her considerably more privileged than her siblings. Then she receives the scholarship to go abroad for study; there she experiences an upward shift in class, but she loses some of the privilege that her lighter skin afforded her in Jamaica. When she returns to the island, her class is once again adjusted as she joins the educated elite in the island, but it is not clear how this initially affects her, since the text skips much of the time between her return and her breakdown in the government yard.

For the periods that she does narrate, Nellie experiences a primarily mental dis-ease in response to her shifts in identity. Early in the text, Nellie gives readers a clue as to the financial status of her family. Although there are six children, she can expect to receive a new dress for her birthday and for Easter Sunday. When her eighth birthday falls on the Saturday before Easter Sunday, however, Nellie lowers her expectations: "Two dresses on two consecutive days was outside of the realms of my reality (though of course it was my due). They would say as they always said when they disappointed me—'The heart is willing but the flesh is weak'"; she asks instead for a "yellow leghorn straw bag" (25). Nellie recognizes the importance of the bag to her ability to "make a distinction between them and us" (51), between her and her siblings and the other children. Even at the early age of eight, she can declare, "On this bag lay my claims to social identity" (25). When she receives *two* dresses *and* the bag, however, Nellie understands that the distinction has become too much and the gulf between herself and "them" too wide: instead of positively establishing her as privileged, the bag, coming as it does with two Easter dresses, will be her "crowning shame." In moderation, such advantages are enviable, but in excess they are shameful. To ease her discomfort, she must bring herself down a peg or two in the eyes of those who confer such "social identity." In compensation, she forgets her lines while performing in her church's Easter service. Her display of intelligence must suffer—publicly—to balance out the material trappings that she gained.

In the rest of the text, however, it is the social weight of this intelligence that becomes too much for her. In her adult years, Nellie's education—particularly the latter, foreign portion of her education—creates the too-wide gap between her "us" and "them." Nellie uses school as her social ladder, and her progress becomes the sign of her higher social status. Here education is divorced from the usual rewards of job security and higher earnings. Education itself—or rather, the academic advancement and degrees that serve as the evidence of education—is the goal. As Merle Hodge states in her introduction to Brodber's *Perceptions of Caribbean Women*, "In order to ensure the best possible life for her children," the Caribbean woman expends "every effort . . . to steer or catapult the next generation out of the sub-culture into which they were born, into the official image-making culture." Thus Caribbean families, mothers in particular, "make every humanly-possible sacrifice to contribute to the grooming of a child who has been singled out by the official educational system as 'promising,' for such a child represents the breakthrough of one's family line into the culture which one does not oneself practice (which one might consciously reject as being contrary to one's own habits and tastes) but which is nevertheless seen as more valid than one's own."[27] It is not unusual, therefore, that in *Jane and Louisa* readers rarely encounter an economic identifier of class; rather, education often signifies the social differences between Jamaicans. Although the parents recognize that it may distance their children from them culturally and geographically, they still encourage the embracing of education. Hodge's parenthetical probability emphasizes the distance between the child's home life and experience at school. This "contrariness" has been described in several other works of West Indian literature, from earlier novels such as George Lamming's *In the Castle of My Skin* and Hodge's own *Crick Crack Monkey*, to more recent works by Michelle Cliff and Jamaica Kincaid. In these as well as in Brodber's other texts, the influence of British colonialism on the anglophone Caribbean educational system creates a peculiar distance between culture and education. In Nellie's case, this opposition between culture and education leads to alienation.

In *Jane and Louisa*'s polyvocal section "Voices," we learn that Nellie has obtained a scholarship—"the best one" (8)—to further her studies. She presents this to her grandmother as a distraction from the lecture on her mother's failure to take her training college exams. Granny Tucker deems her daughter's education fruitless because it ended when Sarah became pregnant with her first of six children. Instead of money or education, the children become what Sarah and Alexander Richmond—and, in turn, Granny Tucker—have "to show for" their lives. This result is not acceptable to Granny Tucker, and Nellie's scholarship is her grandmother's reward, the redeeming factor of what Granny Tucker views as Sarah's "fall." Thus Nellie's success elevates Granny Tucker's social status. In this community, education is so valued that it can create malicious envy in onlookers. Nellie's mother has to warn her: "Don't eat anything from him or anybody else outside of this yard unless you let me see it. You hear me Nellie and Sister. You must be careful" (11). Sweet Boy tells, in section 3 of "Voices," of Mass Stanley's sister "what pass first year and pickney carry poison egg and give her at school and she dead!" (11), and Girlie responds with a story about Mass Cliff, who went "silent mad," although he had been "bright bright . . . and is people do him so" (12). Intellectual ability, which provides access to higher education, is a primary route to social mobility, making education and intelligence objects of scrutiny in Jamaican society; like the yellow handbag, they provide Nellie with another way to socially distinguish herself. Social distinction, however, carries with it the weight of exposure. "Bright," successful students may become the victims of malicious intent or internal turmoil.

Brodber's text, coming as it does after education was made more widely available in Jamaica, offers a larger perspective of V. S. Naipaul's 1962 comment: "[In the Caribbean,] the stories were never stories of success but of failure: brilliant men, scholarship winners, who had died young, gone mad, or taken to drink."[28] Brodber takes a closer look at why such educational success can lead to social failure, particularly for women as they begin to take advantage of greater educational opportunities. Education is a means of increasing the social status of not only the student but also the student's family. As Foner notes, in rural Jamaican communities, "the educational system provides the principal means for achieving mobility," and "an individual's prestige in the local status system is related to his children's educational attainments."[29] So there is a large amount of pressure on the student who shows academic promise. This alone may have been enough to cause the reactions that Naipaul describes, but Brodber focuses on the pressure of social control. *Jane and Louisa* questions the content of the Caribbean curriculum and the reception of education in the community, both of which spring from the same acceptance of colonial values.

Helen Tiffin finds that from the pre- through the postindependence period, "the library, the classroom and sexual relations remain the loci of continuing and complex colonialist erasure and repression."[30] Through the dissemination of knowledge and morality, the various colonizers in the Caribbean attempted to normalize their values in the colonized. By extension, whiteness and all that it entailed were regarded as superior to blackness and all that that entailed. Tiffin does not mention the church, but religion is for her a recognized tool of "colonialist erasure and repression" as well. Institutions such as the classroom and the church move members of a colonized society farther and farther away from any native culture that may have survived slavery or indentureship until it is no longer possible to return to or even to recall a "before they landed" identity. It is not surprising, then, that so many representations of madness in Caribbean literature are figured in relation to religion and education. However, it is also in these arenas that the germs of resistance can be found. As the kumbla can sustain or reject social control, so can institutions of religion and education.

The possibilities for resistance are evident in Nellie's family history, where she pits her father's education with "the pale faces" against the anger of her grandfather. The two are part of her immediate family tree, and she learns different things from each. From her maternal grandfather, "Corpie," she receives anger that should combat the swallowing of religion and education. Nellie likens the anger to "an Adam's apple, an indelicate bulge which appears in the throat" (31); it should work to impede the gobbling of European culture. But this rage "must be trained out of the new generation" through the mix of religion and education that she portrays in this "still life." Brodber's later provocative use of the term *ancestral anger* denotes the passing down of this anger through generations, indicating that such "training" will always be incomplete.[31] But even Granny Tucker, though she talks to the late Corpie daily, resorts to constant prayer and resignation to the will of a Christian God as means of freezing some of the righteous hot rage that Corpie taught her.

While in America, Nellie recognizes the power of this anger in joining blacks across the diaspora. When African Americans embrace her, she thinks, "Strange how a common enemy tightens bonds so that we are people where once we had been men, women, carpenters, cooks, nurse's aides, doctors, light-skinned-curley-haired, black-too-dark-to-make-the TV screen" (33). But Nellie soon realizes that Corpie's anger is not universal; she cannot forget her Caribbeanness. As she begins to revel in the sameness—in thinking herself like Fanon's black man among his own—the anger begins to dissolve and she begins to see herself as "black, taken now for an African, now for a Negro, a nigger, reaching for Corpie's hand to find that I am not home" (33). Corpie's absence makes her realize that she cannot get lost in "her people" but must remember that her enemy, though wearing the same skin, is different and requires a different form of opposition from her. Nellie expresses a stable identity when she returns from America. She can confidently say, "Man, I have a right in this country. I have come home and I have a right to refuse to drink your snail, Mr. Anancy" (34). But during the little-mentioned following years of work in Jamaica, she somehow loses this spirit of resistance.

Brodber opens the text with this opposition on both the educational and religious fronts: "Papa's grandfather and Mama's mother were the upper reaches of our world. So we were brown, intellectual, better and apart, two generations of lightening blue blacks and gracing elementary schools with brightness. The cream of the earth, isolated, quadroon, mulatto, Anglican." The black opposition is immediately reflected in "two wiry black hands up to the elbows in khaki suds," but even this anger has been tempered by religion. Although it may be "hard work that gets a Baptist Amen through lips pursed for the Te Deum," Granny Tucker has been fully Christianized (7). She prays heartily and relies heavily on religious teachings to regulate her children's and grandchildren's behavior. Prominent in her image of proprietary behavior are the sexual mores Tiffin describes. Granny Tucker's daily dressing ritual reflects her belief that female sexuality should be restricted in both body and mind. Although she rebels at first, Nellie inherits this belief, and her descriptions of her later interactions with men indicate that she has incorporated it into her view of the world and herself. The conflicts between these internalized beliefs and her behavior contribute to her "showy" mental breakdown in the government yard.

Carrying the Weight of Gender

During her breakdown, Nellie is guided by her childhood friend Baba, who is grounded by his own success in rejecting the colonial education and expectations of his youth. Baba begins by attacking the restriction of sexuality imposed on Nellie by her education, in which performing intellectuality has meant acting like her male colleagues, and forces her into fully addressing her femininity. After sitting in on a meeting with Nellie and her "brothers" in the government yard, Baba presents Nellie with a doll fashioned from the dried seed of a pear. The doll immediately crumbles in Nellie's lap, a commentary on her own dried-up sexuality. Baba quietly but persistently sets out to crumble Nellie's kumbla of androgyny. In his first appearance in the text, Baba is presented to Aunt Becca to be judged on the basis of his intelligence and success at school. When Nellie wishes permission to go out with Baba, she describes him to Aunt Becca first through his family but then in terms of his education: "You remember him, Mass Stanley's grandson. You know Mass Stanley Auntie. . . . Yes Auntie, you remember Baba. He used to recite well. But he never did come to our Sunday School, so perhaps you really don't remember him. But all the same. You would be proud of him. If you see him! Going up for prizes so often. History prize, Maths prize and with all that, deputy head boy and captain of the cricket team. You would be proud." Part of Nellie's qualification to go to the movies with Baba is that she is "a prefect at school and a patrol leader" (16). All the education and leadership skills in the world, however, cannot make up for the fact that she is a "girl chile" and cannot be allowed to go to the movies alone with a boy at sixteen. In what seems like retaliation, an older Nellie allows herself to be sexually initiated in a movie house by a man that she has either stolen or borrowed from another woman, a man with whom her sexual encounter is, as Carolyn Cooper terms it, "essentially commercial."[32] For this date, she clearly could not say to Aunt Becca, "You would be proud."

Nellie's awareness of the implications of her gender and sexuality begins earlier in her life (though later in her narrative) than the episode with Aunt Becca. At eleven she begins to menstruate, and later she identifies this as the traumatic moment she entered the kumbla. In a section titled "The One-Sided Drum," Nellie considers the "it" that encompasses the different implications of menstruation. She remembers the immediate difference "it" causes between herself and her male friends. When she begins to develop breasts and to experience other aspects of puberty, she loses her easiness with Egbert and other boys, and even with Mass Stanley. This distancing is soon followed by her move to live with Aunt Becca. The bodily evidence of her femininity becomes the cause of her separation from her family and her childhood friends: "I have 'it' in me and Aunt Becca Pinnock has no children of her own. I must go to Town with 'it' and her and Teacher Pinnock to his promotion" (122). Her "coming into womanhood" leads to what seems to her to be a punishment—she is separated from those she depends on for self-definition. When she moves to town to live with Aunt Becca and Teacher Pinnock, Nellie not only is forced outside her immediate family circle but also has to make the country-to-town transition. Her migration to town and the added responsibilities of puberty cause Nellie to begin needing protection: "The circle narrowed, the distance was complete. Go eena kumbla for you need to be cleaned and preserved like peppers in a kilner jar. Go eena Kumbla. I went with Aunt Becca and the sun" (122). Nellie begins to slip into her kumbla as she negotiates her new roles outside the communal base. It is here that Nellie starts to experience the alienation that forces her to begin her mental retreat.

From her family's reaction, Nellie learns that menstruation, or any indication of female sexuality, needs to be cleansed or hidden; she learns that shame is an integral part of being female. Only her father offers fertility as something to be proud of, as an achievement in itself, even as Granny Tucker bemoans Nellie's mother's "spoiled" life. Nellie soon discovers that she is expected to take extra precautions to guard her feminine virtue. Puberty pushes her to exclaim, "What a weight! Slowly it adds up. This bounty. Put it under a bushel or else it will shame you" (24). She refers specifically to menstruation, but the description is also applicable to the subject of the following section: the two new dresses and yellow straw bag. Her "bounty," both her sexuality and her status in the community, must be hidden lest it shame her. Furthermore, this "weight" refers to the communal gaze. Nellie's responses to puberty and its consequences are being judged by those around her. Thus Aunt Becca can warn, "Learn that lest you be weighed in the balance and found wanting. Learn that the world is waiting to drag you down. 'Woman luck de a dungle heap', they say, 'fowl come scratch it up'. But you save yourself lest you turn woman before your time, before the wrong fowl scratch your luck" (17). Nellie is in danger of falling (or being "dragged down") because of her class—measured by her fortune in school and her color—and because of her gender. All these are aspects of her person that are easily weighed and judged by those image-holders surrounding her. During her breakdown, when she feels light enough to levitate, she believes that she cannot be "weighed in the balance" because she refuses to take on the weight of this "bounty." In the kumbla, and in the alternative madness, she can shed both these things, but Baba requires that she face them. She describes his patience with her resistance: "He [Baba] had spent a good long time in teaching me that, in pointing out to me that I was more than a cracked up doll. . . . I was not like Aunt Becca had said, 'wanting.' I had been weighed in the balance and finally found heavy enough to sink" (69). Although she does not yet fully trust Baba—she wonders, for instance, "[Is] this obeah man of an anancy trying to play something else on me!" (69)—she tentatively accepts his diagnosis of her fragmentation. Baba has resisted the results of his promising educational career by turning to a different form of knowledge, which Nellie variously refers to as obeah, Rastafarianism, and Haitian voodoo. When she first recognizes Baba in the government yard, Nellie surmises that his education has not included the alienating effects of colonization, because it has occurred right there on the island. This gives him a grounding that Nellie lost in the period between her return and her breakdown. Although it takes an unspecified "good long time," Baba helps Nellie melt the ice of her anger: the "cracked up doll" begins to "liquefy," coming back to life and awareness.

In this healing process, Nellie attempts to reevaluate and revalue her sexuality, class, gender, and color. Baba's demonstration with the dried doll teaches her that she cannot choose one over the others; she must blend them all together to be a whole person. Evelyn O'Callaghan describes the difficulty Nellie faces as being related to her schizophrenic break because "choosing one model or role of 'femaleness' necessitates a denial of other aspects of womanhood, to the detriment of self-integration."[33] Before Baba's reappearance, Nellie's strategy for sanity was to focus on her role as female intellectual concerned with the plight of "her people," despite having as little to do with "her people" as possible. In the government yard, Nellie joins a group that embraces education to the detriment of everything else, including sexuality. They reduce their lives to such seemingly immaterial things as etymology. Indeed, her boyfriend, Cock Robin, literally reduces himself to such immateriality. His spontaneous combustion brings Nellie partially out of her cocoon of androgynous "brotherhood," further destabilizing her and exposing her to mental decline.

Cock Robin's fiery "transfiguration" is perhaps the most puzzling reference in the otherwise realistic opening of the section "To Waltz with You." Nellie informs the reader that her "young man got caught up in the spirit and burnt to grease like beef suet caught in a dutchie pot" (52), but the event is given very little space in the narrative. Daryl Cumber Dance reads Cock Robin as a figment of Nellie's imagination, representing another part of Nellie herself, but the reactions of the other characters make this reading difficult to accept.[34] The other members of the brotherhood try to console Nellie, and later Nellie describes her reluctance to return to her room where "grease, dust and ash" remain from Cock Robin's burning (65). In this room, she must face the fact that her presence, as a woman, could not ground her man—"After all, how many women's men burn to ash?" (66). Her "young man" however, did not provide much in terms of a mutually supportive relationship. In the shortest of the miniatures in section 1, Nellie speaks of Cock Robin in the present tense, before his "spirit" burned him up (or out): "My young man talks in an unknown tongue . . . words like 'underdevelopment,' 'Marx,' 'cultural pluralism.' I love my young man. He's got the black spirit and it's riding him hard. Lead on Robin. Lead on" (46). Her description of Cock Robin does not indicate a reason for him being her young man. There is no intimacy, only the cause. After his death, Nellie feels intense (and maddening) shame under the watchful eyes of the government yard "gallery." Although they are kind, she feels that they pity her because she was not "woman enough" to hold on to Cock Robin. Again, shame surrounds female sexuality, but now it rests on Nellie's lack thereof rather than her bounty.

When Baba enters the brotherhood's think-in, he judges the "cracked up doll" that Nellie has become. He weighs her in the balance of balance itself and finds her wanting, particularly in sexuality and voice. He recognizes the hypocrisy of the group's ideals and practices; without actually excluding women, the group eclipses females and female sexuality. Nellie does not speak at their meetings, she merely takes the minutes; that is what she considers her contribution to the group, her "small part." Although she has been educated to a high level, she does not have any authority in these think-ins. As she lists them, the speaking members of the group are Egbert, with religious leanings; Errol, the scholar; and Barry, who does not read but leans toward religion. Nellie is one of only two women in the group, and neither of them holds or performs leadership roles. The other woman, Beatrice, is "rough" but "can always find time and cloth to make a bandage or two and to put a patch here and there and she is good with a darning needle" (50). The two women of the group are supportive but silent. Although not quite as domestic as Beatrice, Nellie still occupies a feminine, powerless role in this group of self-proclaimed liberated intellectuals. Paradoxically, she eschewed femininity in joining the group only to fall prey to the group's patriarchal structure.

Baba begins to lead her, however reluctantly, to find her own gendered voice. At first, he needs to separate femininity from sex for Nellie. She attempts to entice him but he refuses her advances, even her blatantly "shameful" act of stripping off her clothes for him. He refuses to begin a sexual relationship with her until he can "meet" her, the whole her. When she offers herself he tells her, "I know you want to give yourself but I fear that you offer yourself because you don't want you. That's no gift love, even if we did need gifts. That's something you throw on a scrap-heap. We won't forage for a thing in a scrap-heap. We need a walking-talking human being" (71). He forces Nellie to realize that in her present state sex is not expression but rather another silencing. Before Baba can know her, Nellie must mentally reintegrate herself and release her psychic dependence on her kumbla.

Throughout the text, and especially in the final section, Nellie has examples of women who, while not exactly embracing their sexuality, do not treat it as shameful. The voices in the beginning provide sketches of Nellie's family tree, including Nellie's mother, who receives little attention in the book otherwise. Sarah, despite the ensuing marriage, is a fallen woman because her first pregnancy ends her educational career. Nellie represents salvation for Granny Tucker, but we never know whether her own mother sees her as such; perhaps Sarah does not feel her actions require exoneration. In addition, Nellie "had seen her cousins rise then fall. Letitia, Teena, B" (142). The fallen women are seen but not heard. One wonders whether they repent their falling or, like Mass Stanley and Miss Elsada, view their children as blessings. The represented Jamaican community, however, has an investment in keeping these fallen women voiceless because the women do not associate their sexuality with shame. They have not been socialized—as Rebecca Pinnock, née Richmond, has been socialized—to deny their sexuality and "[drag] around life on their bottoms like Sirhie, the bitch, in the hope of keeping male dogs at bay" (146) and in hopes of appearing acceptable. What little we are told about these women indicates that their public failure to live within the colonial patriarchal expectations of their society means that, unlike Nellie, they face less risk to their mental health. While conscious of being "seen" as fallen, these women do not appear disturbed by the gap between the reality of their sexuality and the restrictive communal sexual mores.

In Nellie's narrative, it is the "respectable" women, women whose relationships have not led to illegitimate children, who are most susceptible to mental decline—a different kind of fall. Besides Nellie, the clearest example is that of Miss Mal—Mass Stanley's sister-in-law Malvina Psalms—who goes "off her head" because of a failed relationship. Miss Mal is mentioned at several moments in the text, but Nellie does not fully explain who Miss Mal is until two-thirds of the way through the narrative. Nellie relates the story of Malvina's madness as if it were recent history, although it apparently occurred before Nellie was born. Malvina went "clean out of her head" after her love affair with a "Syrian droger" ended; she was taken away in a straitjacket for the government to take care of her. The description of why Malvina was handed over to a governmental institution is evident in the voices that surround her break. Malvina and her sister, Elsada, had migrated from a more rural area of Jamaica and were "stranger[s] in a strange land." Elsada's insistence on virtue for herself and her sister was seen as "too good" by their new neighbors, so when Malvina fell for a fellow stranger who left her, "people laughed" (108). With only Elsada as kin, and as an outsider to the community, Malvina had no resources to help her deal with her madness. Thus she was turned over to the government. In contrast, when Nellie has a similar break in the government yard, she has Baba, sympathetic yard residents, and the spirits of her ancestors there to help her recover.

"Coming Home": Cyclostyled Communal Healing

In *Jane and Louisa*, then, rebirth is a community effort. Although Nellie feels pressure to conform to expectations, there are also positive aspects to the community that play an important role in Nellie's healing process. For while the kumbla effectively protected Nellie from their judging eyes, it also removed her from any communal benefits. A community can provide one with a stable reflection of oneself; in Nellie's case, this helping community consists mostly of her family. Her family serves as the base for her identity, so Nellie needs them to reconnect the split parts of herself. Through her family—a smaller, more tightly knit community—Nellie comes to know herself. At eight, Nellie is capable of claiming herself: she can definitively say, "I am Nellie" after a detailed description of her parents' loving interaction (86). She knows herself through her place within her immediate family. Great-Grandfather Will and Granny Tucker may define the boundaries of her world, but her mother, father, and siblings define her. As she moves outward into the larger community, however, she loses this stable definition and fails to redefine herself, causing her to retreat to her kumbla to survive the changes in her life. At the close of her narrative, when she is ready to fully emerge from her kumbla, she says goodbye to "great grandfather Will, Tia, Granny Tucker, Corpie, aunts and uncles and cousins," but the people she has spoken least about—her parents and siblings—remain with her (147).

Nellie's reinsertion into society is not self-initiated; it occurs in a continuously widening spiral, growing to accommodate more healers. Accordingly, Brodber describes the organization of the text as a "concerto in four movements."[35] The four movements correspond to the four sections of the text, each titled with a line from a child's ring game.[36] Nellie begins her healing in "To Waltz with You" with only Baba. Her kumbla cracks like the hatching eggs under the mother fowl's bottom, and she is reborn in Baba's womblike room. The waltz, a twosome, soon changes to the ring game of the text's title as Nellie takes other partners. Baba gives way to the spirit of Nellie's spinster aunt Alice, who leads Nellie to reflect on her family history in detail. Unlike the negative images they recall in the beginning, the voices now present a larger, multifaceted story. As they surround Nellie, everyone does his or her part to enable her to become a "walking-talking human being."

Both Nellie's psychic breakdown and her healing process, then, are involved in the "continuous circular process" to which the book's title and section subtitles allude;[37] hence Brodber's categorization of the text as "cyclostyled."[38] The implications of her method, however, are constantly shifting from Nellie to her surrounding community. As is evident in her changing perspective and pronoun use, Nellie alternates as symbolic of the individual "I"—which Brodber describes in "Fiction in the Scientific Procedure"—and of the larger communal "I." The text also moves out of the personal with suggestions for postindependence Jamaica. In a 1982 interview, Brodber states, "I'm making the same claim for the history of the nation—that you have to go back and look at it, no matter how your myths have to be destroyed, you still have to go back and look at it. And when you finish, you have to decide whether you're going to live with it, whether you're going to forget it, or—hopefully—you say, well it's so it go and let me do my piece and claim it."[39] In *Jane and Louisa*, then, Nellie's schizophrenic state is symbolic of a nation trapped in its own kumbla, protected from a painful past but also prevented from realizing a productive future. Through her representation of Nellie's madness and healing, Brodber takes the "sociodiagnostic" approach defined by Fanon in *Black Skin, White Masks*. The individual pathology requires not a psychological but a sociological evaluation. Brodber's conclusion, however, is very different from Fanon's. Fanon found that "the tragedy of the man is that he was once a child,"[40] but Brodber asks that that childhood—read, history—be frankly assessed and accepted for all it holds. While Nellie's "disalienation" does in part spring from her stepping out of the kumbla—which is comparable to Fanon's "materialized Tower of the Past"—it also springs from her willingness to face her individual and familial history head on and then to "do [her] piece and claim it."[41] The solution to, and escape from, madness lies with the whole-hearted acceptance of oneself, past and present. Later, in "Fiction in the Scientific Procedure," Brodber finds that in *Jane and Louisa* she was working out "the relationship between history, tradition, and defense mechanisms."[42] Taking the 1982 interview into account, she appears to have been writing about individual, communal, *and* national "history, tradition, and defense mechanisms." Nellie's dissociation, then, becomes representative of not merely a personal or local problem but a national disorder; and the oft-quoted last line of *Jane and Louisa Will Soon Come Home*, "We are getting ready" (147), becomes representative of a national outlook.

Epilogue

Madness and Migration in the New Millennium

Yesterday
Ah was mad mad, mad mad,
Mad mad, mad mad mad, mad mad,
Mad mad, mad!
Stark ravin' mad.
Yesterday was Monday . . .
Yesterday was Tuesday . . .
Today is Wednesday . . . Ash Wednesday,
Jus' like dat . . . O' God!

—Paul Keens-Douglas, "Jus' Like Dat"

In ending, I return to where I began, with Paul Keens-Douglas's "Jus' Like Dat." But here I turn to the closing stanza of the poem, which repeats the beginning of the opening stanza but takes the speaker and his audience in a new direction. This repetition of words, phrases, and in this case the opening lines of the poem primarily contributes to the performative aspect of the poem, but it also makes and remakes the meaning of the speaker's madness. He has been celebrating carnival, he has lost track of time, and now suddenly—"Jus' like dat"—it is time to leave the madness behind and return to reality and respectability. The speaker's "O' God!" can only hint at the massive change in behavior now required for Ash Wednesday church services. Yesterday was women, wine, and wining "down de place." Today . . . today is Ash Wednesday. Keens-Douglas's ellipses, the pauses I imagine present in his performance of the poem, represent the unbridgeable gap between the carnival and the church, between Caribbeanized celebrations and colonial conceptions of respectability. Dramatized in these lines, in the elliptical spaces between words, is the schizophrenic split Frantz Fanon describes in *The Wretched of the Earth*.

Derek Walcott, Sylvia Wynter, and V. S. Naipaul also dramatize this connection between religion and alienation. Across the chapters in *Disturbers of the Peace*, religion plays a large part in the madness of the characters. In chapters 1, 2, and 4 we encounter characters who are described as mad because they imagine themselves as leaders granted power by their gods. Their schizophrenic dreams of power are cited by unspecified official authorities as evidence of their madness, but their followers treat their prophecies as the solution to the madness—the anger, despair, and absurdity—of colonial life. Gender and privilege separate these megalomaniac men and the female protagonists I examine in chapters 3 and 5. That Antoinette and Nellie do not turn to religion to identify themselves as powerful may be due to the patriarchal structure of most religions, even those in which women hold high positions. It may also be due to their social privilege. Both Antoinette's and Nellie's psychic alienation stem, not from the self-destructive effects of poverty singled out by Corporal Lestrade (and Walcott, and Fanon) as the inspiration for religious delusions, but from their inability to meet the expectations of their social class. Given these sometimes stark differences between the main characters above, and between their respective insanities, my collective readings in this project situate such figurations of madness at the center of the texts' grappling with larger questions of Caribbean subjectivity.

In particular, madness provided Caribbean writers with a language for exploring the shifts in subjectivity that necessarily accompanied independence. The images and metaphors of this language—messiahs, dreams, schizophrenias—repeat throughout the texts published in the mid-twentieth century as writers map the internal psychic landscape of the colonized and recently decolonized Caribbean subject. But these images and metaphors also reappear in Caribbean texts published more recently. Though I chose to focus this study specifically on the period most concerned with the problematics of independence, my motivation to begin this project was the larger notion of madness as one of the identifying factors of anglophone Caribbean literature overall. Connections between madness and other concerns—such as racial communities, geographic fragmentation, gender roles—repeatedly surface in Caribbean literatures. To demonstrate some of the ways these connections continue in contemporary Caribbean literature, I close *Disturbers of the Peace* with a look at twenty-first-century narratives from diasporic writers, focusing on three recent first novels by writers from the ever-growing Caribbean diaspora— David Chariandy, Marie-Elena John, and Zadie Smith. In *Soucouyant* (2007), David Chariandy turns to an intimate portrayal of presenile dementia to explore the fragility of personal and cultural memory for Caribbean immigrants in Canada, where immigration laws encourage forgetting. Marie-Elena John's *Unburnable* (2006), set primarily in Dominica, and concerned with the too easily assigned title of "madwoman" as well as with madness as an inherited method of self-defense, echoes Jean Rhys's groundbreaking questioning of madness in *Wide Sargasso Sea*. And Zadie Smith's *White Teeth* (2000) plays on the link between madness and immigration in England—a link that turns on the psychic divide experienced by both the mad and the migrants sharing space in the center of a fallen empire. These novels indicate that in the twenty-first-century literature of the Caribbean diaspora writers still turn to representations of madness to depict their changing worlds. In these new millennial examples, these worlds include not only the perpetual process of decolonization—with its attendant questions of race, gender, and class—but also the distress of displacement and the futility of any notion of return.

The novels under discussion in this epilogue all engage a shift that I argue is occurring in anglophone Caribbean literature toward a reevaluation of what Chariandy calls the "profound socio-cultural dislocations resulting from modern colonialism and nation-building."[1] In the works I examine in my earlier chapters, madness enables the writers to speak to "socio-cultural dislocations" inherent in decolonization at "home"; but in these later texts the "dislocations" are as much literal as sociocultural. Even if we were to grant Frederic Jameson his thesis that "the story of the private individual destiny is always an allegory of the embattled situation of the nation," these three texts do not offer clear options as to which nation we might claim as subject of (or subject to) their allegory making.[2] There is a plurality of battles, a layering of nations as migration spans generations. Chariandy turns to the compound term *postcolonial diasporas* to theorize the fluid combination of hopes, desires, and realities of modern diasporic life. In articulating the term, he considers the "broader political and epistemological stakes" in the utilization of the word *diaspora* while raising a list of concerns about both postcolonial studies' and diaspora studies' abilities to fully articulate the sum of their intersecting parts. He attempts to delineate the problem space of a generation of writers, critics, and diasporic peoples with some definitive questions: "Is there an ideal or original conceptualization of diaspora? Are racial and ethnic groups automatically diasporas? Can diasporas be created through voluntary migration, rather than traumatic exile? Must a diaspora have an extant homeland culture before dislocation, or can it develop or invent one retrospectively? How does generational difference impact the imagining of a diaspora? Must people in a diaspora long to return home?"[3] These last two questions especially frame my approach here to the uses of madness in these twenty-first-century Caribbean narratives.

Chariandy's turn to the plural—diasporas—emphasizes the heterogeneity of experience across locations and across time. Indeed, both space and time must now be reconceptualized, given the epistemology of postcolonial diasporas.[4] These novels are not unique in their questioning of space and time as it connects to diaspora; indeed, some of the texts examined earlier in this book also consider these questions, turning to representations of madness to explore and depict the experiential disjunctures of time and space in the New World. But in these later texts there is a coupling of those explorations with the questions of home and generation Chariandy raises, along with a shift of that "home" from the "Old World" to the Caribbean. That is, despite centuries of migration from the region, forced and voluntary, the Caribbean was formerly conceived of primarily as the *site* of diaspora, or diasporas, with extant and imagined homelands in Africa, India, and Europe for the majority of people settled there. Migration away from the Caribbean was represented as fluid, temporary, or an extension of an earlier migration. Increasingly, however, the Caribbean is being represented as more than a stopping place in generations of dislocation, as not just home but homeland.

This perspective is neither new nor all-encompassing, but it has shifted enough to warrant the search for new language that Chariandy attempts to capture. In the mid- to late twentieth century, work by writers such as Paule Marshall and Audre Lorde raised questions about what counts as "Caribbean literature." At the close of the century, Stewart Brown, in his introductions to *The Oxford Book of Caribbean Verse* and *The Oxford Book of Caribbean Short Stories*, glosses this choice by including "work by any writer with Caribbean connections whose work somehow 'spoke to' Caribbean experience."[5] But for many writers and literary critics, the question is not as easily answered. Yes, exile was a prominent and persistent issue in twentieth-century Caribbean literary production. V. S. Naipaul, Samuel Selvon, Derek Walcott, Jean Rhys—all became problematic as they continued writing and publishing from abroad. But someone born and raised elsewhere? That generation of writers had not yet blossomed, so figures like Marshall and Lorde could be treated on a case-by-case (even text-by-text) basis.

That approach, however, has become insufficient as the ranks of "second-generation" Caribbean writers grow. Raphael Dalleo argues that *White Teeth* has a "distinctly Caribbean sensibility," and his wording captures what I see as one of the major breaks occurring between these twenty-first century novels and the ones I examine earlier.[6] No one has to make an argument for the previous texts' "Caribbeanness." Yes, we may have lost writers to classification despite their birthplace (namely, Naipaul and Rhys) but not their entire oeuvre (again, Naipaul and Rhys present interesting examples here, but even they now occupy secure places in the Caribbean literary canon). However, this new generation of writers, many of them children of various migratory movements, occupy more unsure, inbetween spaces. Like the ill-defined transitory space between colony and nation that preoccupies earlier writers, these spaces lend themselves to variant psychological misfires.

Indeed, the difference in that discourse, place versus space, emphasizes the shift I argue is occurring in the Caribbean literary landscape: on a larger scale, the Caribbean aesthetic is shifting from a regional sensibility to a diasporic one. This is not to say that writers do not exist in the Caribbean itself, or that the generations of writers who are already well known as Caribbean writers were not often speaking from "elsewhere." But there seems to me to be a definite shift in the relationship to the signifier *Caribbean* when it comes to literary production. Perhaps this shift is in content, as writers move significantly beyond the moment of departure or the "enigma of arrival" and no longer consider themselves strangers in a strange land. Or perhaps this shift is in audience, as the writers now imagine their audience in less of a "there" space and more of a "here, there, and everywhere" space. And, of course, there is the ease of transportation back and forth to consider, and the technology that creates an expanded Caribbean space or what some have called a "global Caribbean," though this "globality" has been fairly restricted to the United States, Canada, and England. Whatever the reason, there has been a distinct shift in the Caribbean literary landscape, one that is not necessarily confined to the work of the latest generation of "Caribbean" writers, many of whom were born—or migrated at an early age—away from the region, but is perhaps most easily addressed through their work.

Chariandy, John, and Smith are shaped by the demands of the diaspora they have matured in. This simultaneously groups and divides them. They are of a particular generation, inheritors and negotiators of the preoccupations of the previous generations of Caribbean writers, and are therefore facing similar concerns about Caribbean representation. But they each must also negotiate the twenty-first-century particulars of the metropolis to which they or their parents have migrated. In reading *Soucouyant*, *Unburnable*, and *White Teeth*, I make the connection between madness and this changing Caribbean literary landscape by exploring how—as with the mid-twentieth-century texts I study in the bulk of *Disturbers of the Peace*—madness provides these younger writers with a method of mapping this shifting space.

Soucouyant

As its title indicates, the myth of the *soucouyant* structures David Chariandy's first novel, pulling together its exploration of memory, migration, and belonging. Immigrants, particularly those who live in their host country as visible minorities, continuously balance between retaining and releasing memories of home. Mental imbalance, then, upsets this tightrope of personal and cultural survival. In an interview about *Soucouyant*, Chariandy indicates that one of his primary characters' struggle with dementia allowed him as author to "explore the fragility and endurance of cultural memory."[7] In the novel, the protagonist's mother, Adele, suffers from increasingly severe presenile dementia. An Afro-Trinidadian who migrated to Canada in early adulthood, Adele should be her son's primary entryway to memories of that "other place" that has shaped his life; but Adele's dementia makes her an unreliable source of information about both Trinidad and her life in Canada—inescapable parts of the protagonist's own story. For both herself and her son, Adele's descent into madness results not only in the loss of connection to memory but also in the loss of protection from some of those memories as she progressively forgets to forget some of the trauma of her earlier life. The protagonist must deal with previously uncharted territories of his mother's past while coping with his own increasingly fragmented present (reflected in the novel's nonlinear form). Dementia becomes necessary and formative in not only the telling of a Caribbean immigrant's story but also the extension of that story in the second generation's understanding of place, history, and belonging.

In another interview, Chariandy describes dementia as "this particularly devastating process of unbecoming."[8] *Unbecoming*, as Chariandy uses it here, is a rather fascinating choice of words, particularly because of its traditional definition (as adjective) of "ill-fittingness." Adele is becoming "un"—unbalanced, uncooperative, *undone*. But her very undoing, the slow deterioration and disconnection of dementia, is the becoming of (and is becoming to) the form of her son's story. As with some of the texts I examine in earlier chapters, *Soucouyant* relies on mental illness to structure its narrative. Readers unevenly zigzag between present and past, hearing various characters tell their stories. Everything is filtered through the narrator's story, but we also hear the voices of his mother, of Roger (his father), and of Meera, the young woman he finds taking care of his mother. Perhaps the only main character whose voice we have no access to, who never tells any of his own story, is the narrator's older brother, who deserts the family soon after the father's death to escape the weight of responsibility for his deteriorating mother. The brother, also unnamed, is a would-be poet, yet he is mostly silenced throughout the novel by others speaking for or about him. His voice is present only in the chapter headings, which we later learn come from his notebook that he kept hidden under lock and key. The headings are his attempt at writing the word *soucouyant*, as he too tries to access that foreign past.

Throughout the novel, the narrator is fascinated by the word *soucouyant*, which he has learned from his mother's stories but has to conduct research to define. He finds the definition in a glossary of a tourist-focused Oceanways Cruiseship Company publication on Trinidad, adding irony to an already complex relationship between himself and his heritage. He thinks, "My history is a travel guidebook. My history is a creature nobody really believes in. My history is a foreign word."[9] The word *soucouyant* is foreign to him as a Canadian-born child of Trinidadian immigrants, but also foreign to the now national language of Trinidad—English, marking the island's history as contested colonial space. Although the soucouyant figure is also known in other Caribbean islands (as we will see in the ending of John's *Unburnable*), in Chariandy's novel the legend marks Trinidad as consolidated "elsewhere," forever out of reach for his narrator, whose mother asks him, "What would a nine-year old boy who grow up in Canada know about soucouyants?" (135). *Soucouyant* is a decidedly foreign word in the Canadian landscape, ineluctably connected to elsewhere.[10] Thus, along with the legend it represents, the very word *soucouyant* signifies a split formation of national consciousness: marking the *here* Canadian and the *there* Trinidadian.[11]

Informing himself and his audience while pulling threads of his narrative together, the narrator offers the following definition of a soucouyant: "A soucouyant is something like a female vampire. She lives a reclusive but fairly ordinary life on the edge of town. She disguises herself by dressing up in the skin of an old woman, but at night she'll shed her disguise and travel across the sky as a ball of fire. She'll hunt out a victim and suck his blood as he sleeps. Leaving him with little sign of her work except increasing fatigue, a certain paleness, and perhaps, if he were to look closely on his body, a tell-tale bruise or mark on his skin" (135). The soucouyant myth is, like the mother's madness, a major plot device in the novel. But, given the focus of this epilogue, I would like to put the full particulars of the myth aside for the moment and concentrate on its role in the tangled connections between two major strands in the text: madness and migration. The soucouyant is generally an old woman, marginal to her society. One of the accounts of the origins of the myth is that it grew out of small villages' need to explain strange occurrences, like infant death or general malaise for which the cause was not readily apparent. Old women who were no longer useful to society were blamed, via the soucouyant myth, for the misfortune experienced by the villagers. In a similar manner, immigrants easily become targets when a misfortune befalls a society; even before disaster strikes, there is a fear of these foreigners. "Natives," in this case white Canadians (but interchangeable in other instances with white Americans, or white Britons), whisper to themselves and to each other, as Zadie Smith writes in *White Teeth*, "They should all go back to their own . . ."[12]

In *Soucouyant*, the sentiment appears more boldly, though through the cowardly anonymous writing on the wall, when early in their marriage Adele and Roger return to their first rented apartment after a short vacation to find their apartment ransacked and the words "GO BACK" written in feces across the wall. In an effort to be rid of intruders, as villagers wished to rid themselves of suspected soucouyants, faceless "natives" have attacked Roger and Adele's home, making it as inhabitable as the soucouyant's salted skin. Madness shields Adele from the harsh effects of this attack. She has already begun to show signs of mental deterioration and is perhaps only just beginning to recognize it herself in this moment. She sees the letters G-O-B-A-C-K and is confused, unable to put them back together correctly: "GOB ACK? A clue? She wonders. A name? Some riddle toward an identity?" (77). Adele's confusion is too poignant to be comic, but it does have the benefit of protecting her from the brunt of this violation of the couple's domestic space and their very right to occupy space in Canada.

As they contemplate the damage to their apartment, Adele's failing mind becomes fused with the sense of loss. Indeed, it becomes the method by which the text forces readers to contemplate the mental and cultural alienation involved in immigration as mental and material loss intertwine. Adele becomes increasingly confused when the landlord questions them about what the vandals may have stolen. Although her husband insists that valuable things are missing—"Our china cups, your aunt's pearl earrings, the deya my father give me . . ."—Adele cannot remember. Her son wonders if this is a turning point in her life, the moment she recognizes that her mind is beginning to fail her. He wonders if she recognizes that "something more serious than cutlery or bangles had gone missing? That so many other things were getting lost" (78). These preliminary stages of Adele's dementia combine with the surrounding text to use the loss of individual memory as metaphor for the loss of cultural memory. Although Roger begins by listing the items that have monetary value, he trails off when he realizes that the deya his father gave him is missing. A little clay pot used in the Hindu festival of light—Divali—the deya is not worth much to the robbers. But it is one more piece of Roger's heritage lost in this new country, in the double migration that finds this South Asian born in Trinidad and later resident in Canada.

As the narrator learns more about his parents' past, he draws more links between his mother's madness, her migration to Canada, and the myth of the soucouyant. In particular, his description of how to recognize a soucouyant despite her human disguise provides a context for weaving together these three thematic strands. To discover a soucouyant, you could try

> batting the soucouyant with a stick as she takes the form of a flaming ball. In the morning, you'll only have to look for an old woman in the village who appears to have been beaten. Bruises upon her. Clearly the one to blame.
>
> Or, you might try finding out where a soucouyant conceals her disguise of skin when out on her raids as a flaming ball. Cover her skin with plenty of salt and . . .
>
> Old Skin, 'kin, 'kin,
> You na know me,
> You na know me.
>
> . . . is what she'll chant as she tries to pull on her disguise. The burning of salt under her skin. A guise now strange and painful. The suffering of a monster that deserves no pity at all. (135–36; ellipses in original)

The marking of the soucouyant as "clearly the one to blame" and "a monster that deserves no pity" has clear connections to the outcast Adele as outsider because of her dementia and her marked status as immigrant. One of the functions that mad figures serve in their communities is that of scapegoat, and, as I mentioned earlier, the visible immigrant also serves this scapegoat function. What I am more interested in here, however, is how the other characters and the community imagine themselves through the existence of this figure—mad, mythical, migrant. Adele, who in the novel occupies an intersection of these three spaces, is necessary to the Port Junction community's understanding itself as sane, grounded, *Canadian.*

Near the end of the novel, Meera reveals that Adele has served this function for her as well when she confesses why she has returned to care for her. Years earlier at a high school party, at the moment when she felt herself most separated from the other students and was most at risk of being cast out, Meera prank-called Adele in order to entertain the group. With this act, Meera in some ways rejoined the group because Adele was someone "everyone could openly laugh about" (165). Meera escaped her own marking as other by substituting Adele, who was othered beyond reclamation. Adele's madness situates her as a marginal but hypervisible migrant subject, allowing the community to reassure themselves of their own normality and acceptability. Like the soucouyant returning to a poisoned skin, in Canada Adele must contend with a "guise now strange and painful" as part of the necessary adaptation to a new country. The skin does not fit and at times becomes painful as others metaphorically "throw salt" to incapacitate the immigrant. In several of the Caribbean narratives from the mid- to late-twentieth century, madness is represented as a side effect of trying to make such disguises fit: we can think here most readily and usefully of Frantz Fanon's *Black Skin, White Masks.* But in more recent novels, certainly in the three novels I examine in this epilogue, the emphasis is on madness not as a result of but as a coping mechanism for characters in new spaces.

For the protagonist and for Meera, both second-generation Trinidadian immigrants, there is already a disconnect between themselves, their country, and their heritage elsewhere. Dementia emphasizes this disconnect, further interrupting and complicating the transfer of culture. The two become mixed in the protagonist's mind, as is evident in his attempts to explain his mother's condition to a policeman. He begins with the official diagnosis, "Dementia," but then, finding that inadequate, adds, "It means that she's forgetting . . . or that she's confused, or even . . . even that she's remembering . . ." Although the policeman assures him that he knows what dementia is, the protagonist continues to explain:

> "She . . . she saw a soucouyant."
>
> "A what?"

> "Not literally," I explain. "At least I don't think so. I mean, it's not really about a soucouyant. It's about an accident. It's about what happened in her birthplace during World War II. It's a way of telling without really telling, you see, and so you don't really have to know what a soucouyant is. Well I guess you do, sort of. What I mean is, I'm not an expert on any of that sort of stuff. I was born here, you see, Not exactly here, of course. In a hospital farther west. But here, as in this land." (66; ellipses in original)

His need to explain betrays an anxiety about place and belonging, a recognition of the way, in Canada, his visible difference is "a way of telling without really telling" that he does not have a valid claim on citizenship, despite being born "in this land." And his remaining link to any valid claim on Trinidad is mentally deteriorating before his eyes. Adele's madness leaves him alone to negotiate the space between country and culture with only untold stories, unvoiced hostilities, and unfinished sentences as guides.

Unburnable

Marie-Elena John's *Unburnable* also abounds in these open-ended stories, in a mix of studied "not-telling" and willed forgetting across half a century and three generations. Chariandy's narrator could be speaking directly to the trauma experienced by several characters, particularly *Unburnable*'s female protagonist, Lillian Baptiste, when he explains the advantages and disadvantages of his mother's madness:

> During our lives, we struggle to forget. And it's foolish to assume that forgetting is altogether a bad thing. Memory is a bruise still tender. History is a rusted pile of blades and manacles. And forgetting can sometimes be the most creative and life-sustaining thing that we can ever hope to accomplish. The problem happens when we become too good at forgetting. When somehow we *forget* to forget, and we blunder into circumstances that we consciously should have avoided. This is how we awaken to the stories buried deep within our sleeping selves or trafficked quietly through the touch of others. This is how we're shaken by vague scents or tastes. How we're stolen by an obscure word, an undertow dragging us back and down and away. (32)

Lillian Baptiste spends her adult life fighting this same undertow. She is constantly on guard against memories, inventing strategies for drowning them out when she senses their approach. *Unburnable* begins with her decision to address these memories head on, to question the interpretations of memory and madness that she has been handed. Readers follow Lillian as she returns to her homeland, Dominica, from Washington, D.C. Her grandmother Matilda is a legendary figure in Dominica, variously described as obeah woman, Maroon, or madwoman. She was convicted as a murderer fifty years before the opening of the novel. Lillian's trip to Dominica is ostensibly to clear her grandmother's name, and she convinces her friend Teddy, a black historian and public intellectual in the United States, to accompany and assist her in her quest. The two encounter linguistic as well as cultural barriers to both knowledge and understanding. Teddy is constantly required to release what he believes he knows about the African diaspora in order to grasp the specifics of both past and present life in Dominica. Lillian also experiences difficulty in removing her acquired American perspective as she struggles to dispel the layers of misconceptions and misdirected knowledge that have surrounded her since childhood. She must shed years of psychological protection that she has built up since leaving Dominica, protection that closely resembles Nellie's kumbla in Erna Brodber's *Jane and Louisa Will Soon Come Home*. Lillian too is "brown, intellectual, better and apart," also the result of "two generations of lightening blue-blacks" via racial mixing and "brightening" African minds via colonial religious education.[13] But for Lillian, who has spent her teenage and adult years in the United States, the Caribbean is no longer home, and Dominica proves dangerous to her hard-won sanity and her protective kumbla.

From the white American missionaries who make a home in Dominica to the modern-day Afro-Dominicans, various characters offer the two visitors their readings of the legendary Matilda, her daughter Iris, and Lillian herself. The myriad misconceptions that Lillian and Teddy encounter and generate, particularly in connection with other black characters, engage both the reader and the characters in a reexamination of their own understandings of African "diaspora literacy." Vèvè Clark develops and defines *diaspora literacy* as "the ability to read and comprehend the discourses of Africa, Afro-America and the Caribbean from an informed, indigenous perspective."[14] Although Clark thinks primarily of the readers of texts when framing and utilizing the term, I use *diaspora literacy* more broadly here to encompass the characters themselves "reading" the situations in which they find themselves. For instance, Teddy tries to approach what he learns about Matilda through what he has been taught about "genuine" African practices; but by the end of the novel, he is forced into the realization that, in his haste to claim a connection, he missed the particular influences any Dominican adaptations had on such practices. *Unburnable* reveals most clearly that "diaspora literacy" rests on a complex matrix of race, geography, and memory, both collective and personal.

This matrix manifests itself most clearly in the charges of madness and criminality levied against the three women. As in *Wide Sargasso Sea*, a decree of madness says more about those employing the term than about those it attempts to categorize. *Unburnable* does not directly call on Jean Rhys's novel, but it is undeniably a successor—not simply because of the Dominican setting but more because of the complex negotiation of definitions of madness, cultural misrecognition, and questions of inherited madness. *Unburnable* opens with a subtle genealogy of the uncommon and infamous women of Lillian's line. First her grandmother, then her mother, then Lillian herself are diagnosed casually, communally, or clinically as mad. When Teddy doubts Lillian's memory of her mother's efforts to pass on a message to her, her defense of Iris could very well be Antoinette's defense of her own mother in Rhys's *Wide Sargasso Sea*. Lillian explains, "My mother wasn't crazy. She was destroyed."[15] But like Rochester before him, Teddy cannot hear past his own cultural preconceptions. He instead continues with his nightly consultation about Lillian with a psychiatrist/friend in Washington, D.C., and makes arrangements to enter her into "treatment" upon their return, even as she begins to release what she has been taught about her past and to dig into her own previously blocked memories.

Teddy is not alone in his fear for Lillian's sanity. She has a difficult time convincing other people, including Dominicans, that she is sane because her own actions are read in the light of (or more accurately, in the shadow of) her mother's and grandmother's actions. She cannot turn to her godmother and adopted mother because they "would be even more convinced that she, like her mother, was once again losing her mind—because, they believed, it was inherited madness that had sent her to dig up Iris's grave that night, and madness that made her cut her wrist open. Madness, and Matilda's hand from hell, intervening in her conception" (254–55). And while those around her might read attempted suicide as a sign of mental illness, Lillian sees it as a "logical" route to obtaining "answers to her life from two dead women" (290).

In the end, Lillian returns to suicide as the route to the answers she seeks, but as with Antoinette in the ending of *Wide Sargasso Sea* forty years prior, the narrative ends before Lillian completes the act, leaving yet another story unfinished.[16] In both novels, the women envision a jump that connects them to their past. These visions give them a sense of purpose in an otherwise confused and confusing life. For Lillian, the jump will erase the time away in a foreign land, in "atonement . . . for her inherited sins." Her sacrifice will come to an end when she jumps to join her grandmother's people, an act she thinks of as an indulgence for both herself and Dominicans who will celebrate her death in song: "Let them sing another song about another woman whose life had not fulfilled its promise. Let them sing on her—she wanted her own song, it was her birthright. A *chanté mas* to guarantee her place in history, alongside her grandmother and her mother" (291). She makes a conscious choice to become legend, a legend that will connect her, securely, to the people and future of Dominica through myth. But she wishes to shape this legend in choosing her death. In the midst of what may be deemed an illogical—insane, even—act, Lillian lucidly analyzes various methods of suicide and the resulting legends. Rejecting drowning and wasting away in the mountains in "Creole finery" (deaths corresponding, respectively, to the Mama Glo and La Diablesse myths), Lillian ultimately decides to jump from the cliff where her grandmother lived:[17]

> But Lillian had decided that it would be best to be the worst of the lot, a *soucouyant*: a woman who takes off her skin at night and flies around in search of victims whose blood she sucks. Yes, she would give them that pleasure, and it made sense for her to go back to where the Maroons had jumped; she would fly through the air for her country people—and at the bottom there were enough trees and branches to tear off her skin, so that when they found her she would be exactly what they wanted her to be: their nightmare come true, a *soucouyant*. (292)

While Lillian's choice reflects an intimate knowledge of the folklore of Dominica, the novel itself does not take the diaspora literacy of its audience for granted, explaining each legend as she considers it. Indeed, throughout the novel, the omniscient narrator offers readers explanations of American, African, and Caribbean practices, playing on the characters' ignorance of connections and disconnections, while expecting, as does Chariandy's novel, that much of the Caribbean history and culture may be foreign to readers. Both Chariandy and John are also careful to explain the cultural dimensions of their characters' madness. Though there are what one might call objective indicators that Adele and Lillian suffer from "certifiable" mental diseases, their stories indicate that, in part, their psyches are suffering from the deleterious effects of cultural displacement.

White Teeth

Suicide is often treated as the inclination of the insane or clinically disturbed; but both *Unburnable* and *Wide Sargasso Sea* present the choice, if not the act itself, as a rational ending for their heroines and for the novels themselves. Although adopting a similar perspective of suicide as a sane and logical choice, Zadie Smith's *White Teeth* begins with a decision to commit suicide and follows on what may happen when said decision is thwarted. The novel opens on Archie Jones attempting to follow through on his New Year's resolution of killing himself. In Archie's estimation, he has failed at life and will therefore try his hand at death. (True to his character, however, he makes this decision only after flipping a coin on the subject.) Fate, a character itself in the novel, intervenes and spares Archie, who immediately reverses his idea of suicide as rational, grateful for his second chance.

From then forward, madness seems to permeate *White Teeth*. It begins early on with Archie's main reason for attempting suicide: the desertion and deterioration of his first wife, tellingly named Ophelia, who fails to tell Archie that "lurking in the Diagilo family tree were two hysteric aunts, an uncle who talked to eggplants, and a cousin who wore his clothes back to front" (7). And several hundred pages later the novel ends with a highly contrived scene in which all the main characters' obsessions, compulsions, and neuroses collide spectacularly. In between there are other little insanities that contribute to the narrative: Hortense Bowden's unshakable belief in the impending "End of the World" and Samad Iqbal's obsession with clearing his great-grandfather's name, for example. But there is little sustained treatment of madness. As such, the inclusion of *White Teeth* in a book on representations of madness may, at first glance, seem questionable—after all, there is no extended exploration of *real* madness here, nothing like the delineation of mental alienation that can be found in the other diasporic texts I examine in this epilogue or the earlier texts in previous chapters. But the overwhelming rhetoric of madness—both in the dialogue and in the narrative—and the scattered mad minor characters offer a possible and probable lens through which to read the entire novel and its major themes, particularly the theme of postcolonial migration.

For example, the obsessions cited above (Hortense's religiosity and Samad's obsession with his ancestry) can support, in their repetition throughout the narrative, the novel's preoccupation with the immigrant's fear of "dissolution, *disappearance*" (272; emphasis in original).

Hortense, a lifelong Jehovah's Witness, becomes increasingly incomprehensible in her faith, while Samad doggedly pursues his version of history in the face of disbelieving and bored reactions from his friends and family. Although in some ways opposite types of madness—the first, socializing (with other members of the religion), and the second, ostracizing—both obsessions allow for these immigrants to navigate their way through the maze of cultural and social alienation that threatens them in London. Hortense is empowered by her religion—"This was not a solitary psychosis of the Bowdens. There were eight million Jehovah's Witnesses waiting with her" (27)—and Samad is bolstered by his belief in a glorious ancestor. Both are defensive strategies against invisibility and insignificance. Though other characters and even the narrative itself label these actions with words connected to madness—*psychosis*, *insane*, *crazy*—the novel shows plainly that such madness is a rational response to the world in which these immigrants live.

The novel's insistent narrator also provides some powerful meditations on the wisdom of madness as a response to this world. The most developed passages on madness can be found in the chapter "Molars," where readers also encounter two extended episodes involving characters marked definitively (as opposed to rhetorically) as mad. That the title phrase "white teeth" also occurs most prominently in this chapter is perhaps reason enough to mark it as important in understanding the text;[18] but more significant for my project here is the chapter's reliance on representations of madness to pull together the novel's thematic threads on immigration, hybridity, and the human residues of British colonialism. In what may be a coincidence, in the way of noncoincidental coincidences that drive the plot of the novel, *molar* is also the term for a paradigm in psychology. The molar method approaches behavior as a result of personal history, which must be explored to treat the patient (as opposed to the molecular paradigm, which seeks to address only the individual instance of aberrant behavior). With this in mind, then, the idea of *roots* (via teeth and psychology) becomes even more evident in the chapter title.

The chapter zooms in for a close look at a few hours in Samad Iqbal's and his sons' lives as they separately navigate London, Samad with Poppy (his soon-to-be mistress) and the boys—twins Magid and Millat—with Irie. The three children are the "first descendants of the great ocean-crossing experiment," but they have inherited an immigrant sensibility from their parents (182), much like Chariandy's unnamed narrator, who determines that at some "crucial and early point" in his life, something "seeped into" him: "(Is that how to explain it?) Some mood or manner was transmitted, though my parents tried their utmost to prevent this from happening" (101). So too do these three children exist, split between their claim on their birthplace—London—and the pull of roots buried elsewhere. At nine, however, the children have only vague notions of the geographies of those elsewhere cities (Bangladesh, Kingston), but they believe they *know* London:

> Now, the children knew the city. And they knew the city breeds the Mad. They knew Mr. White-Face, an Indian who walks the streets of Willesden with his face painted white, his lips painted blue, wearing a pair of tights and some hiking boots; they knew Mr. Newspaper, a tall skinny man in an ankle-length raincoat who sits in Brent libraries removing the day's newspapers from his briefcase and methodically tearing them into strips; they knew Mad Mary, a black voodoo woman with a red face whose territory stretches from Kilburn to Oxford Street but who performs her spells from a garbage can in West Hampstead. (145–46)

Here London, center of an ebbing empire, breeds a certain kind of madness. The implications of Mr. White-Face's madness are perhaps too obvious to bear comment, but quite suggestive when placed alongside Mr. Newspaper, who might have appeared in any novel as simply a symptom of modern living. In *this* novel, however, sandwiched between the white-faced Indian and the territorial Afro-Caribbean voodoo woman, the raceless Mr. Newspaper's rejection of packaged knowledge takes on new dimensions: postcolonial dimensions.[19]

The children are relatively comfortable with individuals like these three who are deemed Mad by the raced and gendered cultural norms of London. (Indeed, the capitalization imposes *Mad* upon these characters as a titled category rather than mere description.) But the children's belief in their knowledge of the city is shaken by their discovery that there is a more dangerous kind of madness, a quiet, sinister kind that does not roam the streets or public transportation: Mr. J. P. Hamilton, for instance, who is "half mad and half not" and who reminds the children of their "visitor" status in the country of their birth. For him, and for many white Britons, the children's brown bodies signify that they are not *of* England, only perhaps of her empire. A little background: the children—Irie, the product of a black Jamaican mother and white British father, and Millat and Magid, born to South Asian immigrants from Bangladesh—have a class project to offer charity to an assigned elder during the Harvest Festival (an activity in which their parents have actually forbidden them to participate). The children sneak a few goods from their parents' pantries and secretly visit their "assigned old man," Mr. J. P. Hamilton. At first, Mr. Hamilton tries to shoo the children from his doorstep, closing the door on their gifts while telling them, "I have no money whatsoever; so be your intention robbing or selling, I'm afraid you will be disappointed" (141). Like much that occurs in this scene, Mr. Hamilton's immediate dismissal of the children is based on the combination of visual cues and virulent stereotypes. This misrecognition is previewed during the children's bus ride to visit Hamilton, when an elderly passenger utters what the narrator calls "the oldest sentence in the world": "They should all go back to their own . . ." (137). The sentence is cut off by the noise of the bus stopping and passengers exiting and embarking, but the reader is left with the thought that the children *are* in "their own . . . ": their own city, country, birthplace. They belong there just as much as they belong on Mr. J. P. Hamilton's doorstep.

When they convince the old man of their school-sanctioned mission, he invites them in, offering tea even as he declines their gifts, which are too hard for him to chew. This brings the conversation around to teeth, and the potential significance of the moment is underscored in Smith's choice of *White Teeth* as the title of the novel. Mr. J. P. Hamilton advises the children that they should take care of their teeth, lest they end up without any, like himself. Then he cautions,

> The business has two sides. Clean white teeth are not always wise, now are they? Par exemplum: when I was in the Congo, the only way I could identify the nigger was by the whiteness of his teeth. . . . See a flash of white and bang! . . . All these beautiful boys lying dead there, right in front of me, right at my feet. . . . Beautiful men, enlisted by the Krauts, black as the ace of spades; poor fools didn't even know why they were there, what people they were fighting for, who they were shooting at. The decision of the gun. So quick, children. So brutal. Biscuit? (144)

Mr. Hamilton, therefore, has a deep-rooted history of visual (mis)recognition that he applies to the children now ensconced in his living room. Irie begins to cry silently, whispering that she wishes to go home, but the twins push forward, telling Mr. Hamilton that their father and Irie's fought for England in the war. Mr. Hamilton immediately denies their claim, although they are most likely discussing two different world wars, and informs the children that they must be mistaken: "There were certainly no wogs as I remember—though you're probably not allowed to say that these days –[and] no Pakistanis . . . What would we have fed them?" He is, therefore, somewhat aware of ideas of emerging revisions to socially acceptable language in a changing London but has chosen to reside in his own "Wonderland," kept safe behind a stained-glass door. He assures the children that "the Pakistanis would have been in the Pakistani army, whatever that was" (144). The twins continue to insist that their father really was in the English army, that he has an injury and medals to prove it. But Mr. Hamilton tells them they should not tell fibs because "fibs will rot your teeth." While Mr. Hamilton veers off into a rumination about how to save teeth, the children run away, "tripping over themselves, running to get to a green space, to get to one of the lungs of the city, some place where free breathing was possible" (145).

It is here that the narrative itself runs directly into a consideration of madness and its connection to this city of immigrants. First, the children realize that they prefer the city's public madness. They prefer the kind of Mad who "*announced* their madness—they were better, less scary than Mr. J. P. Hamilton—they flaunted their insanity, they weren't half mad and half not, curled around a door frame. They were properly mad in the Shakespearean sense, talking sense when you least expected it" (146). Overt madness can return those like Mad Mary to an acceptable place in the social order. As displaced persons now residing in the center of the empire that shaped them, people like the voodoo priestess and the white-faced Indian are "properly mad" in the most English of ways, as the most English of writers (Shakespeare) would have them. They have a place *because* they are displaced. And they become the best representation of the cultural, social, and psychological alienation that their less flamboyant migrant brethren feel in the metropole.

Samad meditates on this link between madness and migration when he experiences a feeling of kinship during his confrontation with Mad Mary, just as his sons and Irie are escaping the sinister Mr. J. P. Hamilton:

> Mad Mary was looking at him with *recognition*. Mad Mary had spotted a *fellow traveler*. She had spotted the madman in him (which is to say the *prophet*); he felt sure she had spotted the angry man, the masturbating man, the man stranded in the desert far from his sons, the foreign man in a foreign land caught between borders . . . the man who, if you push him far enough, will suddenly see sense. Why else had she picked him from a street full of people? Simply because she recognized him. Simply because they were from the same place, he and Mad Mary, which is to say: *far away*. (148–49; emphasis in original)

For Samad, the kinship between Mad Mary and himself is built on the twinned identities of mad and migrant. In this scene, the two are inextricable, and, as Samad assures Mad Mary in an attempt to calm her, it bonds not only them but also other postcolonial anglophone subjects now living in London. "Believe me," he tells her, "I understand your concerns. . . . I am having difficulties myself—we are all having difficulties in this country, this country which is new to us and old to us all at the same time. We are divided people, aren't we?" (149). This connection via division, this infinitely reproducible *cleavage*, between Samad and Mad Mary is repeated in the general intertwined form of the narrative. It is aptly described by Samad's wife, Alsana (whose own history is curiously missing in this novel of intersecting individual lives), when later in the novel she considers the intervention of the Chalfen family in her sons' lives: "It is just a consequence of living, a consequence of occupation and immigration, of empires and expansion, of living in each other's pockets. . . . One becomes involved and it is a long trek back to being uninvolved" (363). Involvement, then, serves as a driving force in shaping the narrative of *White Teeth*: not only the current-day involvement of the Iqbals, Chalfens, and Joneses, of the Samads and Mad Marys, of the brown children and the J. P. Hamiltons, but also the historical involvement of their ancestors, the colonizing enterprise that brings them all to this metropole so that their lives rub so intimately and maddeningly against each other, giving the impression of reducing divisions even as it emphasizes them.

On the way to Mr. J. P. Hamilton's house, the children exhibit some of the hybrid results of this intimate involvement as they play the game of "taxing," in which "one lays claim, like a newly arrived colonizer, to items in a street that do not belong to you" (140). As the game continues, Millat ups the ante: "'*Cha*, man! Believe, I don't *want* to tax dat crap,'" he says, "with the Jamaican accent that all kids, whatever their nationality, used to express scorn." After Millat "taxes" two fancy cars, Irie manages to hold her own by claiming a pair of sneakers: "Magid and Millat stopped and looked in awe at the perfectly white Nikes that were now in Irie's possession (with one red tick, one blue; so beautiful, as Millat later remarked, it made you want to kill yourself), though to the naked eye they appeared to be walking toward Queens Park attached to a tall natty-dread black kid" (140). The colors of the Union Jack, propelled by the feet of a "natty-dread black kid," seized colonial-style by a part-Jamaican girl to impress her Bangladeshi friends: the excess of hybridity in this moment is simply an example of the entire novel.[20]

Inherent in this hybridity are multiple levels of both the indoctrination of (former) British subjects into the ideology of colonization and then the enactment of reverse colonization by said subjects. Themselves the residual evidence of the very real acts of appropriation enacted in different regions of the British Empire, the children can now repeat these acts in play, placing themselves in the role of colonizer.[21]

This type of reverse colonization returns in a more subtle form in the later scene between Mad Mary and Samad. Poppy's initial reaction to Mad Mary is that she is harmless, but Samad quickly corrects her: "First of all, she is not homeless. She has stolen every garbage can in West Hampstead and has built quite a significant structure out of them in Fortune Green. And secondly she is not a 'poor woman.' Everyone is terrified of her, from the council downward, she receives free food from every corner shop in North London ever since she cursed the Ramchandra place and business collapsed within the month" (147). Poppy, secure in her middle-class Englishness, would not—*could* not—perceive Mad Mary as anything other than insignificant. It takes an immigrant's perspective to see Mad Mary's abnormal existence as an example of one form of success in London. Mad Mary has a lineage in Caribbean literature: she hails from a tradition that includes characters such as Man-man, Moses, and Makak a strangely alliterative list of characters who have found some power in madness.[22] Within a particular paradigm, one similar to the one Samad employs during this interaction with Mad Mary, these characters are successful models of agency in a world constructed of European concepts that mark their immigrant/colonial/black bodies as inferior. This is perhaps why Caribbean writers continue to create and return to such characters in their work. As a result, madness continues as a notable part of the Caribbean literary aesthetic, appearing in twenty-first-century texts like *Soucouyant*, *Unburnable*, and *White Teeth* to represent the challenges of the Caribbean diaspora—challenges of recognition and reclamation, of revisioning and of re-membering, of making a whole out of the disparate fragments of a dislocated Caribbean.

Notes

Introduction

1. Although I cite a written version of the poem, Keens-Douglas also regularly performs his poetry. So while I refer here to the reader, one can also think of a listening audience.

2. Kenneth Ramchand, *The West Indian Novel and Its Background,* 2nd ed. (London: Heinemann, 1983), 4.

3. Mary Lou Emery, *Jean Rhys at "World's End": Novels of Colonial and Sexual Exile* (Austin: University of Texas Press, 1990), 8.

4. Rex Nettleford, "Introduction: The Fledgeling Years," in *Jamaica in Independence: Essays on the Early Years*, ed. Rex Nettleford (Kingston: Heinemann Caribbean, 1989), 15. Nettleford and the contributors to the anthology capitalize *independence*, and I follow when quoting, but I utilize lowercase in my own text because (1) I discuss independence across several countries and (2) capitalization makes independence into the very event Nettleford's anthology argues against.

5. Franklin W. Knight, *The Caribbean: The Genesis of a Fragmented Nationalism* (New York: Oxford University Press, 1990), 277.

6. As Franklin Knight describes the situation, "By the 1950s, the British West Indies had common regional participation in labor unions, trade and commerce, legal associations, a Civil Service Federation, cricket teams, the Imperial College of Tropical Agriculture (situated in Trinidad but serving the entire British Empire), the West Indian Meteorological Service, and the University College of the West Indies. All these associations, while they did foster some regional consciousness, were weaker than their local units and portrayed less of a coherent view of the West Indies than their names and functions suggested. More often than not, they were out of touch with the masses locally and regionally" (ibid.).

7. Sir John Mordecai, *Federation of the West Indies* (Evanston: Northwestern University Press, 1968), 12.

8. Norman Manley, quoted in Hugh W. Springer, *Reflections on the Failure*

of the First West Indian Federation (Cambridge, MA: Harvard University Center for International Affairs, 1962), 26.

9. Eric Williams, quoted in W. David McIntyre, *British Decolonization, 1946–1997: When, Why, and How Did the British Empire Fall?* (New York: St. Martin's Press, 1998), 54.

10. Barbados gained independence in 1966; Guyana, in 1966; Grenada, in 1974; Dominica, in 1978; St. Lucia, in 1979; St. Vincent, in 1979; Antigua, in 1981; and St. Kitts-Nevis, in 1983.

11. Ramchand, *West Indian Novel*, 4.

12. V. S. Naipaul, *The Mimic Men* (Harmondsworth: Penguin, 1969), 206.

13. Ibid.

14. Michael Thorpe, "'The Other Side': *Wide Sargasso Sea* and *Jane Eyre*," in *Critical Perspectives on Jean Rhys*, ed. Pierrette M. Frickey (Washington, DC: Three Continents, 1990), 180, originally published in *Ariel* 8, no. 3 (1977).

15. Michelle Cliff, *The Store of a Million Items* (Boston: Houghton Mifflin, 1998), 59.

16. Even limiting one's examination to the scientific community, with its investment in bounded definitions, ends in frustration and an inability to pinpoint the meaning of madness. The *Diagnostic and Statistic Manual of Mental Disorders*, the manual utilized by psychologists and psychiatrists (and increasingly by HMOs and private insurance companies) to identify mental illnesses, is now in its fifth edition since 1952. In between the editions, there are changes to definitions, symptoms, and inclusions. One of the most-cited changes is the dropping of homosexuality as a mental illness in 1973, a change that suggests the social nature of defining madness.

17. Erna Brodber, "Socio-Cultural Change in Jamaica," in Nettleford, *Jamaica in Independence*, 58.

18. Ibid., 59, 62, 64.

19. Jean Rhys, *Wide Sargasso Sea (A Norton Critical Edition)*, ed. Judith L. Raiskin (New York: W. W. Norton, 1999), 94.

20. Evelyn O'Callaghan, *Woman Version: Theoretical Approaches to West Indian Fiction by Women* (New York: St. Martin's Press, 1993), 45.

21. Derek Walcott, "What the Twilight Says," in *Dream on Monkey Mountain and Other Plays* (New York: Noonday Books, 1970), 25.

22. Jean-Paul Sartre, preface to *The Wretched of the Earth*, by Frantz Fanon, trans. Constance Farrington (New York: Grove Press, 1963), 17.

23. Bill Ashcroft, Gareth Griffiths, and Helen Tiffin, *The Empire Writes Back: Theory and Practice in Post-Colonial Literatures* (New York: Routledge, 1989), 6.

24. See, for example, V. S. Naipaul, *The Middle Passage: Impressions of Five Societies; British, French, and Dutch in the West Indies and South America* (New York: Vintage, 1981); and Walcott, "What the Twilight Says."

25. Édouard Glissant, *Le discours antillais* (Paris: Éditions du Seuil, 1981),

212, 359. These sections of *Le discours antillais* are not included in *Caribbean Discourse*, J. Michael Dash's 1989 translation. All translations here are my own, unless otherwise noted. I would like to thank Renée Larrier and Brent Hayes Edwards for their assistance with the French.

26. There are published autobiographies by Walcott, Naipaul, and Rhys.

27. Antonio Benítez-Rojo, *The Repeating Island: The Caribbean and the Postmodern Perspective* (Durham: Duke University Press, 1992), 271 (emphasis in original).

28. J. Michael Dash, *The Other America: Caribbean Literature in a New World Context* (Charlottesville: University Press of Virginia, 1998), x.

29. Ibid., 20.

30. Ramchand, *West Indian Novel*, 241.

31. Claude McKay, *Banana Bottom* (New York: Harcourt Brace Jovanich, 1933), 6. Subsequent page citations to this work are to this edition and are given parenthetically in the text.

32. Ramchand, *West Indian Novel*, 260, 262.

33. Hugh Dalziel Duncan, *Language and Literature in Society* (Chicago: University of Chicago Press, 1953), 24.

34. Michelle Cliff, *Claiming an Identity They Taught Me to Despise* (Watertown, MA: Persephone Press, 1980), 18–19.

35. Walcott, *Dream on Monkey Mountain*, 208.

36. Brodber, "Socio-Cultural Change," 60.

1. Manias and Messiahs

1. V. S. Naipaul, *The Middle Passage: Impressions of Five Societies; British, French, and Dutch in the West Indies and South America* (New York: Vintage, 1981), 19.

2. Ibid., 35.

3. These words are from the foreword to the Vintage edition. Although not marked, the later pagination points to the foreword being on page 5.

4. Derek Walcott, "The Garden Path: V. S. Naipaul," in *What the Twilight Says: Essays* (New York: Farrar, Straus, and Giroux, 1998), 127.

5. V. S. Naipaul, "Without a Place: V. S. Naipaul Interviewed by Ian Hamilton," in *Critical Perspectives on V. S. Naipaul*, ed. Robert Hamner (Washington, DC: Three Continents, 1977), 47, originally published in *Savacou* 9–10 (1974).

6. V. S. Naipaul, "Conrad's Darkness," in Hamner, *Critical Perspectives*, 59, originally published in *New York Review of Books*, October 1974.

7. Naipaul, *Middle Passage*, 42.

8. Naipaul provides this term in "The Pyrotechnicist," where he tells Morgan's story. In an aside, the narrator informs the reader: "One of the big words I learnt from Morgan is the title of this sketch." V. S. Naipaul, *Miguel Street* (New York: Vintage, 1987), 80. Subsequent page citations are to this edition and are given parenthetically in the text.

9. Walcott describes this appreciation as an "idealization of History and Order" ("Garden Path," 126).

10. V. S. Naipaul, *The Mimic Men* (Harmondsworth: Penguin, 1969), 104.

11. Ibid.

12. Karl Miller, "V. S. Naipaul and the New Order," in Hamner, *Critical Perspectives*, 113, originally published in *Kenyon Review*, November 1967.

13. Hayden M. Williams, "Reactions to Entrapment in 'Backward Places': V. S. Naipaul's *Miguel Street* and Ruth Jhabvala's *A Backward Place*," in *A Sense of Place in the New Literatures in English*, ed. Peggy Nightingale (St. Lucia, AU: University of Queensland Press, 1986), 69.

14. V. S. Naipaul, corrected TMs draft (1955) of *Miguel Street*, V. S. Naipaul Archive, University of Tulsa, Tulsa, OK.

15. R. H. Lee, "The Novels of V. S. Naipaul," in Hamner, *Critical Perspectives*, 71, originally published in *Theoria* 27 (October 1966). Lee names *The Suffrage of Elvira* as the other "least impressive" work. Lee here refers to *Miguel Street* as a novel, as many critics do, but because of the self-contained nature of each sketch I treat it as a collection of stories.

16. Naipaul, *Mimic Men*, 127.

17. Derek Walcott, "The Muse of History," in *What the Twilight Says*, 42.

18. Naipaul reflects on this chaotic appearance of his early work in an interview: "If you are trained by your reading and inclination to see the novel as one particular thing and if when you look at what you have, your material, and you are aware only of its shallowness and its disorder" ("Without a Place," 42).

19. Derek Walcott, *The Collected Poems, 1948–1984* (New York: Farrar, Straus, and Giroux, 1986), 364; Kamau Brathwaite, *Contradictory Omens: Cultural Diversity and Integration in the Caribbean* (Mona: Savacou, 1974), 64.

20. Naipaul, *Middle Passage*, 216. Naipaul is writing specifically of the Rastafarians in Jamaica here.

21. Édouard Glissant, *Le discours antillais* (Paris: Éditions du Seuil, 1981), 706, translated by J. Michael Dash as *Caribbean Discourse: Selected Essays* (Charlottesville: University Press of Virginia, 1989), 212. Glissant later drops the quotes surrounding *delirium*.

22. Naipaul, *Mimic Men*, 248. Ralph often uses "twenty" as a limit of excess. By the twentieth occurrence, we somehow have validated the commonness of a thing, but the twenty-first renews the sense of the extraordinary.

23. John Thieme, "Calypso Allusions in Naipaul's *Miguel Street*," *Kunapipi* 3, no. 2 (1981): 19.

24. Gordon Rohlehr, "Sparrow and the Language of Calypso," *Savacou* 2 (September 1970): 87.

25. Thieme also notes this split in connection with the text's use of calypso, but he focuses on the cultural, rather than linguistic, differences: "As an art form of the people calypso, then, represents an opposite pole to the metropolitan

culture and, on one level, *Miguel Street* explores this cultural divide" ("Calypso Allusions," 21).

26. Garth St. Omer, "The Writer as Naïve Colonial; V. S. Naipaul and Miguel Street," *Carib* 1 (1979): 13–14.

27. Naipaul, *Mimic Men*, 127, 141.

28. Thieme, "Calypso Allusions," 24, 28.

29. The only sketch without Hat's commentary is that of B. Wordsworth, which has an element of fantasy in the narration; by the end of the sketch, it seems to the narrator "as though B. Wordsworth had never existed" (65). Hat's power as a secondary narrator, then, is evident in both his commentary and the absence thereof.

30. Moses, in Sylvia Wynter's *The Hills of Hebron*, also stages a self-crucifixion, but he does not call for his followers to stone him (see chapter 2, this volume). Brief mentions of similarly aborted self-crucifixions (complete with stoning) can be found at the beginning of Earl Lovelace's *The Dragon Can't Dance* and near the end of Samuel Selvon's *The Lonely Londoners*. Doubtless there are more that I have overlooked or not yet encountered. There are claims, difficult to substantiate thus far, that the self-crucifixion story, such as the myth of Prophet Jordan that Wynter draws on for Moses, is based on a true event that occurred in either Trinidad or Guyana.

31. Naipaul, *Mimic Men*, 127.

32. My understanding of Glissant's theories on verbal delirium ("le délire verbal")] in general and "le délire de théâtralisation" specifically stems from Celia Britton's insightful analysis in *Edouard Glissant and Postcolonial Theory: Strategies of Language and Resistance* (Charlottesville: University Press of Virginia, 1999). I use her translations here.

33. Glissant, *Discours antillais*, translated in Britton, *Edouard Glissant*, 93.

34. Derek Walcott makes this participant-observer status of the audience members more explicit in *Dream on Monkey Mountain* (see chapter 4, this volume).

35. Glissant, *Discours antillais*, translated in Britton, *Edouard Glissant*, 93.

36. Naipaul, *Mimic Men*, 127.

37. The biblical parable of throwing the first stone is an interesting connection here because, utilizing outside forms of definition, the followers are just as mad as Man-man.

38. Naipaul, *Mimic Men*, 166, 190.

39. Ibid., 146.

40. William Belcher finds in this speech, and other parts of Man-man's character, a resemblance to Jonathan Swift. See William Belcher, "Jonathan Swift on Miguel Street," *World Literature Written in English* 24, no. 2 (1984): 348.

2. The Necessity for Madness

1. Sylvia Wynter, *The Hills of Hebron* (London: Jonathan Cape, 1962), 21. Subsequent page citations are to this edition and are given parenthetically

in the text. This chapter appeared originally as "The Necessity for Madness: Negotiating Nation in Sylvia Wynter's *The Hills of Hebron*," in *The Caribbean Woman Writer as Scholar: Creating, Imagining, Theorizing*, published by Caribbean Studies Press, © Caribbean Studies Press, 2009, and is reprinted with the permission of the publisher.

2. Sylvia Wynter, "The Re-enchantment of Humanism: An Interview with Sylvia Wynter," interview by David Scott, *Small Axe*, no. 8 (September 2000): 129.

3. Sylvia Wynter, "Beyond the Categories of the Master Conception: The Counterdoctrine of the Jamesian Poiesis," in *C. L. R. James's Caribbean*, ed. Paget Henry and Paul Buhle (Durham: Duke University Press, 1992), 64.

4. Although Wynter utilizes many biblical names, as far as I can determine there is no consistency in their application. For example, Moses's role in leading his followers into a form of exile does correspond with his name, but I cannot discern any connections between Obadiah and Isaac and their biblical counterparts.

5. Frederic Jameson, "Third-World Literature in the Era of Multinational Capitalism," *Social Text*, no. 15 (Fall 1986): 69; Aijaz Ahmad, "Jameson's Rhetoric of Otherness and the 'National Allegory,'" *Social Text*, no. 17 (Fall 1987): 4.

6. See Sylvia Wynter, "Sylvia Wynter," interview by Daryl Cumber Dance in his *New World Adams: Contemporary West Indian Writers* (Yorkshire: Peepal Tree, 1992).

7. Abigail Bakan, *Ideology and Class Conflict in Jamaica: The Politics of Rebellion* (Montreal: McGill-Queen's University Press, 1990), 95.

8. Barry Chevannes, *Rastafari: Roots and Ideology* (New York: Syracuse University Press, 1994), 109.

9. Wynter "Re-enchantment of Humanism," 131–32 (emphasis in original).

10. Bakan, *Ideology and Class Conflict*, 96.

11. Chevannes, *Rastafari*, 146.

12. Michelle Cliff, *Free Enterprise* (New York: Dutton), 52, 55.

13. Wynter, "Beyond the Categories," 85–86.

14. Ibid., 86.

15. V. S. Naipaul, *The Middle Passage: Impressions of Five Societies; British, French, and Dutch in the West Indies and South America* (New York: Vintage, 1981), 219.

16. Wynter, "Sylvia Winter," 280. As I note in chapter 1 (see note 30), which examines the failed attempt at self-crucifixion by Man-man in V. S. Naipaul's *Miguel Street*, Earl Lovelace and Samuel Selvon have also made references to this legend.

17. The 1984 edition of *The Hills of Hebron* uses a different spelling (Pukumina), which loses the connection between the religion and madness. The 2010 edition returns to the original spelling and, like the 1962 edition, does not capitalize the term.

18. In the novel, Wynter names Moses as a forerunner for Bellows and Bellows as a forerunner of men yet to come. In the Dance interview, Wynter elaborates on Bellows's character: "I was touching on what has become a central concern—the distinction between the Marxist approach to revolution and what I see as a Black approach—some of it is cultural nationalist, but it's not only cultural nationalist, popular perhaps, I think it's a different approach to a different kind of transformation. As you notice, this chap Bellows comes, and he speaks, but in the end it's Obadiah who somehow carries whatever it is through. It was a vague positing of the distinction, but there was something of Bustamante in it, of the Marxist-populist distinction, but not really sorted out" ("Sylvia Wynter," 280).

19. Wynter, "Beyond the Categories," 86.

20. In "Novel and History, Plot and Plantation," Wynter writes, "With the novel form, the rupture of the hero and the now inauthentic values of his world begins. The novel form is in essence a question mark." *Savacou* 5 (June 1971): 96.

21. Janice Lee Liddell, "The Narrow Enclosure of Motherdom/Martyrdom: A Study of Gatha Randall Barton in Sylvia Wynter's *The Hills of Hebron*," in *Out of the Kumbla: Caribbean Women and Literature*, ed. Carole Boyce Davies and Elaine Savory Fido (Trenton, NJ: Africa World, 1990), 327.

22. Wynter refers to Kate as Aunt Kate after Maverlyn's death, and, as much as is possible while maintaining clarity, throughout this chapter I preserve this distinction in my own writing about her character.

23. Sylvia Wynter, "Afterword: Beyond Miranda's Meanings: Un/Silencing the 'Demonic Ground' of Caliban's 'Woman,'" in Davies and Fido, *Out of the Kumbla*, 358.

24. Natasha Barnes, "Reluctant Matriarch: Sylvia Wynter and the Problematics of Caribbean Feminism," *Small Axe*, no. 5 (March 1999): 41.

25. Liddell, "Narrow Enclosure," 323.

26. Wynter, "Afterword," 363–64 (emphasis in original).

27. Ibid., 263. The cover of the first edition of the novel would, at first glance, also seem to dispute the claim that this novel is not about women. It does not display simply the male figure, presumably Moses; it also includes the figure of a woman, noticeably prominent in her bright yellow and orange floral dress, albeit overlain by the male figure. This superimposition, however, rather than diminishing the woman's importance, reflects the significance of women in the novel as (back)ground for the male figure.

28. Wynter, "Sylvia Wynter," 276.

29. In the beginning of the novel, Rose remembers saying "Yes" to Obadiah's proposal of marriage, and near the end she calls to Kate that the baby is coming.

30. David Scott, *Refashioning Futures: Criticism after Postcoloniality* (Princeton: Princeton University Press, 1999), 11, 12 (emphasis in original).

31. Ibid., 12.

32. Frantz Fanon, *The Wretched of the Earth*, trans. Constance Farrington (New York: Grove, 1963), 218.

33. With regard to the function of art, I am thinking not only of its commodification but also of Fanon's argument that "to fight for national culture means in the first place to fight for the liberation of the nation," and, further, that during this period of establishing a nation, "many men who up till then would never have thought of producing a literary work, now that they find themselves in exceptional circumstances—in prison, with the Maquis, or on the eve of their execution—feel the need to speak to their nation, to compose the sentence which expresses the heart of the people, and to become the mouthpiece of a new reality in action" (*Wretched of the Earth*, 233, 222–23). Although Wynter does not find herself in such dire situations as those Fanon describes, she does feel the need to "speak to her nation" as it prepares for independence, and the form she chooses for this message positions a period of psychic alienation as necessary preparation for the building of the new nation.

3. "Fighting Mad"

1. Jean Rhys, *The Letters of Jean Rhys*, ed. Francis Wyndham and Diana Melly (New York: Viking, 1984), 157 (emphasis in original).

2. Ibid., 144.

3. Ibid., 149 (emphasis in original).

4. Ibid., 156 (emphasis in original).

5. Rhys, *Wide Sargasso Sea*, ed. Judith L. Raiskin (New York: W. W. Norton, 1999), 105–6. Subsequent page citations are to this edition and are given parenthetically in the text.

6. Elizabeth Abel, "Women and Schizophrenia: The Fiction of Jean Rhys," *Contemporary Literature* 20, no. 2 (1979): 156. Abel quotes Gregory Zilboorg to describe ambulatory schizophrenia: "Since these patients [ambulatory schizophrenics] seldom reach the point at which hospitalization appears necessary, either to the relatives or to the psychiatrist, and since they appear 'to walk about life' like any other 'normal' person—although they remain inefficient, peregrinatory, casual in their ties to things and to people and tenacious only in their inability to be productive and independent—they pass as 'difficult people,' as 'problem children" (156 n. 4).

7. See Kenneth Ramchand's discussion of the early Caribbean debate about Rhys in *An Introduction to the Study of West Indian Literature* (Middlesex: Thomas Nelson and Sons, 1976). Later, Elaine Savory provides a thorough reading of the criticism of Rhys in "The Helen of Our Wars: Cultural Politics and Jean Rhys Criticism," ch. 9 of *Jean Rhys* (Cambridge: Cambridge University Press, 1998).

8. A. Alvarez, "The Best Living English Novelist," *New York Times Book Review*, March 17, 1974, 6–7.

9. Michael Thorpe, "'The Other Side': *Wide Sargasso Sea* and *Jane Eyre*," in *Critical Perspectives on Jean Rhys*, ed. Pierrette M. Frickey (Washington, DC: Three Continents, 1990), 180, originally published in *Ariel* 8, no. 3 (1977) 179.

10. Evelyn O'Callaghan, *Woman Version: Theoretical Approaches to West Indian Fiction by Women* (New York: St. Martin's, 1993), 34.

11. Helen Tiffin, "Mirror and Mask: Colonial Motifs in the Novels of Jean Rhys," *World Literature Written in English* 17, no. 1 (1978): 328.

12. Carine M. Mardorossian, "Shutting Up the Subaltern: Silences, Stereotypes, and Double-Entendres in Jean Rhys's *Wide Sargasso Sea*," *Callaloo* 22, no. 4 (1999): 1077. Mardorossian borrows the phrase from an unnoted article by Gayatri Spivak.

13. Pierrette M. Frickey, introduction to Frickey, *Critical Perspectives*, ix.

14. Michelle Cliff, "Adrift in Female Terrain," *Ms*, July/August 1993, 77.

15. Michelle Cliff, *No Telephone to Heaven* (New York: Vintage, 1987), 117.

16. Cliff, "Adrift in Female Terrain," 78.

17. Opal Palmer Adisa, "Journey into Speech—A Writer between Two Worlds: An Interview with Michelle Cliff," *African American Review* 28, no. 2 (1994): 275. *Claiming an Identity* also serves as a preface to Cliff's later, longer works.

18. Michelle Cliff, "Clare Savage as a Crossroads Character," in *Caribbean Women Writers: Essays From the First International Conference*, ed. Selwyn Cudjoe (Wellesley, MA: Calaloux, 1990), 264.

19. Cliff, *Claiming an Identity*, 44.

20. Adisa, "Journey into Speech," 275.

21. Cliff, *No Telephone to Heaven*, 116.

22. M. M. Adjarian, "Between and beyond Boundaries in *Wide Sargasso Sea*," *College Literature* 22, no. 1 (1995): 202.

23. Sandra Gilbert and Susan Gubar, *Madwoman in the Attic: The Woman Writer and the Nineteenth-Century Literary Imagination*, 2nd ed. (New Haven: Yale University Press, 2000), 359. Though it was first published in 1979, and though it includes an epigraph from Rhys's *Good Morning, Midnight*, Gilbert and Gubar's text does not mention *Wide Sargasso Sea*.

24. See Tiffin, "Mirror and Mask," and Gayatri Chakravorty Spivak, "Three Women's Texts and a Critique of Imperialism," *Critical Inquiry* 12, no. 1 (1985): 243–61.

25. Tiffin, "Mirror and Mask," 330.

26. Sandra Drake, "'All That Foolishness/That All Foolishness': Race and Caribbean Culture as Thematics of Liberation in Jean Rhys's *Wide Sargasso Sea*," in Rhys, *Wide Sargasso Sea*, 194, originally published in *Critica* 2, no. 2 (1990).

27. Mardorossian, "Shutting Up the Subaltern," 1085. In another article, Mardorossian notes that "the social and political meanings of a text are not solely determined by the ideologies of the time of its production but are constantly reformulated in the process of their reproduction by critical discourses." Carine Melkom Mardorossian, "Double [De]Colonization and the Feminist Criticism of *Wide Sargasso Sea*," *College Literature* 26, no. 2 (1999): 79.

28. O'Callaghan, *Woman Version*, 46.

29. Ibid.

30. Rhys, *Letters of Jean Rhys*, 263.

31. Ibid., 297.

32. Ibid., 263.

33. Mardorossian, "Shutting Up the Subaltern," 1079–80.

34. Rhys, *Letters of Jean Rhys*, 157.

35. Determining who is speaking in each part of the novel takes a moment for the reader because both narrators use the first person; but after a few lines the alternation becomes clear. Antoinette narrates part 1 and most of part 3. Her husband narrates part 2, but about halfway into part 2 Antoinette narrates for one scene. Part 3 is more difficult because of the italicized opening paragraphs, but later the reader realizes that Antoinette is relating a conversation she has overheard between Grace Poole and Leah. However, the last paragraph of this italicized section complicates this reading because it offers Poole's thoughts, which would not be available to Antoinette.

36. Mary Lou Emery, *Jean Rhys at "World's End": Novels of Colonial and Sexual Exile* (Austin: University of Texas Press, 1990) 17 (emphasis in original).

37. Joya Uraizee, "'She Walked Away without Looking Back': Christophine and the Enigma of History in Jean Rhys's *Wide Sargasso Sea*," *CLIO* 28, no. 3 (1999): 265.

38. Mardorossian, "Shutting Up the Subaltern," 1079.

39. The abbreviation of Christophine to "Pheena" is first made by the Rochester figure, but then Antoinette begins referring to her with this shortened name. Antoinette's use of "Pheena" securely places the power of naming in the hands of the Rochester figure.

40. In a letter, Rhys worried that she may have made Christophine too articulate, and the much-cited discrepancy between Gayatri Spivak's and Benita Parry's readings of this character shows that the novel offers Christophine as more than mere convenience. She has a voice and clear opinions of her own. She occupies a privileged position in the narrative. Of course, it is only to talk about Antoinette, but Christophine is there nonetheless, and in the process, other ideas about the Caribbean, slavery, marriage, and women's lives are articulated through her.

41. Mardorossian, "Shutting Up the Subaltern," 1074.

42. Kathy Mezei, "'And It Kept Its Secret': Narration, Memory, and Madness in Jean Rhys' *Wide Sargasso Sea*," *Critique: Studies in Modern Fiction* 28, no. 4 (1987): 196, 197.

43. Ibid., 197.

44. Rhys, *Letters of Jean Rhys*, 24.

45. Italics are my additions to Rhys's words.

46. Rhys, *Letters of Jean Rhys*, 157.

47. Ibid., 254, 233, 254, 233.

48. Jean Rhys, *Voyage in the Dark*, in *Jean Rhys: The Complete Novels* (New York: W. W. Norton, 1985), 3, originally published as *Voyage in the Dark* (London: Constable, 1934).

49. Ibid., 112.

50. Ibid., 115.

51. Michelle Cliff, "Contagious Melancholia," in *The Store of a Million Items* (Boston: Houghton Mifflin, 1998), 36.

52. Cited in Uraizee, "'She Walked Away,'" 267.

4. Shared Dreams and Collective Delirium in Derek Walcott's *Dream on Monkey Mountain*

1.Derek Walcott, "Bajans Are Still Very Insular and Prejudiced," interview by Carl Jacobs, in *Conversations with Derek Walcott*, ed. William Baer (Jackson: University Press of Mississippi, 1996), 8, originally published in *Trinidad Guardian*, July 23, 1967, 5.

2. Édouard Glissant, *Caribbean Discourse*, trans. Michael Dash (Charlottesville: University Press of Virginia, 1989), 209.

3. The term *hallucination* is appropriate here because it encompasses visions from both dreams and mental illness.

4. Derek Walcott, "The Art of Poetry XXXVII: Derek Walcott," interview by Edward Hirsch, in *Conversations with Derek Walcott*, 106, originally published in *Paris Review* 101 (Winter 1986): 196–230.

5. While he does not live there year round, Walcott has maintained a home in St. Lucia and has consistently returned to St. Lucia or Trinidad for long periods every year, even while holding a full-time position at Boston University. For fifteen years his participation in the Trinidad Theatre Workshop was a major reason for his returning.

6. Derek Walcott, "Comments from Derek Walcott," *Caribbean Writer* 8 (1994): 96–97.

7. Derek Walcott, "An Interview with Derek Walcott," interview by Edward Hirsch, *Contemporary Literature* 20, no. 3 (1979): 288.

8. Ibid.

9. Glissant, *Caribbean Discourse*, 196. He explains further: "a. Theater is the act through which the collective consciousness sees itself and consequently moves forward. At the beginning, there can be no nation without a theater. b. Theater involves moving beyond lived experience (dramatic time takes us out of the ordinary so that we can better understand the ordinary and the everyday). The ability to move beyond can only be exercised by the collective consciousness. There is no theater without a nation at its source" (196).

10. Derek Walcott, *Dream on Monkey Mountain and Other Plays* (New York: Noonday Press, 1970), 208. Subsequent page citations are to this edition and are given parenthetically in the text.

11. John Thieme, "Beyond Manicheism: Derek Walcott's *Henri Christophe* and *Dream on Monkey Mountain*," in *Comparing Postcolonial Literatures*, ed. Ashok Bery and Patricia Murray (New York: St. Martin's Press, 2000), 224.

12. The *Oxford English Dictionary* provides several options for the definition

of *dream*. A few, relevant to a discussion of this play, are: 1) "a vision during sleep; the state in which this occurs"; 2) "a similar involuntary vision occurring to one awake"; 3) "a vision of the fancy voluntarily or consciously indulged in when awake"; 4) "a visionary anticipation"; and 5) "a national aspiration or ambition; a way of life considered to be ideal by a particular nation or group of people." *OED Online*, November 2010, Oxford University Press, www.oed.com/view/Entry/57600?rskey=BCNY3h&result=2.

13. Paul Breslin, *Nobody's Nation: Reading Derek Walcott* (Chicago: University of Chicago Press, 2001), 140.

14. Ibid., 131.

15. Breslin designates Corporal Lestrade as the surrogate playwright, which would place even more authority in Lestrade's claiming of the dream for himself and others (ibid., 135).

16. Lloyd Brown, "Dreamers and Slaves: The Ethos of Revolution in Walcott and Leroi Jones," in *Critical Perspectives on Derek Walcott*, ed. Robert D. Hamner (Washington, DC: Three Continents Press, 1993), 195 (author's emphasis).

17. Walcott, "Comments from Derek Walcott," 96.

18. This passage is reminiscent of a speech by Titus Hoyt in Miguel Street: "Look, boys, it ever strike you that the world not real at all? It ever strike you that we have the only mind in the world and you just thinking up everything else? Like me here, having the only mind in the world, and thinking up you people here, thinking up the war and all the houses and the ships and them in the harbor. That ever cross your mind?" V. S. Naipaul, *Miguel Street* (New York: Vintage, 1987), 100.

19. Derek Walcott, "Reflections before and after Carnival: An Interview with Derek Walcott," interview by Sharon Ciccarelli, in *Conversations with Derek Walcott*, 38, originally published in *Chants of Saints: A Gathering of Afro-American Literature, Art and Scholarship*, ed. Michael S. Harper and Robert S. Stepto (Urbana: University of Illinois Press, 1979), 296–309.

20. Derek Walcott, "Meanings," *Savacou* 2 (September 1970): 47. Walcott also finds that "some of the best dramatic moments [are born] out of pure necessity. These have happened to me. Sometimes we have to put in a speech, right out of desperation because a guy has to go backstage and change. The pressure of that moment has made you create." Derek Walcott, "Conversation with Derek Walcott," interview by Robert Hamner, in *Conversations with Derek Walcott*, 23, originally published in *World Literature Written in English* 16, no. 2 (1977): 409–20.

21. Walcott, "Comments from Derek Walcott," 96.

22. Frantz Fanon, *The Wretched of the Earth*, trans. Constance Farrington (New York: Grove Press, 1963), 250.

23. Derek Walcott, "Man of the Theatre," interview, in *Conversations with Derek Walcott*, 18, originally published in *The New Yorker*, June 26, 1971, 30–31.

24. Jean-Paul Sartre, preface to Fanon, *Wretched of the Earth*, by Frantz Fanon, trans. Constance Farrington (New York: Grove Press, 1963), 12.

25. Ibid., 19, quoted in Walcott, *Dream on Monkey Mountain*, 211.

26. Walcott, "Man of the Theatre," 18.

27. Shoshana Felman, *Writing and Madness: (Literature/Philosophy/Psychoanalysis)* (New York: Cornell University Press, 1985), 89.

28. Walcott, "Man of the Theatre," 18.

29. Fanon, *Wretched of the Earth*, 168.

30. In "The Muse of History," Walcott criticizes this approach to history and "forward progress." He writes, "The vision of progress is the rational madness of history seen as sequential time, of a dominated future. Its imagery is absurd." Derek Walcott, "The Muse of History," in *What the Twilight Says: Essays* (New York: Farrar, Straus, and Giroux, 1998), 41.

31. *Dream on Monkey Mountain* also has the following quote from a Noh play on the dedication page: "If the moon is earth's friend, how can we leave the earth?"

32. The essay has been reprinted as the title piece in a collection of Walcott's essays and in an anthology of critical pieces on black drama. See Walcott, *What the Twilight Says*, and Paul Carter Harrison, Victor Leo Walker II, and Gus Edwards, eds., *Black Theatre: Ritual Performance in the African Diaspora* (Philadelphia: Temple University Press, 2002).

33. Walcott stresses that "no play could be paced to the repetitive, untheatrical patience of hunger and unemployment. Hunger produces enervation of will and knows one necessity. Although in very few of the islands are people reduced to such a state, the empire of hunger includes work that is aimed only at necessities" (19).

34. Those who access the electronic version of the play from *Black Drama* (Alexander Street Press) also do not have access to these quotations or the "Note on Production."

35. Walcott, "Man of the Theatre," 18.

36. Sartre, preface, 19–20, quoted in Walcott, *Dream on Monkey Mountain*, 277, emphasis in original.

37. Fanon, *Wretched of the Earth*, 249.

38. Derek Walcott, "An Interview with Derek Walcott," interview by J. P. White, in *Conversations with Derek Walcott*, 156, originally published in *Green Mountain Review*, 4, no. 1 (Spring-Summer 1990): 14–37.

39. J. Laplanche and J.-B. Pontalis, *The Language of Psycho-Analysis* (W. W. Norton: New York, 1974), 408.

40. Mary Boyle, *Schizophrenia: A Scientific Delusion?* (Routledge: London, 2002), 59.

41. Ibid., 99.

42. Louis A. Sass, *Madness and Modernism: Insanity in the Light of Modern Art, Literature, and Thought* (New York: Basic Books, 1992), 12.

43. Gilles Deleuze and Félix Guattari, *Anti-Oedipus: Capitalism and Schizophrenia*, trans. Robert Hurley, Mark Seem, and Helen R. Lane (New York: Viking Press, 1977).

44. Rachel Manley, "Thoughts on Writing from Exile," *Small Axe* 12 (September 2002): 202.

45. Quoted in Sass, *Madness and Modernism*, 76.

46. Quoted in Felman, *Writing and Madness*, 11. There is some indication of depression affecting Caribbean writers, particularly women, and there have been suicides (or suspected suicides). There has also been some mentions of writers suffering from clinical mental diseases like schizophrenia (Jean "Binta" Breeze, for example), but little has been written or recorded to move these beyond the equivalent of whispers.

47. Walcott, "Reflections," 39.

48. Ibid.

49. Walcott, "Interview with Derek Walcott" [interview by White], 156.

50. Patrick Colm Hogan, "Mimeticisim, Reactionary Nativism, and the Possibility of Postcolonial Identity in Derek Walcott's *Dream on Monkey Mountain*," *Research in African Literatures* 25, no. 2 (Summer 1994): 104.

51. Ibid.

52. Sass, *Madness and Modernism*, 50–51.

53. Walcott, "Reflections," 36–37.

54. Derek Walcott, "Walcott on Walcott," interview by Dennis Scott, in *Conversations with Derek Walcott*, 11. Originally published in *Caribbean Quarterly* 14, nos. 1–2 (1968): 77–82.

55. Jan Urbach, in her "Note on Language and Naming in *Dream on Monkey Mountain*," casts a different light on the idea of the play as a physical poem. For her, "*Dream on Monkey Mountain* dramatizes the impossibility of fixity and therefore, at least to some extent, the impossibility of writing. As a text then, the play must be, almost by necessity, both confused and confusing. Everything constantly changes: the characters' identities; the balance between reality and dream; the meanings of words, phrases, symbols and images. In order to illustrate this difficulty with definition and fixity of meaning, the work must be in the form of a play. As a play, it is a living work." Jan R. Uhrbach, "Note on Language and Naming in *Dream on Monkey Mountain*," *Callaloo* 29 (Autumn 1986): 578.

56. Derek Walcott, "This Country Is a Very Small Place," interview by Anthony Milne, in *Conversations with Derek Walcott*, 73, originally published in *Sunday Express*, March 14, 1982, 18–19.

57. Walcott, "Conversation with Derek Walcott," 24. The rest of the quote, interesting with regard to this point, reads, "In the case of Yeats, that is a literary thing in a sense, forcing the material on to the contemporary stage. It is a nostalgic revival. The great thing about this is all these rites are authentic performances and one is simply absorbing what is physically existing in the country."

58. Walcott has also discussed changing accents for performances in different regions of the Caribbean in order to make the plays more accessible to the audiences. Walcott, "Reflections," 43.

59. Theodore Colson, "Derek Walcott's Plays: Outrage and Compassion," in Hamner, *Critical Perspectives*, 125.

60. Glissant, *Caribbean Discourse*, 195

61. Ibid., 195.

62. Like madness, the dream can also be a catalyst. Lloyd Brown finds that "the romantic fantasies about an African "home" royal lions act as a catalyst, enabling Makak and his people to come home to their human selves. The dream-fantasy about revolution involves and confirms a very real revolutionizing of self-perception." Brown, "Dreamers and Slaves," 195.

63. Arguably, it is a collective theatralization during a performance because Walcott's "Note on Production" leaves space for, and almost demands, changes that involve the audience during each performance.

64. Walcott, "Interview with Derek Walcott" [interview by White], 166.

65. Ibid., 168.

66. Critics have responded in various ways to this troubling ending of scene 3. Urbach concludes that the woman Makak beheads is not the same as the woman who first appeared to him in a vision. Her argument is convincing, especially in light of her contention that the theater offers a lack of fixity. Daizal Samad similarly wishes to make the ending more acceptable by reading the death of the moon woman as merely symbolic, representing Makak's past. Patrick Hogan, however, suggests that the white woman be accepted as a real body on stage and her beheading as a reference to Fanon's "linking violence with catharsis." Thieme views the ending as freeing both Makak and Lestrade "from their roles as mimics, liberating them into an emergent Caribbean consciousness, in which local subjectivity frees itself from the strait-jacket of being constructed in terms of otherness." See Urbach, "Note on Language," 581; Daizal R. Samad, "Cultural Imperatives in Derek Walcott's *Dream on Monkey Mountain*," *Commonwealth* 13, no. 2 (1991): 19; Hogan, "Mimeticisim," 116; and Thieme, "Beyond Manichaeism."

5. "Claims to Social Identity"

1. At sixteen, Nellie asks her aunt for permission to go to the Globe to see *Jack the Ripper*, which was released in 1959. Even given time for the movie's distribution to Jamaica, we can assume that Jamaica received independence very soon afterward; but readers are never told this outright, though Nellie does mention Emancipation Day, which the government joined with the celebration of Independence Day in 1962. Brodber's 2006 reference to the importance of Emancipation Day in her description of ancestral anger sheds some light on why Nellie and her colleagues continue to celebrate Emancipation Day after its abolition. (See my introductory chapter to this volume.)

2. Erna Brodber, *Jane and Louisa Will Soon Come Home* (London: New Beacon, 1980), 70. Subsequent page citations to this work are to this edition and are given parenthetically in the text.

3. For Brodber's brief discussion of the influence of her social work on *Jane and Louisa Will Soon Come Home*, see Erna Brodber, "Fiction in the Scientific Procedure," in *Caribbean Women Writers: Essays from the First International Conference*, ed. Selwyn Cudjoe (Wellesley, MA: Calloux, 1990), 164–68.

4. See chapter 4, this volume, for my discussion of the difficulties of diagnosing schizophrenia and Walcott's metaphorical use of the term.

5. In short, Anancy and his son Tucuma are caught poaching by King Dryhead. Anancy, being the trickster that he is, convinces Dryhead that he has several children with him and offers them to the king in exchange for his own freedom. Dryhead, who has poor daylight vision, watches as Anancy says goodbye to his children individually—really Tucuma hiding and then reappearing as another child. Each time Tucuma appears, Anancy gruffly tells him to "go eena kumbla." The phrase is as misleading as Anancy himself because Dryhead understands it as an insult while Tucuma understands it as an order to disguise himself as another child. In the end, Dryhead grants Anancy's request that one of his children make the journey back with him, so both Anancy and Tucuma escape (123–30).

6. The critical scholarship on *Jane and Louisa Will Soon Come Home* has yet to catch up to the scholarship on similar paradigm-shifting texts from the anglophone Caribbean, but there have been some attempts to define the kumbla. Evelyn O'Callaghan's early review of *Jane and Louisa Will Soon Come Home* refers to the kumbla as evidence of "linguistic skill" based on the Anancy story. Joyce Walker-Johnson connects the kumbla to "the strategies women adopt to protect their offspring." Michael Cooke compares the kumbla to the garden imagery of the text but states that whereas "the garden gives space, the kumbla goes one better by giving both space and time." For Rhonda Cobham, the kumbla "becomes a symbol for the manifold strategies by which black women throughout the ages have ensured their own survival and that of the race." Most readings of Brodber's use of the kumbla, therefore, understand it as a form of camouflage, but they vary on the source and use of this camouflage. See Evelyn O'Callaghan, "Rediscovering the Natives of My Person," *Jamaica Journal* 16, no. 3 (1983): 63; Joyce Walker-Johnson, "Autobiography, History, and the Novel: Erna Brodber's *Jane and Louisa Will Soon Come Home*," *Journal of West Indian Literature* 3, no. 1 (1989): 56; Michael G. Cooke, "The Strains of Apocalypse: Lamming's *Castle* and Brodber's *Jane and Louisa*," *Journal of West Indian Literature* 4, no. 1 (1990): 37; Rhonda Cobham, "Revisioning Our Kumblas: Transforming Feminist and Nationalist Agendas in Three Caribbean Women's Texts," *Callaloo* 16, no. 1 (1993): 49.

7. Farah Jasmine Griffin, "*Who Set You Flowin'?*": *The African-American Migration Narrative* (New York: Oxford University Press, 1995), 111.

8. Ibid., 103.

9. Erna Brodber, *Perceptions of Caribbean Women: Towards a Documentation of Stereotypes* (Cave Hill, Barbados: Institute of Social and Economic Research, 1982), 2.

10. Griffin, "*Who Set You Flowin'?,*" 102.

11. Ibid., 103.

12. Ibid., 111.

13. Ibid., 107.

14. Evelyn O'Callaghan, *Woman Version: Theoretical Approaches to West Indian Fiction by Women* (New York: St. Martin's Press, 1993), 47 (emphasis in original).

15. Brodber, "Fiction in the Scientific Procedure," 166, 167.

16. Ibid., 166.

17. Front cover of the 1998 paperback reprint.

18. Shoshana Felman, *Writing and Madness: (Literature/Philosophy/Psychoanalysis)* (New York: Cornell University Press, 1985), 41.

19. Ibid., 221, 54.

20. Brodber, "Fiction in the Scientific Procedure," 166.

21. Ibid.

22. Frantz Fanon, *Black Skin, White Masks*, trans. Charles Lam Markmann (New York: Grove, 1982), 86. Fanon's text also challenges generic boundaries. Like Brodber, Fanon disrupts the assumed barrier between objective/subjective writing. He adds autobiographical information, literary criticism, and case studies, making *Black Skin, White Masks* difficult to classify.

23. Ibid., 225, 109.

24. Trinh Minh-ha, "Not You/Like You: Postcolonial Women and the Interlocking Questions of Identity and Difference," in *Making Face, Making Soul*, ed. Gloria Anzaldua (San Francisco: aunt lute, 1990), 375.

25. Brodber, "Fiction in the Scientific Procedure," 168.

26. Nancy Foner, *Status and Power in Rural Jamaica* (New York: Teachers College Press, 1973), 37–38.

27. Merle Hodge, introduction to *Perceptions of Caribbean Women: Towards a Documentation of Stereotypes* (Cave Hill, Barbados: Institute of Social and Economic Research, 1982), xii.

28. V. S. Naipaul, *The Middle Passage: Impressions of Five Societies; British, French, and Dutch in the West Indies and South America* (New York: Vintage, 1981), 42.

29. Foner, *Status and Power*, 37, 60.

30. Helen Tiffin, "Cold Hearts and (Foreign) Tongues: Recitation and the Reclamation of the Female Body in the Works of Erna Brodber and Jamaica Kincaid," *Callaloo* 16, no. 4 (1993): 910.

31. For more on ancestral anger, see the introduction to this volume.

32. Carolyn Cooper, "Afro-Jamaican Folk Elements in Brodber's *Jane and*

Louisa Will Soon Come Home," in *Out of the Kumbla: Caribbean Women and Literature*, ed. Carole Boyce Davies and Elaine Savory Fido (Trenton, NJ: Africa World, 1990), 283.

33. O'Callaghan, *Woman Version*, 63.

34. Darryl Cumber Dance, "Go eena Kumbla: A Comparison of Erna Brodber's *Jane and Louisa Will Soon Come Home* and Toni Cade Bambara's *The Salt Eaters*," in Cudjoe, *Caribbean Women Writers*, 174.

35. Brodber, quoted in ibid., 182 n. 12.

36. The game is generally referred to by the opening line—"Jane and Louisa Will Soon Come Home"—and the sections of Brodber's text transpose the order of the verses. Rhonda Cobham provides a brief summary of the verses and structure of the game. See Cobham, "Revisioning Our Kumblas," 48.

37. Denise deCaires Narain, "The Body of the Woman in the Body of the Text: The Novels of Erna Brodber," in *Caribbean Women Writers: Fiction in English*, ed. Mary Condé and Thorunn Lonsdale (London: Macmillan, 1998), 101.

38. Brodber, "Fiction in the Scientific Procedure," 166.

39. Brodber, quoted in O'Callaghan, *Woman Version*, 66.

40. Fanon, *Black Skin, White Masks*, 231.

41. Ibid., 226.

42. Brodber, "Fiction in the Scientific Procedure," 167.

Epilogue

1. David Chariandy, "Postcolonial Diasporas," *Postcolonial Text* 2, no. 1 (2005–6), journals.sfu.ca/pocol/index.php/pct/article/view/440/839.

2. Frederic Jameson, "Third World Literature in the Era of Multinational Capitalism," *Social Text*, no. 15 (Fall 1986): 69.

3. Chariandy, "Postcolonial Diasporas."

4. Later in the article, Chariandy offers an additional set of questions that he recommends potential future critical projects address, some of which include: "How is time represented in a diaspora, and what is its relationship to the 'homogenous empty time' associated with national imaginary, or the compressed time/space of globalization, or the disjunctive histories and re-memberings that constitute the postcolonial moment (See Benedict Anderson, Homi Bhabha)? Finally, how do we understand space in the diasporic imaginary, and its relationship to both contemporary developments in cultural geography, as well as emergent non-Euclidian theories of space (See Derek Gregory, Arjun Appadurai, Richard Cavell via Marshall McLuhan)?" (emphasis in original).

5. Stewart Brown, introduction to *The Oxford Book of Caribbean Short Stories*, ed. Stewart Brown and John Wickham (Oxford: Oxford University Press, 2001), xv. Also in Stewart Brown, introduction to *The Oxford Book of Caribbean Verse*, ed. Stewart Brown and Mark McWatt (Oxford: Oxford University Press, 2009), xxii.

6. Raphael Dalleo, "Colonization in Reverse: White Teeth as Caribbean Novel," in *Zadie Smith: Critical Essays*, ed. Tracey Walters (New York: Peter Lang, 2008), 91.

7. Kit Dobson, "Spirits of Elsewhere Past: A Dialogue on Soucouyant," *Callaloo* 30, no. 3 (2007): 813.

8. Charles Demers, "Forgotten Son: David Chariandy on Soucouyant," *Tyee*, October 17, 2007, thetyee.ca/Books/2007/10/17/Soucoyant/.

9. David Chariandy, *Soucouyant* (Vancouver: Arsenal Pulp, 2007), 137. Subsequent page citations are to this edition and are given parenthetically in the text.

10. Indeed, it is so foreign that Chariandy added the subtitle "A Novel of Forgetting" to keep "Soucouyant" as the title while diminishing the foreignness of the word itself. Personal interview with the author, October 27, 2010.

11. Norma Alarcon contends that legends "contribute to the formation of national consciousness." Quoted in Giselle Anatol, "Transforming the Skin-Shedding Soucouyant: Using Folklore to Reclaim Female Agency in Caribbean Literature," *Small Axe*, no. 7 (March 2000): 44.

12. Zadie Smith, *White Teeth* (New York: Vintage, 2000), 137. Subsequent page citations are to this edition and are given parenthetically in the text.

13. Erna Brodber, *Jane and Louisa Will Soon Come Home* (London: New Beacon, 1980), 7.

14. Clark continues: "In such an environment, names such as *Sundiata*, *Bigger Thomas*, and *Marie Chauvet* represent mnemonic devices releasing learned traditions." Vèvè A. Clark, "Developing Diaspora Literacy: Allusion in Maryse Condé's *Hérémakhonon*," in *Out of the Kumbla: Caribbean Women and Literature*, ed. Carole Boyce Davies and Elaine Savory Fido (Trenton, NJ: Africa World, 1990), 304. In a later essay, Clark proposes an expanded definition of *diaspora literacy*, but her refined definition narrows down to "the reader's ability to comprehend the literatures of Africa, Afro-America, and the Caribbean from an informed, indigenous perspective." Although she notes that readers can now "observ[e] the protagonists as they develop diaspora literacy," she returns her focus to the reader in the same sentence by clarifying, "We become voyeurs reading the characters reading events." Vèvè A. Clark, "Developing Diaspora Literacy and Marasa Consciousness," in *Comparative American Identities: Race, Sex, and Nationality in the Modern Text*, ed. Hortense Spillers (New York: Routledge, 1991), 42, 46. I rely on Clark's first definition of the term because it is more amenable to broadening for my own uses here. I keep, however, her limitation to the African diaspora, though I acknowledge that the term carries in itself the possibilities for application to other diasporas.

15. Marie-Elena John, *Unburnable* (New York: Amistad, 2007), 255. Subsequent page citations are to this edition and are given parenthetically in the text.

16. In *Wide Sargasso Sea*, Antoinette wakes from a dream in which she jumps from the top of Thornfield Hall. Upon waking, she heads out into the

passage in a repetition of her dream, thinking that now she knows what she must do. The implication is that she will, like Bertha Mason in Jane Eyre and herself in her dream, set the house on fire and jump from the roof. (See my discussion of this ending in chapter 3, this volume.) In *Unburnable*, the narrative closes with Teddy rushing to save Lillian, who has already decided to jump from Matilda's mountain.

17. Drowning, she believes, would lead to songs about her as a Mama Glo, a deadly river siren, while rotting in Creole finery would lead to songs about her as La Diablesse, an enchanting devil woman who leads men to insanity or death. Lillian rejects these because the former legend already belongs to her mother and the latter to her grandmother.

18. For sample discussions of the significance of the particular scene in "Molars" that produces the title of the novel, see John Clement Ball, *Imagining London: Postcolonial Fiction and the Transnational Metropolis* (Toronto: University of Toronto Press, 2004); Pilar Cuder-Dominguez, "Ethnic Cartographies of London in Bernadine Evaristo and Zadie Smith," *European Journal of English Studies* 8, no. 2 (2004): 173–88; and Jan Lowe, "No More Lonely Londoners," *Small Axe*, no. 9 (2001): 166–80. This chapter may also be read as Smith's indication that such readings are reductive and ultimately useless. For this latter perspective, see Ulka Anjaria, "On Beauty and Being Postcolonial: Aesthetics and Form in Zadie Smith," in Walters, *Zadie Smith*, 31–55. Anjaria "wonders whether the passage may not be satirizing the critic's impulse to identify a formal or conceptual unity through the instantly identifiable, and therefore potentially misidentifiable, metaphor contained within the title. Might the 'white teeth,' the root canals, and other 'teeth' imagery operate as empty signifiers that proliferate unendingly yet remain unintelligible within a novel clearly skeptical of the political assumptions behind conventions of meaning-making?" (36–37).

19. Zadie Smith published a short story titled "Mr. Newspaper," in *The May Anthology of Oxford and Cambridge Short Stories*, ed. Penelope Fitzgerald (Oxford: Varsity/Cherwell, 1996), but I have been unable to obtain a copy to determine if there is a connection to the character mentioned here.

20. The very excess of *White Teeth*, exemplified by the comic narrator and the surplus of events, might tempt readers to classify it as a "mad, mad novel." This excess can be connected to theories of excess in the postcolonial novel. For a general discussion of the idea, see Bill Ashcroft, "Excess: Post-Colonialism and the Verandahs of Meaning," in *De-Scribing Empire: Post-Colonialism and Textuality*, ed. Chris Tiffin and Alan Lawson (New York: Routledge, 1994), 33–44; see Anjaria, "On Beauty and Being Postcolonial," 31–56, for a short but specific application of this theory to *White Teeth*.

21. At the beginning of this chapter, the narrator groups together these postcolonial subjects of England in their experience of repetitive trauma: "This is like watching TV in Bombay or Kingston or Dhaka, watching the same old

British sitcoms spewed out to the old colonies in one tedious eternal loop. Because immigrants have always been particularly prone to repetition" (136).

22. When discussing names for her as-yet-unborn children, Alsana declares: "Ems are good. Ems are strong. Mahatma. Muhammad, that funny Mr. Morecambe, from Morecambe and Wise—letter you can trust" (Smith, *White Teeth*, 64). Man-man is a character in V. S. Naipaul's *Miguel Street* (see chapter 1, this volume); Moses is a character in Sylvia Wynter's *The Hills of Hebron* (chapter 2); and Makak is a character in Derek Walcott's *Dream on Monkey Mountain* (chapter 4).

Index

Recent Books in the New World Studies Series

Nick Nesbitt, *Universal Emancipation: The Haitian Revolution and the Radical Enlightenment*

Doris L. Garraway, editor, *Tree of Liberty: Cultural Legacies of the Haitian Revolution in the Atlantic World*

Dawn Fulton, *Signs of Dissent: Maryse Condé and Postcolonial Criticism*

Michael G. Malouf, *Transatlantic Solidarities: Irish Nationalism and Caribbean Poetics*

Maria Cristina Fumagalli, *Caribbean Perspectives on Modernity: Returning the Gaze*

Vivian Nun Halloran, *Exhibiting Slavery: The Caribbean Postmodern Novel as Museum*

Paul B. Miller, *Elusive Origins: The Enlightenment in the Modern Caribbean Historical Imagination*

Eduardo González, *Cuba and the Fall: Christian Text and Queer Narrative in the Fiction of José Lezama Lima and Reinaldo Arenas*

Jeff Karem, *The Purloined Islands: Caribbean-U.S. Crosscurrents in Literature and Culture, 1880–1959*

Faith Smith, editor, *Sex and the Citizen: Interrogating the Caribbean*

Mark D. Anderson, *Disaster Writing: The Cultural Politics of Catastrophe in Latin America*

Raphael Dalleo, *Caribbean Literature and the Public Sphere: From the Plantation to the Postcolonial*

Maite Conde, *Consuming Visions: Cinema, Writing, and Modernity in Rio de Janeiro*

Monika Kaup, *Neobaroque in the Americas: Alternative Modernities in Literature, Visual Art, and Film*

Marisel C. Moreno, *Family Matters: Puerto Rican Women Authors on the Island and the Mainland*

Colleen C. O'Brien, *Race, Romance, and Rebellion: Literatures of the Americas in the Nineteenth Century*

Kelly Baker Josephs, *Disturbers of the Peace: Representations of Madness in Anglophone Caribbean Literature*